EMERGENCY, CONSTITUTION AND DEMOCRACY

EMERGENCY, CONSTITUTION AND DEMOCRACY

AN INDIAN EXPERIENCE

Dr. N.M. Ghatate

SHIPRA

ISBN: 978-81-7541-578-2

2012 Revised Edition
(First Published in India in 2001)

Emergency, Constitution and Democracy: An Indian Experience

Published by:
SHIPRA PUBLICATIONS
H.O.: LG 18-19, Pankaj Central Market, Patparganj,
I.P. Ext., Delhi-110092, Tel: 91-11-2223 5152, 2223 6152
Br.Off.: 4617/18, Ansari Road, Darya Ganj,
New Delhi-110002, Tel: 6594 6453, 9810522367
E-mail: info@shiprapublications.com
www.shiprapublications.com

PREFACE

Since the adoption of the Constitution in 1950, Emergency had been declared thrice on the grounds that the security of India was gravely threatened by external aggression. This was when the Chinese hostilities erupted in 1962 and when the Indo-Pak War of 1971 was fought and on grounds of internal disturbance in 1975, better known as Internal Emergency.

The Constitution also provides for a takeover of the administration of State Governments when there is a breakdown of the constitutional machinery such. Emergency has been proclaimed more than a hundred times. It also provides for financial Emergency whereby the financial stability and credit of India is threatened but such an Emergency has never been proclaimed.

The net effect of the Proclamation of any one of the Emergencies mentioned above is that the central government becomes all powerful and the federal character of the government of the country is kept in cold storage.

It is significant to mention that in the 44th Constitutional amendment, the Presidential proclamation from suspending right to life and liberty and to prevent a person from being prosecuted twice for the same offence has been deleted and checks on use of preventive detention laws are incorporated to put civil liberty on stronger ground.

The focus of this book is to study the Emergency powers when Emergency is proclaimed on ground of a grave security threat to India with emphasis on the Internal Emergency of 1975. The experience of working this Constitution for six decades has shown that Emergency powers are used longer than conditions warrant its and were abused, particularly during the 1975 Emergency. Every time during such emergencies preventive detention laws and the Defence of India Rules were employed to silence opposition.

This book begins with an Introduction–Chapter-I; Constitutional Assembly Debates on Emergency Provisions are included in Chapter-II; Emergency in Operation with emphasis on Internal

Emergency is analyzed in Chapter-III, followed by Condition of Detention and Martial Law in Chapters-IV and V. The 44th Constitutional Amendments the 59th Constitutional Amendments to combat the unprecedented explosive situation in Punjab are dealt with in Chapter-VI. Preventive Detention and Constituent Assembly Debates on the subject are examined in Chapter-VII. The final chapter—Conclusion, includes recommendations.

During the operation of Internal Emergency, I was in the midst of filing and arguing a number of *habeas corpus* petitions, in the various High Courts and the Supreme Court and met various political leaders inside and outside jails. I have recorded my experiences and wit and humour during the nineteen dark months. Asterisks are given about the wit I was told by others. I may be forgiven as my name often appears particularly during the Operation of Internal Emergency in Chapter-III.

The notes are given at the end of each chapter. Four Appendices are given in the end; Appendix-I contains Emergency Powers in the Government of India Act of 1935, the Constitutional Amendments from time to time to the Constitution of India and the Preventive Detention Law, *viz.*, the Maintenance of Internal Security Act and the Conservation of Foreign Exchange and Prevention of Smuggling Act during the Internal Emergency, for ready comparison. Appendix II is the text of my argument reported in *The Times*, London. Appendix-III is the text of the editorial in *The New York Times* and the analysis of the three judgments during the Internal Emergency are given in the Appendix-IV.

I will be failing in my duty if I do not record my appreciation and gratitude to late Justice A.C. Gupta of the Supreme Court who despite his heavy Court schedule read the manuscript and made several useful recommendations. I am also obliged to T.K. Viswanathan, then the Law Secretary of India who took out precious time to go through the manuscript and made valuable suggestions.

I appreciate the hard work put in by Subhash C. Agarwal and Gopal Chandra Das for typing and re-typing the manuscript. And above all, to D. Kumar of Shipra Publications to bring out this book of the era gone by, but which has not lost its relevance even now.

Needless to say I take full responsibility for any omission and commission.

N.M. Ghatate

Contents

CHAPTER ONE

INTRODUCTION

> In all the three Emergencies there has been an abuse of power, but the Emergency of 1975 takes the cake.

The prime objective of every country whether it is a democracy or a dictatorship, monarchy or republic, federal or unitary, secular or theocratic, is to protect its sovereignty and integrity. To this end, apart from maintaining the armed forces and police forces it also provides for arming the executive with extraordinary powers to meet emergent situations. Proclamations of emergency, state of siege or martial law are some of the prevalent nomenclatures.

India has a democratic, federal and republican Constitution. Part VIII of the Constitution contains Emergency provisions. It contemplates three types of emergencies. First, under Article 352, when the security of India is threatened by war, external aggression or armed rebellion. The phrase "by internal disturbance" copying from Section 102 of the Government of India Act of 1935 used in the first Draft Constitution was first replaced by the phrase "armed rebellion" but again replaced by "internal disturbance" by the Drafting Committee. It was deleted by the 44th Constitutional Amendment by imposing the Internal Emergency in 1975, because of the abuse of this nebulous phrase. Second, under Article 356 President's Rule is imposed, when the government of the State cannot be carried out in accordance with the provisions of the Constitution, and third, under Article 360 when the financial stability or credit of the country is threatened.

The net consequences of the proclamation issued under any of the three types of emergencies are that it impairs the federal structure and the Central Government becomes supreme. It also empowers the Central Government to give directions to the States, distribute revenue and legislate for the States. In a nutshell the Central Government becomes unitary. However, the independence of the judiciary, insulated under clause 2 of Articles 125 and 221, cannot be affected either when the security of India is threatened or when there is a failure of the constitutional machinery in the State. During a financial emergency however salaries and allowances of Judges of the High Court and Supreme Court apart from that of the bureaucracy can be adversely affected. Secondly, grave threat or eminent danger cannot be a ground for proclaiming President's Rule in the States unless there is a breakdown of the constitutional machinery, unlike when the security of India is threatened and there is a proclamation of the emergency before its actual occurrence if there is an imminent danger thereof.

The Emergency under Article 352 is the most serious of all the three emergencies because firstly under Article 358, Article 19 which forms the bulwark of democracy, such as freedom of expression and association, freedom to move throughout the country, are suspended. Under Article 359, the President is empowered to suspend enforcement of any of the Fundamental Rights like Right to Equality, Right to Life and Liberty and fair trial and right to judicial remedies. Secondly Parliament is empowered to make laws in violation of Fundamental Rights during the continuance of emergency and the executive power is extended to give direction to any State as to how the executive power should be exercised. Parliament is also empowered to make laws relating to subjects which are reserved for the States—Article 353. The President can also pass orders determining the share of the States regarding duties levied by the executive but collected by the States or allocation of taxes and duties to the States—Article 354. Of course such laws are not permanent but elapse within six months after the withdrawal of Emergency. But before the 44th Constitutional Amendment, the executive was empowered to continue this Emergency as long it wished and there was no time limit to the duration, unlike in Article 356, where democracy in the State has to be restored within three years by holding elections. To top it all, the life of the Lok Sabha and the State's Legislature can be prolonged for one year at a time vide Articles 83 and 174, during the operation of this Emergency. The Constitution makers vested the executive with these vast powers to preserve the Constitution and to meet the emergent danger facing the country. But if those who do not have faith in democratic ethos, come to power, temporary 'Constitutional Dictatorship' contemplated by the Constitution can degenerate into absolute despotism. History is replete with such instances. In fact this is what happened during the internal Emergency of 1975 declared by the then Prime Minister Indira Gandhi on grounds of 'internal disturbance'. This was the darkest period of Indian democracy. The 44th Constitutional Amendment of 1979 by the Janata Government has put fetters so that people can not be denied Fundamental Rights indefinitely and put the democracy in deep freeze as long as the executive desired.

Since the implementation of the Constitution in 1950, Emergency was proclaimed three times on grounds that the security of India was threatened and each time the Fundamental Right to equality—Article 14, democratic freedoms—Article 19, right to life and liberty—Article 21 and Article 22 which provided for preventive detention, were suspended. Furthermore each time powers under preventive detention were abused and the executive continued to prolong the emergency long after conditions for the issuance of such declaration had ceased to exist.

This along with the conditions of detention and the Martial Law, as it also figures under Fundamental Rights–Article 39 and which finds support in Justice P.N. Bhagwati's majority judgment in *ADM, Jabalpur's case*[1], form the scope of discussion. So also is the Preventive Detention discussed which was the main weapon to detain and silence all opposition during the National Emergency, particularly that of 1975. Moreover, the 44th Constitutional Amendment which proposed to check the misuse of emergency provisions and to put on secure footing the right to life and liberty, is analyzed.

It is therefore, necessary to scrutinize the nature of constitutional power which enables the executive to declare national emergency, its limitations as well as its scope. Also, possible remedies to prevent its abuse in the light of our experience with three emergencies, two external and one internal, we have had so far, are examined.

In this context it is worthwhile to mention the conditions formulated by the International Commission of Jurists and Carl J. Fredrich in his book *Constitutional Government and Democracy*:

(a) the authority that creates the constitutional dictator should be outside the control of the constitutional dictator;
(b) the Emergency should be declared only when the circumstances make it absolutely necessary to do so in the interest of the country;
(c) there shall be a fixed time limit for duration of authorization of power;
(d) the period of Emergency should not be prolonged further than what is absolutely necessary;
(e) the restriction placed on fundamental rights and freedoms should be only such as the particular situation demands; and
(f) judicial review by ordinary courts to ensure such dictatorial powers, Emergency legislations and orders are continued to defend the democratic constitution.

To put it briefly, the Emergency powers should be as wide as necessary but their exercise must be strictly controlled.

However, the provisions of the Constitution which pose four more latent threats to democracy are: President's Rule in the States, the Financial Emergency, Ordinance making Power, and Presidential discretion. Though important, they do not form the scope of this book and are, therefore, briefly discussed.

Article 356 provides for the imposition of what is generally known as President's Rule in the States which affects the functioning of democracy in the States and upsets the federal character of the Constitution, does not form a part of this work because much has already been written about it. However, it may be mentioned when this Article was discussed by the Constituent Assembly many members expressed fears that the party at the Centre would use this Article to subvert federal democracy, where different parties would rule in the Centre and the States. Dr. Ambedkar in the Constitutional Assembly Debates is on record for stating that this Article would become the 'dead letter of the Constitution". The experience of the working of the

Constitution has shown that it has been the most abused Article of the Constitution and has been used more than 100 times in the last six decades. It may be mentioned that the nine Judges Bench of the Supreme Court in *S.R. Bomai's case*[2], realized the inadequacy of parliamentary control of the executive in the abuse of power under Article 356 and unanimously held that satisfaction of the President about taking over the administration of a State is justiciable.

The Supreme Court further provided a check on the Central Government stating that the power to dissolve the State Assembly should be deferred till the Parliament approves the declaration of imposition President's Rule. Besides, the Court could decide on the validity of the proclamation even after it was approved by the Parliament, and quash it provided it came to the conclusion that it was a malafide or an unconstitutional exercise of power. In that case, *status quo-ante* could be restored reinstating the dismissed Government and the dissolved Assembly. Furthermore, the court could direct the Election Commissioner not to hold fresh elections till (this case adjudicated) the question of dissolution of the Assembly, so that the case does not become infructuous. The Supreme Court in this case also suggested that the floor test was the best method of ascertaining a majority ruling.

However, the finding of the Supreme Court in this very case was that the imposition of President's Rule in the BJP-ruled States of Rajasthan, Madhya Pradesh, Himachal Pradesh and Uttar Pradesh after the Babri Masjid demolition in 1992, was justiciable in view of the apprehension of a breakdown of the constitutional machinery is not correct. The wording of Article 356 requires the breakdown of the constitutional machinery as a pre-condition for imposition of President Rule. Secondly, according to the minority judgment a political party which does not believe in the basic principles of secularism of the Constitution can be dismissed by the Central Government is justified. The minority judgement should have dealt with what will happen if such government came to power in the Centre as there is no provision for dismissal of the Central Government in the Constitution.

Article 360 which provides for financial Emergency also does not form the scope of this study because it has never been proclaimed. It may however, be mentioned that although India has passed through several financial crises, the most acute being the Foreign Exchange crisis of 1957 and the almost financial bankruptcy the country faced in 1991, the country has been able to overcome them without declaring a financial emergency. Nevertheless, the executive is armed with this power under Article 360 which may also affect the federal structure of the Constitution as also the independence of the judiciary. For nearly six decades, the country has survived without the exercise of power under Article 360, which nevertheless contains a latent threat to federal as the democratic structure of the Constitution, as well as the independence of the judiciary. It, therefore, seems that the emergency Powers under Article 360 should be deleted.

The Ordinance making power of the President and the Governors under Articles 123 and 213 respectively, also make deep in-roads into the parliamentary system of the Constitution if the President or Governor, as the case may be, is 'satisfied' that immediate legislation is necessary when the legislature is not in session. The primary law making body being the legislature, the Ordinance has to be laid before the legislature when it assembles and it ceases to operate unless it is approved within six weeks. However, the right of the legislature to critically examine a legislation by referring it to a Select Committee or Joint Parliamentary Committee, becomes a casualty. The usual plea of the Government is that any delay would result in the Ordinance lapsing, and there would be a legislative vacuum, and therefore, it would not be possible to refer the Ordinance to a Parliamentary Committee. The frequent use of this extraordinary power has not only eroded legislative power but has resulted in much hasty, ill-conceived and defective legislation. Sometimes, Ordinances are issued just after the session is over to avoid a debate in the legislature or just before the session when there could be no pressing urgency. For example, the Bank Nationalization Ordinance was issued by the President late in the afternoon of Saturday, July 19, 1969, that is, after banking activity had closed; as the Parliament was to meet on Monday, July 21, there could be no conceivable urgency. The Supreme Court in the *Bank Nationalization case* (and the eveven Judge Bench of the Court) noticed the timing of the Ordinance but as it had become an Act, it did not go into this aspect. But the majority held that the determination by the President of the existence of circumstances and the necessity to take immediate action, on which the satisfaction was based, was not declared final.[3]

This question of satisfaction, which occurs seven times in the Constitution, particularly in relation to Emergency situations is discussed in the Conclusion part of the volume.

There are also a number of instances when the same Ordinance has been promulgated again and again. In Bihar, one Ordinance had been replaced by another as many as seventeen times. It may be mentioned that though an Ordinance has the force of law it is qualitatively different from law enacted by the legislature because as mentioned earlier it is provisional and lapses unless it is approved by the Legislature. The Ordinance therefore, lacks the standard 'procedure established by law' required by Article 21 to deprive a person of his life or liberty. Justice S.C. Gupta noticed this aspect in *A.K. Roy's case*, and his minority view has correctly held that Article 21 is beyond the Ordinance making power.[4]

The Constitutional position of the President and the powers that they flow from has been the subject of much heated discussions during the Constituent Assembly Debates. Despite judicial pronouncement and constitutional amendments, the position is far from settled. The President has tampered with the federal and democratic fabric of the country and powers and which continues to pose potential danger.

Having adopted the Cabinet system of government with the President at its head, Jawaharlal Nehru and Alladi Krishna Swamy Iyer in the Constituent Assembly Debates stated that the President's position was like that of the British Monarch, who does not have any executive power which rests with the government. This view was contested by K.M. Munshi. If that had been so, there was no need to burden the Constitution with power to impeach him under Article 61, which shows that he has certain discretionary powers; more so, when his office is not hereditary and he is elected by the entire country though indirectly. Not only that he takes oath to 'preserve, protect and defend the Constitution' under Article 60 and the Supreme Command of the Defence Forces is vested in him under Article 53; while other high Constitutional functionaries take oath to 'Bear true faith and allegience to the Constitution' (Article 69). Though the Governor also takes oath like the President vide Article 159, his position is qualitatively different from that of the President as much as he is not elected and can be removed without any impeachment proceedings. Considering all these aspects, Dr. Ambedkar concluded that the President has certain discretionary powers. Nehru also accepted this view when he said, 'we do not want to make the President just a mere figurehead, like in the French Constitution'. R.K. Sidhawa pointed out that India had 'bitter experience of the British Governors under the Government of India Act, 1935, choosing the Prime Minister to suit their own ends and that they "created hell and mischief in appointing the Prime Minister who lacked the majority support".[5] The Drafting Committee had tabled the Instrument of Instructions for the President in the exercise of his discretion; but later, it was withdrawn without giving any reasons. This however, underscores the discretionary powers of the President and the Governors.

The Supreme Court had on several occasions considered the scope and powers of the President and the Governor in relation to their role to 'act' on the aid and advice of the Council of Ministers under Article 74 (1) and 163 (1) respectively. And it has consistently been held that they are under a Constitutional obligation to act on the advice of the Council of Ministers as established in *Ram Jawaya's case*[6] in 1954 and *Shamsher Singh's case*[8] in 1977.[7] The reason for such interpretation of the un-amended Articles 74 (1) and 163(1) respectively, is that India has adopted a Cabinet form of democracy and ministers represent the will of the people and command confidence of the Parliament as long as they are of people's representatives. This finding in *Ram Jawaya's case* was affirmed in *Sanjeev Naidu's case* and *U.N. Rao's case*.[7] The Seven Judge Bench in *Shamsher Singh's case* reiterated this principle. However, Chief Justice A.N. Ray and four other Judges held that the discretionary powers did not vest in the President. In the concurring judgment by Justice Krishna Iyer, however, it was held that the President had certain discretionary powers in choosing the Prime Minister and in the dissolution of the Lok Sabha.[8]

Amendments of Articles 74 and 163 clause 1 which stated that the President and Governor 'shall' act on the advice of the Council of Ministers, emphasized his obligation; but the 44th Constitutional Amendment added clause 2 to these Articles which clause vested them with one time discretion to the Council of Ministers to reconsider the advice tendered. These amendments, however, do not change the original position of the obligation of the constitutional heads to act on the advice of the Council of Ministers which is predicated upon the Council of Ministers enjoying the confidence of the Legislators. But this too is not always so. When the question arises, as to whether one of the Members of the Legislature is disqualified, the question has to be referred to the Election Commission by the President or the Governor as the case may be under Articles 103 and 192 respectively, and they have to act on the advice of the Election Commission and not that of the Council of Ministers. Furthermore, the Governor has the power to refer certain Acts passed by the Legislature to the President, under Article 200. Above all, there is no time limit within which the Constitutional head has to give his assent to the Bill as passed by the Legislature. For instance, President Zail Singh did not give his assent to the Postal Bill nor did he return it to the Parliament for reconsideration. This was the first veto of the President uncontemplated by the Constitution. R. Venkatraman, who succeeded him, did return the Bill after a lapse of years, but the Government finally withdrew it.

In 1959, the Parliamentary democracy was rudely shaken when President Neelam Sanjeeva Reddy ignored the claim of Jagjivan Ram to be invited to the Prime Minister though he had the support of 203 of the Members of the Lok Sabha. He swore in Charan Singh, who had only 74 Members, as the Prime Minister, dissolved the Lok Sabha and even promulgated the draconian preventive detention ordinance *viz.*, Smuggling and Hoarding Ordinance, although 22 out of 24 Chief Ministers had communicated to the President that ordinary laws were sufficient to deal with such problems. For six months, the Constitutional head had thus acquired virtual autocratic powers.

With the emergence of the era of hung legislatures in the Centre and the States, the President and the Governors have acquired arbitrary discretionary powers in appointing Prime Ministers and Chief Ministers who in their opinion could provide stable governments. But often they were not sure of their opinion and asked the appointees to demonstrate their majority on the floor of the House within a certain period. But again there is no time limit prescribed so they are not strictly bound to follow the advice of the Prime Minister or the Chief Ministers during this interregnum.

It may be mentioned here that the President when he appoints a Prime Minister who fails to demonstrate his majority, can legally dismiss the Prime Minister, impose President's Rule and also declare an emergency under Article 352, suspend Fundamental Rights of the people and thwart impeachment proceedings against him by dissolving the Lok Sabha as existence of both the Houses is a pre-condition for his impeachment. All this can be done without violating the provisions of the Constitution as pointed out by Allan Glendhill in his book, *The Republic of India, the Development of Law and Constitution.*. This however, is no doubt an important subject deserving in-depth study and is also excluded from the scope of this work.

Conclusion is given at the end of this work and contains some suggestions for the future.

ENDNOTES

1. *Additional District Magistrate, Jabalpur etc. Vs. Shivkant Shukla etc.* 1976 (2) SCC 521.
2. *S.R. Bomai etc. Vs. Union of India etc.* 1994 (3) SCC 1.
3. *R.C. Cooper Vs. Union of India* 1970 (1) SCC 248.
4. *A.K. Roy etc. Vs. Union of India etc.* 1982 (1) SCC 271.
5. See discussion on Article 74 (Article 61 of the Draft Constitution) *Constituent Assembly Debates*, Vol. VII (New Delhi: Printed by Lok Sabha Secretariate) December 30, 1948, pp. 1141-1161 and Article 163 (Article 142 of the Draft Constitution) Ibid., Vol. IV, June 1, 1949, pp. 489-503.
6. *Ram Jawaya Kapoor Vs. State of Punjab* 1955 (2) SCR 225.
7. *Sanjeev Naidu Vs. State of Madras* 1970 (1) SCC 443; *U.N. Rao Vs. Indira Gandhi* 1971(2) SCC 63.
8. *Shamsher Singh Vs. State of Punjab* 1974 (2) SCC 831.

CHAPTER TWO

Emergency Provisions of the Constitution

"People have not given us their sanction to make the Constitution for them. It is the British who gave us this sanction... we are making this Constitution. And this Constitution is going to be inflicted on the people without their express consent or legal sanction."

—Mahavir Tyagi

EMERGENCY IN THE 1935 ACT

The origin of Emergency Powers can be traced to Section 102 of the Government of India Act of 1935. The Governor-General was given power to issue Proclamation of Emergency if a grave situation arose in which the security of the country was threatened by war or internal disturbance. In 1937, this section was amended to proclaim Emergency before the actual occurrence of war or internal disturbance if the Governor-General was satisfied that there was imminent danger, thereof. The Federal Legislature was empowered to make laws for the provinces or any part thereof in respect of matters enumerated in the Provincial List. But the Federal Legislature was not empowered to introduce a Bill without the sanction of the Governor-General unless he thought it was necessary in view of the nature of the emergency. The Governor-General, however, was required to communicate the Proclamation of Emergency "forthwith" to the Secretary of State in London, who then was required to lay it before both the Houses of the British Parliament. Unless it was approved by resolution by both the Houses of Parliament it ceased to operate within six months. However, if approved, the Governor-General was empowered to revoke it by subsequent proclamation.[1]

Thus, the British Parliament, which was outside the control of the Governor-General, was the final authority to approve the proclamation of an emergency. Further, the Governor-General, who was outside the control of the Federal Assembly, could veto any legislation affecting state subjects.[2]

However the India Independence Act of 1947 specifically deleted the power of the Governor-General to declare an emergency. It is equally important to mention that no sooner had India gained independence, she was faced with grave threats to her security but she overcame these by the use of normal powers. She not only had to combat external threats of Pakistani aggression over Kashmir, but also had to deal with internal threats as the Princely States of Hyderabad and Junagarh declared open rebellion. But with the restrained use of force and statesmanship, the Central Government was able to prevent the balkanization of India.

The Drafting Committee of the Constitution, however, felt that to protect the very existence of a country as an independent nation and to prevent democracy itself from being destroyed, the Constitution should provide for emergency powers. But it was also thought necessary to provide safeguards against the abuse of such powers.

The provisions of the Draft Constitution dealing with the emergency when the security of India was threatened, were Articles 275, 276, 277, 279 and 180 corresponding to Articles 352, 353, 354, 358 and 359 respectively. It is significant to note that the phraseology of some of the clauses in the Draft Constitution, which was circulated to the members, was radically different from those presented for debates.

In the Draft Constitution, the President could issue a proclamation of emergency when the security of India was threatened by war or domestic violence; and the time given for approval of the Proclamation was six months. The draft that was presented was modified to reduce this period from six to two months. But the most important change was the substitution of the phrase "domestic violence" by a nebulous phrase "internal disturbance", which was in the Government of India Act of 1935. This phraseology, as will be seen later, was used with devastating consequences in 1975. Besides, an additional ground for proclamation was added *viz.*, "external aggression". This was an improvement, as an emergency could then be declared if there was an aggression, without the official declaration of war, which has now become a common practice in the post-Second World War period.

In fact, India itself was one of the first victims of undeclared war when Pakistan attacked Kashmir in 1947 without an open declaration of war. Furthermore, emergency could be proclaimed if 'any part' of India was threatened. In this respect it is pertinent to note that under the 1935 Act, the Governor-General could only declare an emergency if the security of the whole of India was threatened, but not if only the security of a part of India was threatened. This was a wholesome approach because India is one country and any part of India includes the whole of India.

But the change in wording might have been felt necessary because when the Draft Constitution was being framed the princely states were not integrated. Immediately after Independence, whether the princely states formed part of India or not was a debated question. The Government of India, to prevent further fragmentation of the country, was of the view after the withdrawal of British rule that that there would be two countries, India and Pakistan. Both countries would inherit the same rights over the princely states within its area as did the British. However, the British were of the view that after the lapse of the paramountcy of the British, only the British provinces would be handed over to the Indian and Pakistani Governments while the princely states would have the choice either to become independent or to join one of the two countries. The princely states like Hyderabad and those bordering Pakistan, including Kashmir, had favoured this British view to gain some bargaining power. The Pakistan Government also encouraged the British theory and wooed the princely states to join Pakistan and thereby weaken India.

Furthermore, the proclamation of emergency was required to be approved by both the Houses of Parliament within two months. But a proviso was added that in case of the dissolution of the Lok Sabha within two months of this declaration the reconstituted Lok Sabha was required to approve the proclamation within one month. As it will be seen later this provision is pregnant with mischief.

Another important change in Draft Article 280, corresponding to Article 359 which dealt with the suspension of Fundamental Rights, was the enlargement of its scope in the Draft Constitution. According to this Article, pending cases of the enforcement of Fundamental Rights were also suspended by this Presidential Order. Moreover, the application of the Order suspending Fundamental Rights did not nessarily apply for the whole of India but could be restricted to any one part of India. Thirdly, unlike the Draft Constitution, the President was required to lay it before each House of Parliament. Thus, while the Drafting Committee gave vast powers to the Executive during an Emergency, safeguards against their misuse were not adequate.

CONSTITUENT ASSEMBLY DEBATE

When these Articles came for approval before the Constituent Assembly, as expected, they provoked long-drawn debates and several amendments were moved. Their relevance is not lost by the passage of time and they still provide food for thought for those interested in saving our independence and democracy through thick and thin.

T.T. Krishnamachari, a Member of the Drafting Committee, who initiated the debate stated that the allocation of Emergency Powers was a "necessary evil" while Alladi Krishnaswamy Ayyar, another Member, belittled the critics by saying, "We cannot fight war with Magna Carta".[3]

The critics, on the other hand, led by H.V. Kamath and Sibban Lal Saxena, not only questioned the grant of wide powers to the Executive but also criticized the weakness of the safeguards provided against abuse by those in power.

ARTICLE 352

H.V. Kamath pointed out that the country had faced the crisis of Partition, communal strife of the worst magnitude, aggression by Pakistan on Kashmir, an attempt by the State of Hyderabad to secede from India without the emergency power, being available and wondered if they were at all necessary. He also reminded the Constituent Assembly that the Constitution can be subverted not only be rebellions, conquest or revolutions but also by the people in power. He pointed out that Article 48 of the Wiemiar Constitution of Germany paled into insignificance when compared with the emergency provisions of the Draft Constitution and they had no parallel in any other democratic constitution. Hitler using the provisions of Article 48 of the Wiemar Constitution was able to establish dictatorship of the worst kind and that too without violating any of the provisions of the Wiemar Constitution.[4]

Kamath was also totally opposed to the phrase "internal disturbance" as one of the grounds for declaring an emergency, and demanded its substitution by phrases like "internal violence, rebellion or insurrection," as a ground for declaring an emergency. According to him, "this was a 'flimsy ground". He feared that the emergency could be proclaimed if different parties came to power in the Centre and the States. There could develop natural tension between them, and it could provide an excuse for proclaiming an emergency. As a result provincial democracy would become a mockery. An intra-party dispute could be considered as "internal disturbance" to proclaim an emergency and could be used even to crush a party which was likely to come to power. Therefore, Kamath strongly pleaded for the substitution of the word 'disturbance' with "internal rebellion".

Kamath was also against the declaration of an emergency when there was a grave threat but suggested its proclamation only on the actual outbreak of war, or aggression. According to him, a threat was always there and Clause (3) which provided for the declaration of an emergency before an actual occurrence, if the President was satisfied that there was "imminent danger", should be deleted.[5]

K.T. Shah, who supported Kamath, said that the Clause (3), coupled with the phrase, "internal disturbance", was pregnant with "grave mischief". He also submitted that if a real emergency had arisen and the Council of Ministers did not rise to the occasion, the President should be empowered to use this power.[6]

Mahavir Tyagi was, however, of the opinion that power to declare an emergency before the actual occurrence of eventuality which permitted such a declaration should be there as contemplated by Clause (3), so that a threat to the security of India could be effectively averted by timely action.[7]

As regards the President's power to declare an emergency, H.V. Kamath, Dr. Punjabrao Deshmukh, Tajmul Hussain and Kazi Syed Karimuddin wanted that a specific clause should be inserted so that this vast power should not be used without the advice of the Council of Ministers.[8] However, Mahavir Tyagi argued that since the President was elected by the whole of India, he was the sole custodian of the rights and freedom of the country. He is a person in whom the entire country has vested its confidence and he should be allowed to declare an emergency.[9] Supporting this view, Tajmul Hussain and Kazi Syed Karimuddin argued that if the Council of Ministers did not rise to the occasion, when an emergency had arisen, the President should be allowed to use this power.[10] T.T. Krishnamachari speaking for the Drafting Committee's Recommendations however felt that amendment was not necessary as it was implicit that the President would act on the advice of the Council of Ministers according to the constitutional theme.[11] This controversial question of the President's Emergency Powers deserves special treatment and the same has been dealt with subsequently.

Tajmul Hussain felt that the two months period allowed for laying the proclamation for approval before both the Houses was much too long. He wanted that it should be laid immediately before Parliament for approval.[12] K.T. Shah wanted that Parliament should also be armed with the power to disapprove the Proclamation and as proposed by the Draft Article the Executive alone must not have the power to revoke an Emergency so that Parliamentary control was not eroded.[13] It may be mentioned here that, in France, when a State of Siege, i.e., emergency, is proclaimed Article 16 of the Constitution of the Fifth Republic provides that the National Assembly "shall meet as of right and it cannot be dissolved during emergency" so that the legislature continuously supervises the exercise of extraordinary power vested with the Executive.[14]

T.T. Krishnamachari, who replied on behalf of the Drafting Committee, stated that the Emergency Power was given to save the Constitution. It was a "safety valve"; if safeguards to protect the Constitution were not provided, the Constitution framers would be "guilty of a grave dereliction of duty". They have at the same time provided enough safeguards to see that the people's voice would be heard and popular will would dominate whatever might be the conditions under which we have to function under the emergencies. Rejecting the proposed amendments, Krishnamachari also said that if Parliament's powers were not curtailed and if Emergency Powers were abused, Parliament could "throw the Government".[15]

This safeguard, in view of Parliamentary democracy based on party discipline, is wholly inadequate. Due to party discipline members of the party have to support the policies of their leaders. Clause 5 of the 52nd Constitutional Amendment introduced the anti-defection provision by which legislators face disqualification if they vote against the party directive. Also, the safeguard of the popular voice controlling the executive is no safeguard at all. It could be effectively scutled as rights to the freedom of speech, association and movement throughout the country stand suspended under Article 358 when emergency is declared.

ARTICLE 353 AND ARTICLE 354

There was not much debate over Draft Articles 276 and 277 corresponding to Articles 353 and 354 which strengthened the hands of the Union Executive during an Emergency. The former Article 353 extended the power of the Union Executive to give direction to any State as to how it should exercise its powers and enable Parliament to frame laws regarding State subjects. The latter, Article 354, authorised the President by order to alter the distribution of revenue among the States but provided that such an order shall be laid before Parliament as soon as thereafter.

Hridayanath Kunzru, however, felt that too much power was being vested with the Centre, and wanted some parliamentary control over financial matters even during emergency.[16] Sibanlal Saxena's only grievance was that Article 277 did not provide a machinery to implement the financial policies mentioned therein.[17] It is these two articles which made Graville Austin observed that during an emergency "the distribution of powers can be so drastically altered that the Constitution becomes unitary rather than federal."[18]

ARTICLE 358 AND ARTICLE 359

As the Draft Article 275, i.e., Article 352, was approved in the present form, it was presented and amendments seeking to strengthen the safeguards against its abuse were rejected. These

Draft Articles 279 and 280, i.e. Articles 358 and 359, which proposed to remove all fetters against the Executive and Legislature in the matter of Fundamental Rights evoked unprecedented criticism, and strenuous attempts were made to amend these articles to control the Executives Power.

As pointed out earlier, as soon as an emergency was declared, the State under Draft Article 279 (Article 358) could pass laws and the Executive could take action in violation of Fundamental Rights contained in Draft Article 13 (Article 19) and such laws or action could not be challenged in court. In other words, power was proposed to be given to suspend democracy. While under Draft Article 280 (Article 359) the right to move any court for the enforcement of Fundamental Rights were mentioned in the Presidential Order as also pending proceedings for the enforcement thereof remained suspended.

Dr. P.R. Deshmukh felt that Draft Article 279 (Article 359) by which Article 19 was suspended was unnecessary. According to him Parliament had all powers to frame laws imposing reasonable restrictions, as freedoms contained in Article 19 were not absolute.[20]

Sibanlal Saxena, seeing the mood of the Constituent Assembly, moved an amendment that the suspension of Fundamental Rights should only be done by an Act of Parliament and not by the Executive. But according to him also there was no need to suspend freedoms mentioned in Article 19 as none were absolute but laden with provisos, and Parliament was already empowered to make laws restricting them in public or national interest. He appealed for deletion of this Article or to at least accept his amendment, and asked: "Can we not trust Parliament in emergency?"[21]

H.V. Kamath, supporting Sibban Lal Saxena's amendment, argued that there was no need for Draft Article 279 i.e., Article 358, as all articles which guarantee Fundamental Rights could be suspended under Article 280 i.e., Article 359. Pointing out that no democratic constitution ever gave such a sweeping power to the executive, he asked, what was meant by "State could make laws", whether it meant Parliament, State legislature or an Executive and emphasized that Parliament alone, and not the President, must have the power to suspend Fundamental Rights. H.V. Kamath, in a well studied speech, cited from the Constitutions of the U.S.A., Italy and the Defence Realm Act of the U.K. of 1920, how safeguards to avoid tyranny were added. For example, the Defence of Realm Act that provided Regulation under the Act were withdrawn, and Act would cease to have effect unless both the Houses of Parliament approved it. In the U.S.A. the Fundamental Rights to *habeas corpus* is suspended only if there is a rebellion or war and not a threat of war, and that too could be done by the U.S. Congress and not by its President.[22]

Also under the Italian Constitution, which was framed in similar situations as in India, it was stipulated that in an extraordinary urgency the Government could make a provisional law but it must be laid before the Chamber on the same day for approval and if the Chamber was not in session it could be called within five days.[23]

When Sibanlal Saxena's amendment, that Parliament instead of the President should be empowered to suspend Fundamental Rights, was rejected, Kamath moved another amendment that the Presidential Order suspending Fundamental Rights should be subject to the "approval of the majority, of a total membership of each House of Parliament." So that as, K.T. Shah put it, Parliament could discuss the Order threadbare and only give that power which was absolutely necessary.[24]

Thakurdas Bhargava also expressed similar views and as the Order under Article 359 "vitally affected citizens, Parliament must meet immediately after the Order suspending Fundamental Rights were issued.[25]

B.M. Mauval wanted that no discretion should be granted to the Executive in placing the Order before each House for approval.[26]

B.M. Gupte, who felt that the period of two months to place the Order before Parliament was too long, said that it must have the sanction of Parliament.[27]

Sibban Lal Saxena wanted the period to be reduced from two to one month and Parliament have the power to approve, vary or disapprove the Order suspending Fundamental Rights.[28]

Several Members opposed the blanket powers given to the Executive to suspend all Fundamentals Rights during the emergency, as several Fundamental Rights had no nexus with the security of the State.

According to H.V. Kamath, Sibban Lal Saxena and Mahavir Tyagi had advocated that if Article 32 which guaranteed Right to approach the Supreme Court for any violation of Fundamental Rights was suspended, all Rights would become paper rights. Tyagi warned that a future Government might misuse the power and the only remedy people had against the highhandedness of the Government was to approach the court. If the power to suspend all Fundamental Rights was given to the Executive, they could override the Judiciary and then "there will be nothing but a law of the jungle." To stress his indignation he said that he would oppose Draft Article 280 even if the whole House supported it. He stressed that the Right to move the court cannot be taken away under any circumstances and that the supremacy of the Judiciary must be maintained even in an Emergency. He warned the Constituent Assembly:

> "The Government may tend to become tyrannical and beastly, the opposition will have no safety, and "for God's sake", he pleaded, "let not individuals, let not your opponent be deprived of their basic right of approaching the Supreme Court for the protection of their life, honour and liberty". He emphasized that this power to suspend the Fundamental Rights should be reconsidered "in the interest of democracy, in the interest of future freedom. It may be revised so that the future governments might not be able to misuse it."

The grave consequence of these provisions provoked Mahavir Tyagi to question the very power of the Constituent Assembly to enact such a Constitution. He reminded the Constitution Assembly:

> "We were elected long ago to fight with the British, and now by indirect election we have come here; people have not given us their sanction to make the Constitution for them. It is the British who gave us this sanction and with the borrowed sanction of the foreigners we are making this Constitution. And this Constitution is going to be inflicted on the people without their express consent or legal sanction."[29]

In the same vein, H.V. Kamath pointed out that during the Emergency it was said the Centre must be strong and that included Parliament as well as the Judiciary. The Executive could not be made strong at the cost of the other two limbs of the State. All the limbs of the State should be made strong in an emergency.[30] The Liberty of the individual was not a thing to be trifled with at the behest or arbitrary fiat of the Executive and, "as an autocratic negation of liberty this article [Article 359] takes the palm over all other Constitutions. It has no parallel in the world." He was firmly of the opinion that the writ of *habeas corpus* should never be suspended. Even the British Government did not take away this right to move the court although they resorted to several repressive measures to preserve their empire.[31]

Nazir Uddin Ahmed correctly pointed out that there was no point in saying that the Rights would remain if one could not go to courts if they were violated and "If you can't vindicate a right it is not there". According to him it was wrong to give needless power to the President. He also analysed various Fundamental Rights and asked what was the need to suspend Fundamental Rights that dealt with untouchability or equality before the law and giving the power to the government to discriminate during an Emergency or whether the government was going to restore titles abolished by Article 18. Similarly he contended that freedoms under Article 19 were hedged with such limitations that one could not use them for any purpose detrimental to national interest. And as regards Article 20, he said that if it was suspended a person could be punished for the same offence again and again. He wanted Article 358 to be amended so that only clause (g) of Article 19 which dealt with the right to carry on trade or business and Article 16 which dealt with equality of opportunity and right of permanency of tenure in government service could be suspended during an emergency as these rights might hamper effective dealing with the emergency situation.

He further pointed out that even during the Second World War the doors to court were never closed and quoted Lord Atkin's words: "War or no war, justice must go on. His Majesty's justice cannot be curtailed or in the least affected by the existence of war." And he reminded the Constituent Assembly that when the phrase emergency itself was not defined, people's liberty could be "in peril at the slightest pretext".[32]

Similarly, K.T. Shah opposed the suspension of the right to move the Supreme Court guaranteed by Article 32, however grave an emergency may arose. If the Right was suspended all other

Rights would become meaningless. "Even if there is war," he said, "Justice of the people, justice in this land shall not be stopped or suspended." Furthermore, he wanted that no action of the officers in violation of Fundamental Rights should be protected unless it was done bona fide and that too, by an Act of Parliament passing indemnity laws. This was so because in a democracy officers must know that they cannot act unjustly and violate the Fundamental Rights of the people. According to him, the power to suspend Fundamental Rights was too important a matter to be decided by the Parliament by a simple majority.[33]

H.V. Kamath's strong dissent had a ring of prophecy. He quoted from various Constitutions and pointed out that even the Wiemar Constitution of the Third Reich of Germany had better safeguards. But authors of the Constitution felt "no use of such safeguards".[34] He eloquently pointed:

> We are told that the Assembly should trust the Executive implicitly. But if the executive wants the trust [of the people] why should the Executive not trust the judiciary and Parliament... Is our Judiciary bereft of all wisdom, integrity and conscience that the executive should snap their figures at them? This is a most disgraceful state of affairs. I do not see how we can build up an egalitarian or democratic state on such a foundation. It is said that at a time of emergency the state has to be preserved. By all means preserve it but not at the unjust sacrifice of individual liberty. The most serious emergency should not empower the state to unjustly deprive a person of his liberty. This should be the lodestar of our Constitution. Article 280 by given power to suspend *habeas corpus* destroys this principle.
>
> The argument is we want peace and order so that the state is preserved... But the peace may be of the graveyard the void of the desert. If that is the peace the Drafting Committee's wise men have in mind, I would rather die than live in such a peaceful situation... This Article is fraught with disastrous consequence for rights and liberties of the people by this Chapter XV we are seeking to lay the foundation of the totalitarian state, a police state a state completely opposed to our deals.[36]

To R.K. Sidhava's intervention that in an emergency the government should have all the power,[37] Kamath said that he agreed but he wanted safeguards against its abuse.[38] Thakurdas Bhargava expressed reservation about the power given to the Executive to suspend any Article in the chapter of Fundamental Rights and asked, "Is Parliament your enemy?"[39]

Even Alladi Krishnaswamy Ayyer, who replied to the debate on behalf of the Drafting Committee had to concede that some of the Fundamental Rights mentioned in Part-III had no nexus with emergency and could not be suspended, but he felt it was better to leave it to the government and weakly tried to defend Article 359 by saying that Parliament and in the parliamentary system the Executive was responsible to the Parliament. "The Security of the State," he concluded, "was more important as the liberty of the individual which is based upon the security of the State" and such provision was necessary in a country of "multitudinous types of people with probably diverse loyalities.[40]

When this Article 359 was adopted Kamath remarked: "This is the day of sorrow and shame. May God help the Indian people!"[41]

ARTICLE 83 (DRAFT ARTICLE 68A)

Coupled with the power of the executive to indefinitely continue the emergency with colossal powers to deny Fundamental Rights, make laws in violation of Fundamental Rights, and convert the federal structure into a unitary one, was the proviso to the Draft Article 83 which authorised the President to extend for one year at a time during an emergency.

When this article came up for discussion, Ambedkar himself proposed a change in the Draft Article stating that the life of the Legislature would be extended during an emergency not by the President but by the law enacted by Parliament. It is pertinent to note that not only the life of the Lok Sabha could be extended but also the life of the State legislature, as similar proviso is provided in Article 172(1) of the Constitution.

Sibban Lal Saxena was opposed to the proviso as it permitted indefinite extension of the life of Parliament. Sighting the American example, that war or no war, elections had to be held at the scheduled time, he said that people must have the right to elect their representatives every five years and no emergency should take away this valuable right. But if in extraordinary circumstances the life of the legislature had to be extended, there must be a period beyond which it could not be extended and then elections must take place.[42] This view was in accordance with Article 355 and 356 where during President's rule the life of the legislative assembly could be extended for six months at a time, but not beyond three years after which holding of elections is mandatory. But this sound proposal was unfortunately not accepted.

The net result of this debate on Emergency Powers was that Articles 352, 353, 358, 359 were adopted as proposed by the Drafting Committee.

This provoked H.V. Kamath to observe:

> Through Fundamental Rights a great edifice of democracy is built. Surrounding that edifice is the arch of great negation and Article 280 is the keystone of this arch of autocratic reaction... the weight of negation will be so heavy that I am afraid the whole edifice will collapse.[43]

The fears expressed by the Members were genuine while replies given by the Members of the Drafting Committee were hardly satisfactory. The only safeguard, if at all they can be called safeguards, was that the proclamation of an emergency and Presidential Order suspending Fundamental Rights had to be laid before Parliament for approval. Thus while the Drafting Committee gave vast powers to the Executive during an Emergency, the safeguards against their misuse were not at all adequate.

ENDNOTES

1. This Article 102, of the Government of India Act, 1935 along with relevant provisions of the Draft Constitution, and of the Constitution as was adopted along with the amendments to this date, are given in Appendix I, for ready reference.
2. See, p. 5.
3. The Draft Article 275 (352) was debated on August 2, 1949. See *Constituent Assembly Debates,* Vol IX, (New Delhi: Printed by Lok Sabha Secretariat) p. 103 to 127; T.T. Krishnamachari; Alladi Krishnamachari Ayyar, *Ibid.* August 20, 1945, p. 545.

4. See Article 48 of the Constitution of the German Reich of August 11, 1949 – popularly known as the Wiemar Constitution reads as under: "In the event of the State not fulfulling the duties imposed on it by the constitution or laws of the Reich, the President of the Reich may make use of the armed forces to compell it to do so.

   Where the public security and order is seriously distrubed or endangered within the Reich, the President of the Reich may take measures necessary for their restoration, intervening in case of need with the help of armed forces. For this purpose he is permitted for the time being, to abrogate either wholly or partially fundamental rights laid down in Articles 114, 115, 117, 123, 124 and 153.

   The President of the Reich must without delay, inform the Reichstag of any measures of the kind in paragraph No. 2 of this Article. Such measures should be abrogated upon the demand of the Reichstag.

   Where there is a danger in delay, the State Government may take provisional measures of the kind indicated in paragraph 2, for its own territory. Such measures may be abrogatted upon the demand of the President of the Reich or Reichstag.

   Details are to be determined by the law of the Reich."
5. H.V. Kamath, *Ibid.*, pp. 105-107 and 125.
6. K.T. Shah, *Ibid.*, p. 113.
7. Mahavir Tyagi, *Ibid.*, p. 120.
8. H.V. Kamath, loc cit., Dr. Punjabrao Deshmukh, *Ibid.*, p. 115.
9. Mahavir Tyagi, *Ibid.*, p. 120.
10. Tajmaul Hussain, *Ibid.*, p. 118; Kazi Sayyed Karimuddin, *Ibid.*, p. 115.
11. T.T. Krishnamachari, *Ibid.*, p. 124.
12. Tajmaul Hussain, *Ibid.*
13. K.T. Shah, *Ibid.*
14. See Article 16 of the Constitution of the Fifth Republic of France.

   "When the institution of the Republic, the Independence of the Nation, the integrity of territory or fullfilment of its international commitment are threatened in a grave and immediate manner and when the regular function of the constitutional government authorities is interupted, the President of the Republic shall take measures commanded by these circumstances, after official consultation with the Prime Minister, the President's of the Assemblies and Constitutional Council.

   He shall inform the nation of these measures in message.

   These measures must be prompted by the desire to ensure the constitutional government authorities, in the shortest possible time, the measures of fullfilling their assigned functions. The Constitutional Council shall be consulted with regard to such measures.

Parliament shall meet by right.

National Assembly may not be dessolved during the exercise of emergency powers by the President."

15. T.T. Krishnamachari, *Ibid.*, pp. 122-125.
16. Pt. Hridaynath Kunzru, Articles 272, 276, (353 and 354) were debated on August 3, 1949, *Ibid.* pp. 157-158.
17. Sibban Lal Saxena, *Ibid.*, pp. 508-509.
18. Granville Austin, *The Indian Constitution: the Corner Stone of a Nation* (Oxford: Clarendon Press 1966), p. 207.
19. The Draft Articles 280 and 280A (359 and 360) were debated on August 4 and 20, 1949. There was a long-drawn debate when these Articles came for approval. See *Constituent Assembly Debates* Volume IX, *Ibid.;* pp. 180-198 and pp. 523-554.
20. Dr. Punjabrao S. Deshmukh, *Ibid.*, August 4, 1949, pp. 183-184.
21. Shibban Lal Saxena, *Ibid.*, pp. 180-181.
22. H.V. Kamath, *Ibid.*, pp. 180-187.
23. *Ibid.*, pp. 387-388.
24. K.T. Shah, *Ibid.*, pp. 196-97.
25. Thakur Das Bhargava, *Ibid.*, pp. 527-528.
26. B.M. Munavalli, *Ibid.*, August 20, 1949, p. 529.
27. B.M. Gupte, *Ibid.*, p. 541.
28. Shibban Lal Saxena, *Ibid.*, pp. 541-542.
29. Mahavir Tyagi, *Ibid.;* August 4, 1949, pp. 541-542.
30. H.V. Kamath, *Ibid.*, August 20, 1949, p. 535.
31. H.V. Kamath, *Ibid.*, p. 535.
32. Naziruddin Ahmed, *Ibid.*, pp. 529-531.
33. *Ibid.*
34. K.T. Shah, *Ibid.*, pp. 539-540.
35. H.V. Kamath, *Ibid.*, pp. 535-539.
36. H.V. Kamath, *Ibid.*
37. R.K. Siddhava, *Ibid.*, p. 543.
38. H.V. Kamath, *Ibid.*, p. 543.
39. Pt. Thakurdas Bhargava, *Ibid.*, p. 543.
40. Alladi Krishnaswamy Ayyar, *Ibid.*, pp. 545-546.
41. H.V. Kamath, *Ibid.*, p. 546.
42. Shibban Lal Saxena, Draft Article 68A, (Article 83) *Constituent Assembly Debates*, Vol. III *Ibid.*; May. 18, 1949, pp. 87-88.
43. H.V. Kamath, *Constituent Assembly Debates*, Vol. IX, *Ibid.* August 20, 1949, pp. 545-547.

CHAPTER THREE

EMERGENCY IN OPERATION

"Autocratic power everywhere tends to perpetuate and entrench itself in the name of public good."

—***Chief Justice K. Subba Rao***

During the sixty years of Independence the security of India was threatened by external forces no less than four times. Soon after Independence in 1947, India was attacked by Pakistan in an attempt to conquer Kashmir. Simultaneously, the Nizam of Hyderabad geared his forces to seek independence along with the Nawab of Junagarh, while the other princely states demanded special status. The Government of India was able to deal with these grave problems effectively by foresighted statesmanship, restrained use of force and protected the security and integrity of India without resorting to emergency powers although the security and integrity of the country was threatened both from inside and outside. If it was a remarkable achievement, it also goes to the root of the matter. It raises an important question: Whether the existing normal powers are enough, or extraordinary powers in the form of emergency powers are necessary to protect the security of India.

EMERGENCY OF 1962

Nevertheless, the Constituent Assembly, despite reservations expressed by several members, adopted the emergency provisions in the Constitution. On September 7, 1962, China invaded the northern border of India. On October 25, 1962, orders were issued under the Foreigner's Act restricting the movement of Chinese nationals. On the next day i.e. October 26, 1962, the President of India issued a Proclamation under Article 352 that a grave emergency existed whereby the security of India was threatened by external aggression. Simultaneously, the President promulgated the Defence of India Ordinance as Parliament was not in session. The Proclamation of Emergency was approved by Parliament and the Ordinance was replaced by the Defence of India Act of 1962 and the Defence of India Rules of 1962 (DIR) framed under this Act were also adopted.

Four days after the declaration of emergency, the Presidential Order was issued under Article 359, which suspended the enforcement of the Right to move court under Articles 21 and 22 of the Constitution. But it was only applicable to foreigners and those also who were citizens by birth but not of Indian origin, subjects of the other country committing aggression against India or assisting such a country. Thus even persons who were Indian citizens by birth but of Chinese origin were deprived of the Right to Liberty under Articles 21 and 22. It was a notorious Order. It reminded one of the shameful incarceration of American citizens of Japanese origin when Japan attacked America during the 2nd World War.

During the Emergency a large number of communists were put under preventive detention under Rule 30(1)(b) of the Defence of India Rules. A group of 26 appeals by communists detained by the States of Punjab and Maharashtra came before the Supreme Court, and a special bench of seven judges was constituted as it involved the Right of Liberty during an Emergency. In the judgment delivered by the then Chief Justice, P.B. Gajendragadkar, with Justice K. Subba Rao dissenting, the majority held in the famous *Makkhan Singh Tirsika etc. Vs. State of Punjab etc,*[1] that the validity of the Presidential Order under Article 359 came for judicial scrutiny before the Supreme Court. Those under detention also questioned the validity of the Defence of India Act and the Rules under which they were being detained as these contravened Articles 14 and 21 and some provisions of Article 22. In this landmark judgment, the Supreme Court for the enforcement of Rights under Articles 14, 21 and 22, held that the detention under the Defence of India Act and Rules could not be challenged on the ground that the relevant provisions contravened the said Fundamental Right. But it also held that notwithstanding this bar, the Presidential Order left open the door for deciding (a) whether a person is deprived of any of his fundamental rights not covered by the order, (b) whether it is made under any law other than the Defence of India Act and Rules, (c) whether the detention order had been made in violation of mandatory provisions of the law, and (d) whether the order of detention was *mala-fide*? It was, therefore clear that the Presidential Order did not bar remedy in all cases and the court could interfere when there was abuse of power or the detention order was in violation of the provisions of the Act and Rules, or was *malafide*.

Justice K. Subba Rao in his dissent held that Article 359 empowered the President only to suspend the remedy to enforce Fundamental Rights. But it did not empower Parliament to enact law in violation of Fundamental Rights.[1]

Although the Chinese withdrew soon after and in a year's time conditions for the proclamation ceased to exist, Emergency was not withdrawn. And when Pakistan committed an aggression in August 1965 there was no need to proclaim a fresh emergency as the earlier one had not been revoked. The 21-day Indo-Pak War was over in September 1965, with the declaration of cease-fire and the Tashkent Agreement of 1966 between the two countries marked the official termination of hostilities. However, the emergency declared in 1962 was not withdrawn and the Executive continued to retain extraordinary powers.

Retention of such extraordinary emergency powers, when not required, have a corrupting influence. Instead of following the normal law, the officials of the Executive tend to use shortcuts and exhibit dangerous impatience to the normal process of law. The spirit of accountability of the Executive is eroded. But what is more harmful is that the general public gets used to accepting abnormal law as normal and meekly submits to the whims of the Executive. This in turn threatens the very foundation of the democratic ethos of India's Constitution.

In 1966, P.L. Lakhanpal, a journalist, and Gulam Sarwar[2] were detained under DIR. They challenged the continuance of the Proclamation of Emergency of 1962 on the grounds that the conditions justifying it had long ceased to exist and the continuance of the Emergency was intolerable and was *mala fide* exercise of power.[2] So did Bhutnnath Methe in 1974[3]. The Supreme Court in all these cases, rejected the contention on the ground that enough facts were not placed to prove the allegations, but the question whether the emergency could be challenged i.e. whether it is justiciable, was left open.[3]

To cite a few examples of abuse of emergency powers: a veneer factory in Assam, TV sets in Delhi were acquired under the DIR on the pretext that they were needed for the defence of India. In Kerala, an Esso dealer S. Sadanandan was detained under the DIR. When this action of the Executive was challenged in the Supreme Court, quashing the order of detention as having nothing to do with the security of India, and noticing the casual manner the emergency powers were being used, the Chief Justice, Gajendragadkar in 1966 issued a warning:

> We feel rudely disturbed by the thought that continuous exercise of the very wide powers conferred by the rules on several authorities is likely to make the conscience of the said authorities insensitive if not blunt to the paramount requirement of the Constitution that even during emergency the freedom of Indian citizens cannot be taken away without the existence of the justifying necessity specified in the rules themselves. The tendency to treat matters in a casual and cavalier manner which may conceivably result from the continuous use of such powers may ultimately pose a serious threat to the basic values on which the democratic way of life in this country is formed. It is time that cases of this kind though are rare, but even presence of such rare cases constitutes a warning to which we think it is our duty to invite attention of the appropriate authorities.[4]

EMERGENCY OF 1971

Perhaps, because of the aforesaid warning, the Government became aware that the emergency powers were being abused and withdrew the emergency on January 10, 1968, only to re-imposed it in 1971. The situation was grave. East Pakistan was smoldering under the terror let loose by the Pakistani forces. Thousands of refugees were coming into India. The proclamation of emergency in 1971 was followed by a Presidential Order under Article 359 suspending the enforcement of Fundamental Rights under Articles 14, 21 and 22. The Proclamation was approved by the Parliament unanimously. The entire nation stood behind the Government and gave it whatever powers it wanted to repulse the aggressor, in the hope that as soon as the threat ceased, the emergency would be revoked.

The Proclamation stated that a grave emergency existed whereby the security of India was threatened by external aggression. It was obvious that as soon as the aggression ceased the *raison d etre* for its continuance also ceased. It was equally clear that "internal disturbance" could not be a ground for the continuance of emergency. Furthermore, the expression "grave emergency" in Article 352 (1), "imminent danger" in Article 352 (3) shows that their existence is a pre-condition for the declaration as well as the continuance of an emergency.

A chronology of the events would show that this emergency was not only continued beyond the time that the Constitution warranted, but was also used for purposes other than mentioned in the Proclamation.

Within a fortnight of the Proclamation, Bangladesh was liberated and India announced a unilateral ceasefire on December 16, 1971. On the following day, Pakistan accepted India's offer of the ceasefire and the hostilities ceased.

Within two months of the cessation of hostilities, conditions were so normal that general elections for State Assemblies were held in several States, such as Madhya Pradesh, Maharashtra and even in the border States of Rajasthan and Punjab. The Shimla Pact, which was a peace treaty, and which marked the official conclusion of hostilities between India and Pakistan, was signed on June 3, 1972.

As per Clause 3 of this agreement, both India and Pakistan agreed to normalize their relations. There was also progressive normalization of Indo-Pakistan relations. Within a month of the treaty the conquered territories were returned. The agreement to exchange prisoners of war was signed on August 28, 1972 and their repatriation was completed by April 30, 1974. Both the countries resumed postal and telecommunication services, signed a Visa Agreement and Protocol on Visits to Religious Shrines on November 4, 1974.

Furthermore, on November 24, 1974, a trade agreement was signed lifting the trade embargo following the Indo-Pakistan War of 1965 after a period of nine years. The two countries also agreed to give "the most favoured nation treatment to each other".

In this four-year intervening period there had also been general elections in U.P. in February 1974, and the Presidential election. All this was conclusive proof of the return to normalcy.

Even Prime Minister Indira Gandhi, could not justify the continuance of the Emergency on the basis of reasons given in the Proclamation of December 3, 1971. In a reply to a question at a press conference held on June 15, 1974, she admitted "...There may not be a war emergency but I think the economic emergency is just severe for a country as it ought to be in war time." Similarly the Deputy Home Minister in the Lok Sabha on August 21, 1974 stated, "The question of continuance of the Emergency was being reviewed in the light of security considerations, progress of normalization of relations with Pakistan and *overall economic situation* in the country."

The Home Minister, Uma Shankar Dixit stated in the Lok Sabha on September 9, 1974, that the Government was taking recourse to the "provisions of DIR for dealing with anti-social elements whose activities were prejudicial to the larger *economic* interests of the nation." He asserted that several quarters, including Members of Parliament, advocated the use of DIR for dealing with economic problems.

As Article 352 does not permit the declaration of Emergency for economic reasons, or for progressive normalization of relations, the continuance of emergency was *ultra vires,* besides being a *mala fide* abuse of powers. Extraordinary powers were given to meet an extraordinary situation created by the Pakistani aggression. To retain and use these powers in violation of Fundamental Rights, for reasons unconnected with the Proclamation, was not only a clear subversion of our democratic Constitution, but also a betrayal of the trust people reposed in the government to meet an external threat to the security of India.

This enlargement of the scope of the Emergency by the Executive without the consent of Parliament further indicates the respect that the Government had for this august body. It needs to be mentioned here that even Parliament could not enlarge the scope of the emergency or permit its continuance for reasons extraneous to either Article 352 or the Proclamation of Emergency of December 3, 1971.

In view of the fact that the Constitution specifically provides for financial emergency, *vide* Article 360, economic grounds could not be a justification for continuing the emergency proclaimed under Article 352 (1). Moreover, the reading of Article 360 shows that when a financial emergency is proclaimed, the democratic process is not suspended as it does not contemplate suspension of Article 19; nor does the executive have the powers to suspend the enforcement of any of the Fundamental Rights. The fact that the Government tried to justify the continuance of the Emergency for economic grounds and yet did not proclaim emergency under Article 360 shows its ulterior motive to retain its power of violating Fundamental Rights.

The Emergency was continued not because of any threat to the security of India but to avert any threat to the ruling party. It was a cloak to achieve indirectly what one could not do directly and as such the continuance of the Emergency was not only unconstitutional and *mala fide* but also an intolerable exercise of power by the Executive in violation of the Fundamental Rights enshrined in the Constitution.

By 1975, restlessness against the abuse of emergency powers was growing. In 1973, DIR was used to break the railway strike. In 1974, Nanaji Deshmukh, General Secretary of the Bharatiya Jana Sangha, was externed from Bihar because he supported a rally held under the leadership of Jayaprakash Narain. As he was externed under Rule 11 of the Defence of India Rules, which owed its existence to the Emergency, he challenged the Externment Order and the continuance of the Emergency of 1971 as a *mala fide* and unconstitutional exercise of power, before the Supreme Court. Instead of meeting the challenge, the Government revoked the Externment Order and the petition became infructuous.

Similarly, the continuance of the Emergency was challenged by one detenue, Bhutnath Mehte, and the Supreme Court held that the petitioner had not discharged the burden that there are no grounds whatever for the satisfaction of the President to continue the Emergency. However, in this case Justice Krishna Iyer observed, "Appeal should be to polls and not courts."[3] Just as in *Makhan Singh's case* Chief Justice Gajendragadker had said, "Public opinion was the best safeguard against this abuse of emergency powers.[2]

These observations, however, presume that the right of creating public opinion is available during an Emergency. But this is not so.

The instrumentalities, through which public opinion is created, like the freedom of expression, association, movement etc., contained in Article 19, stand suspended during an emergency under Article 352. The Executive has the power to prevent the creation of public opinion on a subject it does not approve. This being so, it is an illusory, and not a guaranteed remedy available to the citizens during an Emergency.

Similarly, when Article 19 is not available the right of "appeal to the poll" as suggested by Justice Krishna Iyer can also become an academic solution. How can there be elections, as we understand them, if the Government tampers with Fundamental Rights under Article 19 and opposition workers are not allowed the freedom of expression, movement, etc.?

In our Constitution, the Judiciary is made a watchdog of the Constitution and has a duty to protect the citizen against infringement of his Fundamental Rights by the Executive, as well as by legislative action. When the action of the Executive is an unconstitutional exercise of power or *mala fide* abuse of power, as has been shown above, by the continuance of the Emergency amounted to abridgment of Fundamental Rights. There is nothing to prevent the Judiciary coming to the rescue of the citizen.

By early 1975, it had become obvious that the Government was not prepared to revoke the Emergency declared in 1971, and was abusing the emergency powers to suppress the voice of dissent. Opposition to unjustified and indefinite continuance of Emergency began to grow. Not only the opposition political parties, but also the press, the legal community, students and labour unions began to demand its revocation. In March 1975, a seminar, *Emergency in the Constitution and Democracy*, attended by former judges of the Supreme Court, jurists, lawyers, journalists and leaders of several political parties passed a resolution that the continuance of the Emergency of 1971, was an unjustified and unconstitutional exercise of power. The former Chief Justice of India, K. Subba Rao, who inaugurated the seminar, warned the country, "Absolute despotism is within the realm of probability" and Jayprakash Narain gave a national call to observe April 6, 1975 as *Revoke Emergency Day* and led a massive rally in the Capital.

INTERNAL EMERGENCY OF 1975

On June 20, 1975, the Allahabad High Court gave a historic judgment setting aside the election of Prime Minister Indira Gandhi on the ground of corrupt practices. Immediately, the opposition parties demanded her resignation. This demand had sympathisers in the ruling Congress also. In fact Indira Gandhi herself had made Dr. Chenna Reddy, Chief Minister of Andhra Pradesh, and D.P. Mishra, Chief Minister of M.P., relinquish their Chief Ministerships when their elections were set aside for corrupt practices by the High Courts, pending the decision of their appeals in the Supreme Court.

As expected, Indira Gandhi appealed to the Supreme Court against the judgment of the Allahabad High Court and prayed for absolute stay. On June 24, 1975, Justice Krishna Iyer, then a Vacation Judge, following the well established practice granted only conditional stay of the judgment of the High Court as she was unseated for corrupt practices. However, he observed that being a Prime Minister she could still participate in the proceedings of Parliament. Nevertheless demand for her resignation continued to grow and the Sangharsha Samiti led by Jaiprakash Narain called a public meeting on June 26, 1975, to protest against Indira Gandhi's continuance as the Prime Minister. There was no violence or even a law and order problem anywhere in the country.

For the first time in the history of independent India, on the night of June 25-26, 1975, the President proclaimed an emergency on the ground that the security of India had been threatened by 'internal disturbance'. The President also issued the Defence of India Internal Security Ordinance. This was the darkest period in Indian democracy. All opposition leaders all over the country, including persons like Jaiprakash Narain, Morarji Desai, Atal Bihari Vajpayee, L.K. Advani, Charan Singh, Madhu Dandavate, Jyotirmoy Basu, Madhu Limaye, Piloo Modi were arrested alongwith hundreds of political leaders and workers and were detained under the Maintenance of Internal Security Act—MISA. Even the M.Ps. of the ruling party, like Chandra Shekhar, Ram Dhan and Sher Singh, also the editors and artists who wanted Indira Gandhi to step down till the Supreme Court decided her appeal, were not spared. Electricity in the capital was deliberately shut off so that press could not report the events of that fateful night. Unprecedented press censorship was imposed. The country was kept in the dark about the happenings in the country. Moreover, the emergency was proclaimed without consulting the Council of Ministers who were presented with the *fate accompli* on the morning of June 26, 1975. An atmosphere of suspicion and fear pervaded the country. Within four months, Justice Subba Rao's prophecy, "Absolute despotism is within the realm of probability", became a reality. The Maintenance of Internal Security Act (MISA) which empowered preventive detention and press censorship were the main weapons used to silence all the opposition and voice of descent. This was the bleakest period of our democracy.

As an Advocate, I represented more than 300 detenues and visited more than 12 jails. If I was a witness to some poignant movements, I also shared many a humorous occasion.

K.R. Malkani, the Chief Editor of *The Mother Land* was the first to be arrested. Nobody knew his whereabouts or the order under which he was taken into custody. On the same day i.e., June 26, I filed the *habeas corpus* petition under Article 32 in the Supreme Court on behalf of his wife Mrs. Sundari Malkani with an application for legal interview. When the petition came for hearing before the Bench presided by Justice V.R. Krishna Iyer, he issued notice. At that time the Solicitor General Lal Narain Sinha appearing for the government stated that Malkani was arrested under the MISA and detained in the Hissar Jail. He also pointed out that Clause-3 of Article 22 specifically denied him the right to engage and defended by a lawyer of his choice to a person detained under preventive detention laws or in contrast to others arrested for criminal offences under Clauses 1 and 2 of Article 22. However, he said that Dr. Ghatate would be allowed legal interview with Malkani in jail, "As a grace not as a right". I (author) immediately applied to the government for permission to meet Malkani. After about one month, I was given the permission.

Next day on June 27, 1975, Fundamental Rights under Articles 14, 21 and 22 were suspended by a Presidential Order under Article 359 of the Constitution. Two days later on June 29 an ordinance amending the MISA was issued, adding Section 16A, which amongst other things added that if a person was detained under MISA on 25th of June or after, and the authorities were satisfied that his detention was necessary for dealing effectively with the emergency, the order of detention had to be reviewed every four months and he was not entitled to get grounds of detention or make representation to the Advisory Board to obtain his release. Furthermore, the grounds of detention and material on which the detention order was passed shall be treated as confidential and no one shall be allowed to disclose them to any authority,[1] thereby stripping the defence of his right to make representation to the Advisory Board as guaranteed by clauses 4 and 5 of Article 22. Thus detenues could not seek their liberty either by challenging the grounds of detention through filing a *habeas corpus* petition in the Supreme Court or by making representation against their detention to the detaining authority or the Advisory Board.

When Malkani's petition came after notice before the Supreme Court, the Solicitor General Lal Narain Sinha informed the Court that as the above Articles were suspended, the petition under Article 32 was not maintainable. I therefore took the permission to withdraw the petition of Mr. Malkani and file it before the High Court, under Article 226.

When the Internal Emergency was declared, Atalji, Advaniji, Shri Shyam Nandan Mishra and Shri Madhu Dandavate, all M.Ps., were in Bangalore in connection with Parliamentary work and were staying in the MLA Hostel. When Karnataka police came to arrest them, Shyam Babu was doing his morning yoga. When the police entered his room, he was doing his *sirsasan* (head stand, a yoga exercise) and when he was informed about his arrest, Shyam Babu staying in the same position asked the police, "Where is the arrest warrant?" As the Police did not have any such warrant, they said they were arresting him under Section 151 of Cr.P.C. where the police have the power to arrest without warrant if they have an apprehension that a person is likely to commit a cognizable offence such as murder, dacoity, house breaking etc. Shri S.N. Mishra objected to such an arrest as they were respected leaders of political parties and asked them to get the proper arrest warrants. He said, "I will not come unless you bring the warrant." So they went back and prepared the warrant which read "Shri S.N. Mishra, M.P. son of so and so, ..." There was another S.N. Mishra who was also an M.P. from U.P. whose father's name was inserted in the warrant.

When Shyam Babu read the warrant, he said, "I am not that father's son." So the police respectfully asked, "What is your father's name Sir?" He replied, "Why should I tell you? Find it from the Parliament's Directory."

It was 10 O'clock by then, and the police had not even taken their morning tea. The Police Inspector then told Atalji, "If Shri Mishraji does not come, we will have to physically take him to the Police Station." At that time Atalji said, "Shyam Babu let us go to our *sasural.*" (father-in-law's house). In the Indian culture the son-in-law gets a royal treatment at his in-laws place.*

On the same evening of his arrest on 26th June, Shri L.K. Advani wrote a letter (Plate 1) to me along with a copy of the order of detention under MISA which was signed by the Police Commissioner and served at 7 P.M. (Copy of the facsimile of this letter is produced). It may be mentioned that these four detenues in Bangalore were the only detenues who were detained for activities prejudicial to the security of India in contrast to others who were detained for activities prejudicial to public order.

I informed Shri Advani that I would come to see him in Bangalore. On July 1, 1975, Shri Advani sent a telegram to me stating, "Kindly bring woollens from residences of Atalji, Mishraji and Dandvate. Also Atalji's medical reports." (Copy of the facsimile is produced). It may be mentioned that Bangalore becomes quite chilly after the rains even in June.

When I went to Bangalore jail to see them, I was surprised to see Atalji wearing warm jail clothes. I exclaimed, "Atalji what is all this" and he replied, "Now Indira Gandhi will feed me and Indira Gandhi will give me clothes. I am not going to spend a penny from my pocket."

I told him that I had drafted a *habeas corpus* petition challenging the detention, as also the MISA Ordinance of 1975 and also the Emergency of 1971 and 1975. But there was difference of opinion among the then Opposition parties whether we should approach the court. Some leaders thought that as in the 1942 Quit India Movement, we should not. His immediate reaction was:

> This is 1975, not 1942. We are in an independent country. Courts are ours. If we do not knock at the doors of the Judiciary, tomorrow the judges might say, "We would have given relief, if you had approached us." We must make the judiciary face and acid test.

But whatever his personal opinion he believes in decision by consensus and immediately he said, "Let me consult others also." They all decided to approach the High Court. Hegde and I, who later retired as a Judge of the Supreme Court, redrafted the *habeas corpus* petition which was settled by Justice K. Subba Rao, former Chief Justice of India, and Justice K.S. Hegde, former Supreme Court Judge, who was superseded; and was also living in Bangalore and these four writ petitions were filed by Santhosh Hegde in the Karnataka High Court.

In these four *habeas corpus* petitions the detenues challenged the orders of the Police Commissioner as the orders of detention were *malafide* and illegal as there could be no incriminatory material before the Police Commissioner to warrant their detention. It was also contended that he had ordered the detention not on the basis of his personal satisfaction as required under the MISA but on the orders of the Central Government because hundreds like them had been arrested all over the country on the night of June 25-26, 1975. These petitioners also challenged the MISA Ordinance which deprived them of their right to know the grounds of detention and of making representation to the Advisory Board as invalid as Ordinance could not be made in violation of Fundamental Rights.

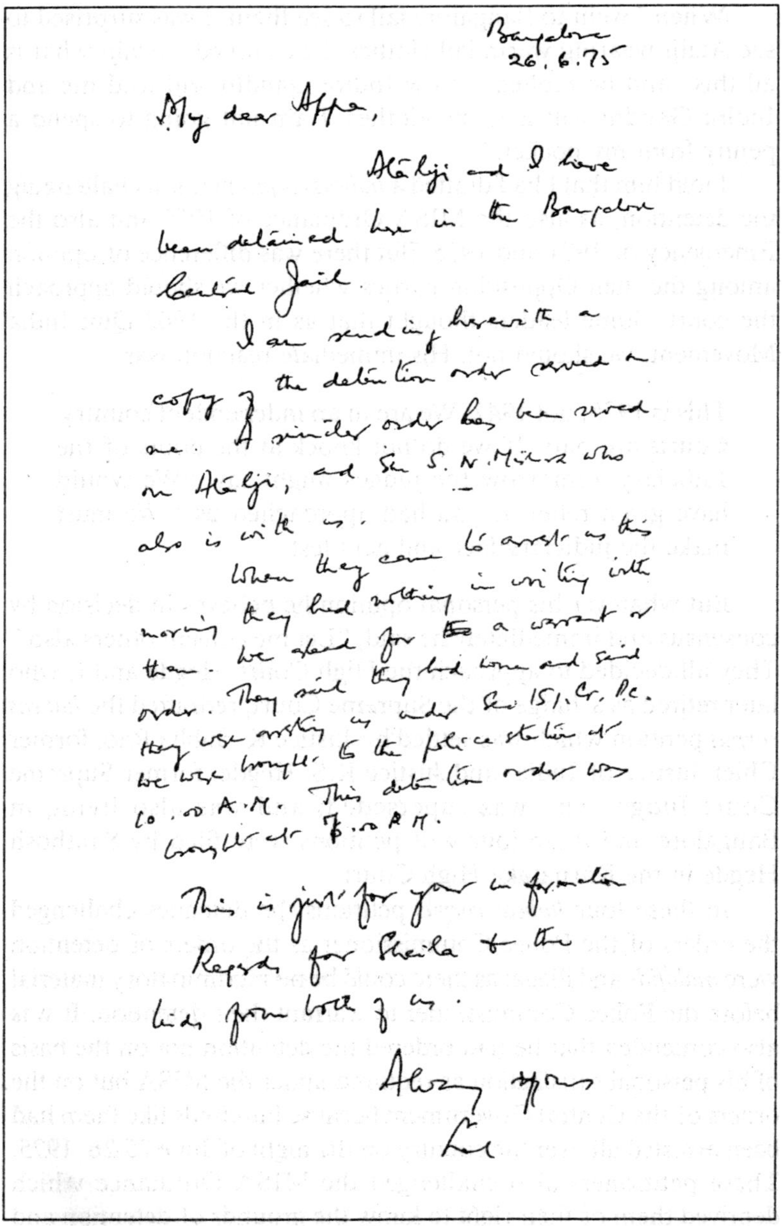

Bangalore
26.6.75

My dear Appa,

Atalji and I have been detained here in the Bangalore Central Jail.

I am sending herewith a copy of the detention order served on me. A similar order has been served on Atalji, and Shri S. N. Mishra who also is with us.

When they came to arrest us this morning they had nothing in writing with them. We asked for a warrant or order. They said they had come and said they were arresting us under Sec 151, Cr. P.C. We were brought to the police station at 10.00 A.M. This detention order was brought at 7.00 P.M.

This is just for your information.

Regards for Sheila & the kids from both of us.

Always yours
Lal

Plate 1: Advani's letter dated 26.6.75 (see typed version on next page)

Bangalore
26.6.75

My dear Appa,

Atalji and I have been detained here in the Bangalore Central Jail.

I am sending herewith a copy of the detention order served on me. A similar order has been served on Atalji, and Shri S.N. Mishra who also is with us.

When they came to arrest us this morning they had nothing in writing with them. We asked for a warrant or order. They said they had none and said they were arresting us under Sec. 151 Cr.PC. We were brought to the police station at 10.00 A.M. This detention order was brought at 7.00 P.M.

This is just for your information.

Regards for Sheila and the kids from both of us.

Affectionately yours,

Sd/-
(L.K. Advani)

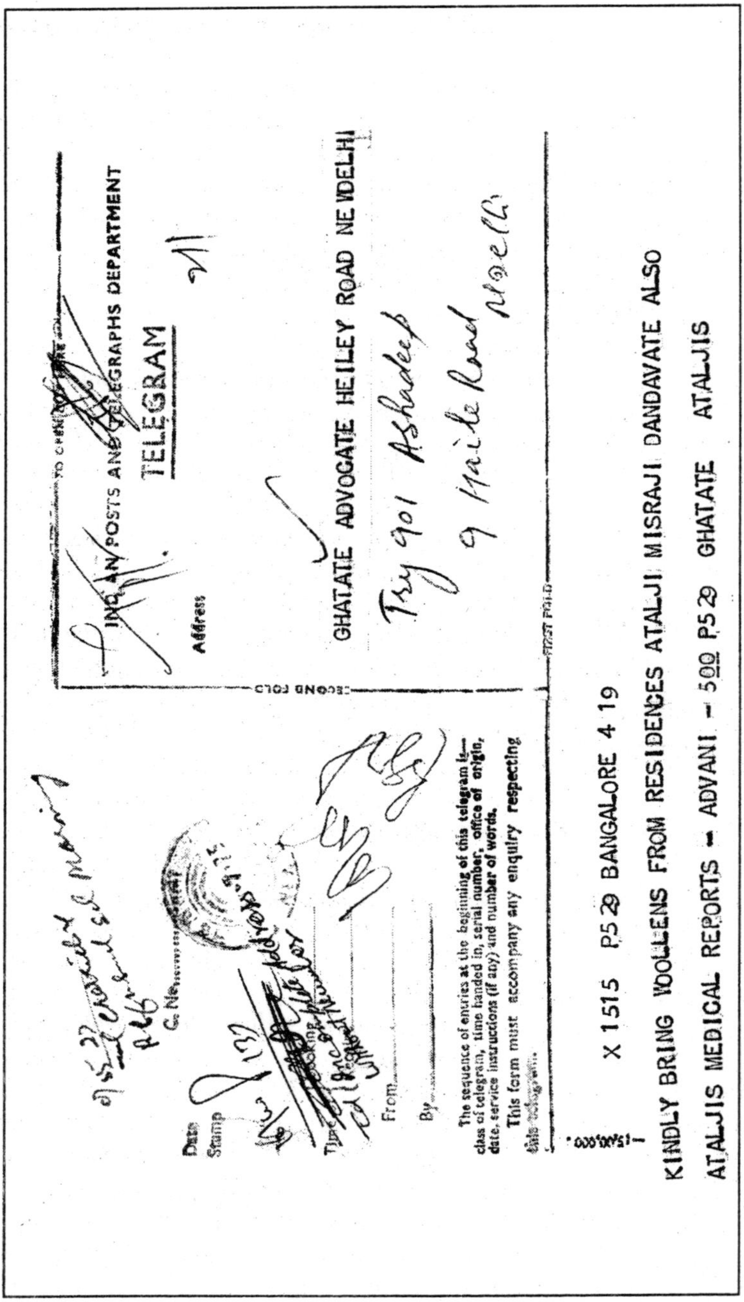

INDIAN POSTS AND TELEGRAPHS DEPARTMENT

TELEGRAM

Address

GHATATE ADVOCATE HEILEY ROAD NEWDELHI

X 1515 P5 29 BANGALORE 4 19

KINDLY BRING WOOLLENS FROM RESIDENCES ATALJI MISRAJI DANDAVATE ALSO ATALJIS MEDICAL REPORTS - ADVANI - 500 P5 29 GHATATE ATALJIS

The sequence of entries at the beginning of this telegram is—class of telegram, time handed in, serial number, office of origin, date, service instructions (if any) and number of words.

This form must accompany any enquiry respecting this telegram.

Plate 2: Advani's telegram dated 26.6.75 (see typed version on next page)

Indian Posts & Telegraphs Department

Telegram

I.7.75

Ghatate Advocate Heiley Road New Delhi

TRY, 901 Ashadeep
9, Hailey Road
New Delhi

X 1515 P529 Bangalore 49

Kindly bring woollens from residences Atalji Misraji Dandavate also Ataljis medical reports—
Advani—500 P 529

They squarely challenged the continuance of the Emergency of 1971 and also the Proclamation of Emergency of 1975 as being *mala fide*, gross abuse of power and unconstitutional. All the facts beginning from 1971, which have been mentioned earlier, were cited to support their contention regarding the continuance of the Emergency of 1971, while the history of political developments beginning with the Allahabad High Court Judgment were narrated to show the *malafide* intention in proclaiming Internal Emergency. The Proclamation of Emergency of 1975, was also challenged on the ground that it was made without the advice of the Council of Ministers as required by Article 74 of the Constitution. Following their cue, hundreds of *habeas corpus* petitions were filed in various High Courts. In some petitions, the power to issue second proclamation under Article 352 was also challenged as one was already in force.

On June 4, the Rashtriya Swyamsevak Sangha (RSS), Jamait-e-Islami and about twenty other organizations were banned under the Defence of India Rules (DIR) and hundreds of their workers and their leaders were detained under the MISA multiplying the number of *habeas corpus* petitions in the High Courts. Some detention orders were issued in the names of persons who were long dead. For example in the name of Shri Bhayyaji Dani, late General Secretary and Shri Appaji Joshi, a prominent leader of RSS of Vidharba. Detention of hundreds of persons all over the country on the night of June 25-26 coupled with the facts that even detention orders were issued in the names of dead persons further underscored that detention orders were issued without verification hurriedly and were not made on the satisfaction of the detaining authorities as required by the MISA, but on the orders of the Central Government.

During the 1975 Emergency, it had become a common practice to revoke the detention order as soon as it was found to be unsustainable and replace it by a fresh detention order. Similarly, to defeat the bail application of persons arrested under the DIR, the authorities often issued detention orders under the MISA as it did not permit bail.

It was quite obvious that detenues in Bangalore would seriously challenge the Emergency and the MISA which had become the foundation of the dictatorial power of the Prime Minister, Indira Gandhi, and the Government used every available method to thwart the challenge.

When the *habeas corpus* petition of Atal Bihari Vajpayee and other three M.P.s came for admission before the Karnataka High Court, they requested that their petitions be disposed of before 21st July to enable them to attend the session of Parliament, which was scheduled to meet on that day.

The Advocate General, Karnataka asked for an adjournment. The Chief Justice rejected the plea for an adjournment with the telling observation:

> In England, *habeas corpus* petitions are required to be taken up for hearing within 48 hours. In (a) *habeas corpus* petition, in which the liberty of an individual is involved, the State must file its objection forthwith.

These petitions were posted at the top of the list for final hearing on July 17, 1975. On that day the petitions were admitted. Advani filed an additional ground against the proclamation of the second Emergency that it was violative of Article 74 for it was signed by the President on 25th June 1975 but was placed before the Council of Ministers on the next day, i.e. on 26th June 1975. Thus in fact, the proclamation was signed by the President, without any advice from the Council of Ministers in contravention of Article 74.

The Central Government was not prepared to face the Court, and abusing its powers, played an administrative trick. Just a few hours before the hearing of the petitions, the orders of detention on June 26, 1975 were revoked and fresh orders of detention signed by an official of the Union Home Ministry on July 17 of 1975, were served on all the four detenues. They were released and held again under the new orders of detention..

When the High Court assembled to hear the case, the Attorney General, Niren Dey, who had specifically come to appear for this case, took the plea that these petitions had become infructuous since the impunged orders of detention dated June 26, 1975 were already revoked by the Government. The petitioners now were left with only the recourse to file fresh *habeas corpus* petitions and the High Court was prevented from disposing of the petitions before July 21, 1975, so that these detenues could attend the Parliament.

To facilitate the detenues, the Court gave the following orders:

> The detenues who are present before us made a submission that the Superintendent General of Jail, Bangalore, should be directed to afford them all reasonable facility to take the assistance of their lawyers, Sri M. Rama Jois, N. Santosh Hegde and K.G. Maheswarappa.
>
> The Attorney General has no objection to our making an order that all such facilities should be made available to the detenues. It is ordered accordingly. Let a copy of their order be sent to the Superintendent, Central Jail, and Bangalore forthwith.

All that the High Court could do was to allow the prayer of the detenues to take legal assistance to file fresh petitions. But the High Court also recorded that the Attorney General 'has no objection to making such order.'

But this order of the Court was circumvented by the Government by hurriedly transferring L.K. Advani, S.N. Mishra and Madhu Dandavate to Rohtak Jail in Haryana, by a special Air Force plane that very afternoon. The Central Government wanted to shift Vajpayee also, although he had been operated a day earlier. But this could not be done as the doctors of the Victoria Hospital refused to discharge him.

It is relevant to note that under section 5(b) of the MISA, the Government has the power to transfer a detenue from one State to another, but the proviso to this clause requires that prior approval of the concerned State should be obtained. Since the detenues were flown to a Haryana jail within hours of the assurance given by the Attorney General to the High Court, one wonders if prior permission of the Haryana Government had been obtained at all and if it was, why was this fact deliberately concealed from the Court?

Next day, i.e. on 18th July, a fresh *habeas corpus* petition on behalf of Vajpayee was filed in the High Court by M. Rama Joise, explaining the circumstances in which the other three petitioners had been removed from the jurisdiction of the High Court and praying that the government be restrained from shifting Vajpayee from Bangalore.[6]

The Division Bench of the High Court, consisting of the Chief Justice Govind Bhatt and Justice E.S. Venkatramaiah passed an order restraining the Government from 'removing the petitioner from Bangalore city, without the leave of this Court' and also allowed the earlier Vajpayee's advocate to file additional ground for a fresh *habeas corpus* petition since petition had been filed in a hurry to block the Central Government's attempt to delay the hearing of the writ petition by removing Vajpayee outside its jurisdiction. However, since Vajpayee's health deteriorated, the court directed the government on August 6 to remove him to the All India Institute of Medical Sciences, New Delhi, for treatment.

When these three leaders were flown from Bangalore Jail to Rohtak Jail, it was evening and raining cats and dogs. The jailor after taking them into custody started examining Shyam Babu's torn chappal to find if any blade or sharp instrument had been hidden in it. Piloo Modi, who was also in the Rohtak Jail came to the Jailor's office to meet these leaders. He remarked, to the laughter of all present, "Mr. Jailor, Indira Gandhi has said that the opposition should search their soul—SOUL and not their sole—SOLE".*

I visited Advaniji a number of times in the Rohtak Jail. Once, while I was waiting for him to come to the Jailor's office, the Jailor gave me an interesting news that in the morning even Piloo Modi's dogs had come to interview him. And he showed me a copy of the letter written by Piloo Modi to Indira Gandhi. It read:

> "My dear I.G. (*read* Indira Gandhi),
>
> Under the Conditions of Detention Order, I am allowed to meet my family members once in a fortnight. I have a wife and no children except two Irish Setter dogs. They should be treated as my family and also allowed the interview.
>
> Thanking you,
> Yours faithfully,
> Sd/-
> P.M. (*read* Piloo Modi)"

Indira Gandhi knew his background. Besides being a leading architect, who designed Chandigarh with the French architect Corbusier, he was known for his great sense of humour. Piloo Modi was also a close friend of Pakistan's Prime Minister Zulfikar Ali Bhutto and after the 1971 War, during the negotiation Indira Gandhi had invited him to Shimla. Therefore, perhaps Indira Gandhi granted his unusual request to be interviewed by his pets. It may be mentioned that even L.K. Advani admired Piloo Modi—who was used to luxuries for his adjustment to prison inconveniences.

When the Parliament assembled on July 21, 1975, with most of the opposition members behind bars, a willing Council of Ministers, a captive Parliament and the press gagged, the approval of the Proclamation of Emergency was a foregone conclusion. Next, the Government tabled a Constitutional Amendment Bill to amend Emergency Powers, which later came to be known as the 38th Constitutional Amendment Act, 1975. By this amendment two new clauses 4 and 5 were inserted in Article 352, which empowered the President to issue a proclamation when one proclamation was already in operation, and made the satisfaction of the President to proclaim an emergency as "final and conclusive", i.e. the President's satisfaction was made non-justiciable. Furthermore, this clause specifically barred the Supreme Court or any High Court from entertaining the question of the validity of "the Proclamation of the Emergency or continued operation of such a Proclamation on any ground whatsoever". Article 359 was also amended to give Parliament the power to make laws in violation of Fundamental Rights during the operation of the Emergency. Both these Articles were amended with retrospective effect. Similarly, the MISA Amendment Ordinance, which has been mentioned earlier, was replaced by an Act.[7]

The Parliament also passed the government—sponsored motion to delete Rules relating to the Question Hour, Calling Attention and other business initiated by private members. Thus all opposition to Government policies was scotched. To avert any challenge to pre-censorship of the press and publication of any news against the Government, Prevention of Objectionable Matters Act was passed. The Government thus acquired full powers to stop any adverse publication, including the proceedings of Parliament in spite of Parliamentary Proceedings of Publication Act of 1956.

Apprehending that some loopholes might still have been left unplugged, the Constitution was again amended on August 10 and 27, 1975, by the 39th and 40th Constitutional Amendment Act. This measure included the MISA and other detention laws, *viz.,* the Conservation of Foreign Exchange and Preventive of Smuggling Activities Act (COFEPOSA), in the 9th Schedule of the Constitution to forestall any challenge to the provisions of the MISA or COFEPOSA for violation of any of the Fundamental Rights. By these Amendment Acts as many as 102 Acts were put in the 9th Schedule hurriedly, in a day, including the Representation of Peoples Act of 1951. In addition, Prevention of Publication of Objectionable Materials Act Constitutional Amendment Act were included.[8]

If these amendments to the Constitution and MISA show how desperate the Government was to avoid a judicial scrutiny of the emergency and detentions, it also reveals that the legislators had totally abdicated their constitutional duty of controlling the Executive and had become servile. Thus the *de-facto* dictator became a *de-jure* dictator.

Courtsey *The States,* 15-29 March, 1975, Fortnightly

Advaniji asked me to visit him and draft a fresh petition challenging the fresh order of detention dated 17th July, the 38th and 39th Constitutional Amendments and the Amendment of the MISA. When I visited him, he objected to the jail authorities about going beyond hearing distance since he was consulting his advocate. After they left I told him, "Under Clause 3 of Article 22 the person detained under the Preventive Detention Law has no right to engage and be defended by the lawyer of his choice which is available to ordinary prisoners," and showed him the provision. But I was allowed to get a legal interview as a grace of the government and not as a Fundamental Right. This was the position even before the suspension of Fundamental Rights under Article 22. However, it may be mentioned that throughout the Emergency as an Advocate, I was always given permission to meet the detenues.

In early August, 1975, when I went to meet Malkani at Hissar Jail, his wife told me that she had not received any letter from her husband. When Malkani came to meet me in the Jailor's office, he was in a sulky mood and told the Jailor, "Start your tape recorder." He started criticizing the government for imposing a fake Emergency etc. He also told me that he had not received any reply from his wife, though he had sent her several letters.

After he had gone back to his cell, I asked the Jailor why they were not receiving any letters. He replied, "Sir, Mr. Malkani writes 'My dear Sundari' and the letters are full of criticism of Mrs. Indira Gandhi and Emergency which I have to censor and what remains is only 'Your Kewal'. Similar are Mrs. Malkani's letters. So how can I send them to Mrs. Malkani or her letters to Mr. Malkani? But if Mrs. Malkani sends any sweets etc. I will immediately deliver them to Mr. Malkani."

As mentioned earlier, in August, 1975, Atalji was moved from Bangalore jail to AIIMS in Delhi for treatment. On August 13, 1975, he wrote me a letter (Plate 3) asking me to see him. (Copy of the facsimile letter is enclosed). Pradipto Ghosh, who was then the Additional District Magistrate (South) had given me permission to meet him. When I went to see Atalji, he asked., "Who is my *malik* (boss) here?" When I asked what he meant, he said, "When I was in Bangalore, the Jailor would provide daily needed items like soap, toothpaste etc. plus postcards. Here I get nothing." I told Mr. Ghosh about Atalji's grievance and from that time his basic needs were made available to him.

At the AIIMS, Atalji was diagnosed for spinal problem and surgery was recommended. One important underground leader told me to tell him that it was a very delicate operation, and instead he should go to Bombay where there was a Parsi gentleman who kicks and cures spinal problems. When I gave him this message he laughed and said, "Indiraji is already kicking me. Why do you want one more person to kick me?"

Rajmata Scindia who was detained in Pachmarhi in M.P. was transferred to Tihar Jail sometime in September 1975, and kept in the women's ward along with Maharani Gayatri Devi. When I went to see her in the Tihar Jail, she asked me to send clothes, particularly towels as they had to share towels with other female inmates, including sex workers. She narrated a nauseating fact about jail authorities and police officers visiting their ward and ogling at the beauty of Maharani Gayatri Devi as if she was an animal in a zoo.

All the four leaders, Vajpayee from Bangalore with the assistance of M Rama Joise, and Advani, Dandavate and Mishra from Rohtak Jail, filed fresh petitions before the Karnataka High Court challenging the MISA Amendment Act and both the Constitutional Amendment Acts which amended Emergency Powers as violative of the basic structure of the Constitution. They contended that these amendments went beyond the amending power of Parliament as they excluded judicial review which was a basic feature of the Constitution. With a view to forcing the Government to face the High Court, whose orders it had circumvented, the leaders who were transferred to Haryana requested for a personal appearance. The High Court was perhaps rudely disturbed over the circumvention of their order by the Central Government. While posting the case for the final hearing on September 29, 1975, the court ordered that these three leaders in Rohtak Jail be produced before the Court three days before so that they could file a rejoinder to the Government's reply to their petitions.

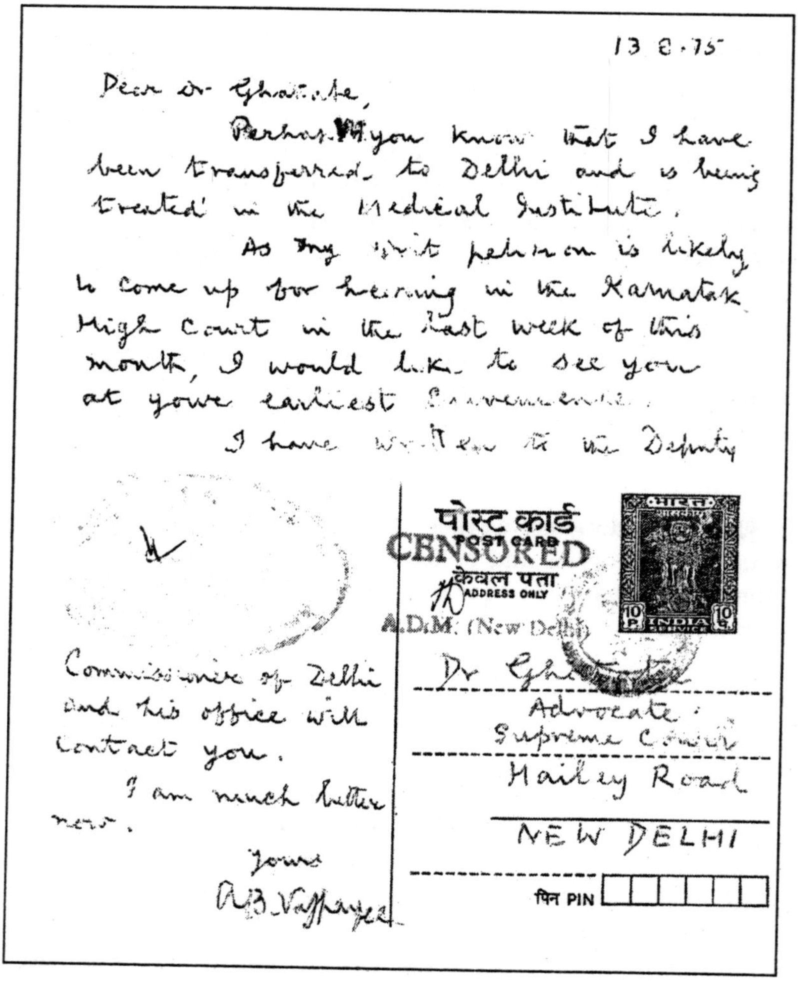

13.8.75

Dear Dr. Ghatate,

Perhaps you know that I have been transferred to Delhi and is being treated in the Medical Institute.

As my writ petition is likely to come up for hearing in the Karnatak High Court in the last week of this month, I would like to see you at your earliest convenience.

I have written to the Deputy Commissioner of Delhi and his office will contact you.

I am much better now.

Yours

A.B. Vajpayee

पोस्ट कार्ड
POST CARD
CENSORED
केवल पता
ADDRESS ONLY
A.D.M. (New Delhi)

Dr Ghatate
Advocate
Supreme Court
Hailey Road
NEW DELHI

पिन PIN

Plate 3: Vajpayee's Letter Dated 13.8.75 (see typed version on next page)

13.8.75

Dear Dr. Ghatate,

Perhaps you know that I have been transferred to Delhi and is being treated in the Medical Institute.

As my writ petition is likely to come up for hearing in the Karnatak High Court in the last week of this month, I would like to see you at your earliest convenience.

I have written to the Deputy Commissioner of Delhi and his office will contact you.

I am much better now.

Yours

Sd/-
(Atal Bihari Vajpayee)

Santosh Hegde and I went to Bombay to request M.C. Chagla to argue for Atalji and others. He readily accepted our request. When we were going with him to Bangalore, he said, "Tomorrow is my 75th birthday, and my family was very keen that I should stay with them to celebrate the birthday, but is there a better way to celebrate the birthday than by fighting for democracy and liberty?" That evening I went to Bangalore jail and told Advaniji that Chagla has come and tomorrow is his birthday. L.K. Advani brought a rose from the jail and giving the rose to Chagla, said, "Roses of September". Obvious reference was to Chagla's book *Roses of December,* which one reviewer had described it, "As all roses without thorns".

When these *habeas corpus* petitions came for hearing before the Karnataka High Court, Niren De for the Government raised a preliminary objection which was raised in every High Court, as to the maintainability of the *habeas corpus* petition in view of the Presidential Order suspending Articles 21 and 22. It was contended that the detenue had no *locus standi* to evoke the jurisdiction of the High Court to obtain his release because the Presidential Order of 1975 under Article 359, as compared to the earlier such order of 1962 was a blanket order as much as it did not specify any law under which a person was detained. Therefore, even if detention was in violation of the law or *malafide*, the detenue could not obtain his liberty.

M.C. Chagla, who led the arguments, appeared on behalf of Atal Bihari Vajpayee before the Division Bench of the Karnataka High Court consisting of Justices D.M. Chandrasekhar and B. Venkataswamy. He argued for two days and was at his brilliant best. He opened the argument by saying, "I have come to Bangalore not to argue a case but to fight for a cause—a national duty I owe to my country."

In reply to the preliminary objection, he submitted that the court could give relief in spite of the Presidential Order, if the detention order was either in violation of provisions of law or *mala fide*, as held by a Bench of seven judges of the Supreme Court in the *Makhan Singh's case* and other cases.[9]

Chagla also submitted that under Article 359, the President could suspend remedy to enforce any of the Fundamental Rights, only when there was a validly proclaimed emergency. But since the Proclamation of both the Emergencies were being challenged they had to be decided first. He further submitted that the preliminary objection was not maintainable without first pronouncing upon the legality of imposing the Emergency under Article 352 and not the nature of orders issued under Article 359 suspending Fundamental Rights. This would be decided only then.

Relying on 7 the judge bench of the Supreme Court he quoted extensively from *Makhan Singh's case* in which Chief Justice B.G. Gajendragadkar had stated:

> The common important questions of considerable importance: The first question is what is the true scope and effect of the Presidential Order which has been issued under Article 359(1)? The answer to this question would depend on fair and reasonable construction of Article 359(1) itself. The second question is: Does the bar created by the Presidential Order issued under Article 359(1) operate in respect of applications made by detenues under section 491(b) of the Code?

We are not concerned here with the second question as Section 491 of the Criminal Procedure Code has been deleted. However, the first question makes it clear that the Supreme Court then was concerned with interpreting Article 359(1) to find the scope and effect of the Presidential Order of 1962. This can be seen from the following observations of the Court:

> We have already seen that the right to move any court which is suspended by Article 359(1) of the Constitution and the Presidential Order issued under it is the right for the enforcement of such of the rights conferred by Part-III as may be mentioned in the order. If in challenging the validity of his detention order, his right to move any Court in that behalf is not suspended, because it is outside Article 359(1) and consequently outside Presidential Order itself. Let us take a case where a detenue has been detained in violation of the mandatory provisions of the Act. In such a case, it may be open to the detenue to contend that his detention is illegal for the reason that the mandatory provisions of

> the Act have been contravened. Such a plea is outside Article 359(1) and the right of the detenue to move for his release on such a ground cannot be affected by the Presidential Order.... Take also a case where the detenue moves the Court for a writ of Habeas Corpus on the ground that his detention has been ordered *mala fide.* It is hardly necessary to emphasize that the exercise of a power *mala fide* is wholly outside the scope of the Act conferring the power and can always be successfully challenged. It is true that a mere allegation that the detention is *mala fide* would not be enough; the detenue will have to prove the *mala fides.* But if the *mala fides* are alleged, the detenue cannot be precluded from substantiating his pleas on the ground of the bar created by Article 359(1) and the Presidential Order. That is another kind of plea which is outside the purview of Articles 359(1).

M.C. Chagla also argued about the continuance of the 1971 Emergency and of the 1975 Emergency as unconstitutional; compared the Presidential Orders of 1962 and 1975 under Article 359 and the meaning of the Order under Article 359 as specifically interpreted. He also cited the subsequent judgment of the Constitution Bench of the Supreme Court in *K. Anand Nambiar's case,* which followed *Makhan Singh's case* and *Jaychand Lal Sethia's case.*[10] The latter judgment specifically held that if "the statutory power was exercised for purposes foreign to those for which it is intended" the Presidential Orders under Articles 358 and 359 did not bar challenge to the order of detention.

The Karnataka High Court rejected the preliminary objection raised by the government to its order dated August 17, 1975. The Government's application to move the Supreme Court against this interlocutory order was rejected because no substantial question of law was involved, and as the *Habeas Corpus* petitions, deserved to be disposed of as expeditiously as possible, refused stay of the hearing.

However, the High Court's interlocutory decision gave the Government a handle to go to the Supreme Court and delay the proceedings. Had the High Court reserved its judgment on preliminary objections and directed the Attorney General to reply to Chagla's arguments on merit, both the matters could then have been decided together in the final judgment, and thus would have disposed off the petitions at the earliest.

After the interlocutory order was passed by the Karnataka High Court, both M.C. Chagla and Justice K.S. Hegde felt that when the case had been argued exhaustively, the High Court ought to have given the judgment on merits instead of passing an interlocutory order.

In the Karnataka High Court there is no practice of mentioning whether a writ petition is civil or criminal. When the High Court decided that the writ petitions were maintainable and refused to stay the hearing, the Government of India was in a hurry to obtain the stay from the Supreme Court and to avoid any delay because of objection by the Registry paid court fees applicable to Civil Special Leave Petition. I had filed four *caveats* on behalf of Atalji, L.K. Advani, Madhu Dandavate and Shyam Nandan Mishra. The Registry told me to file ₹ 16 as court fee in each case. When I told the Registrar that the *habeas corpus* Petition that is always criminal and no court fee is required he said the Government's petitions did not say so. Therefore I paid ₹ 64. After the Supreme Court decided the case I filed an application for refund of court fee. When the application came for hearing, the cause list showed *Union of India Vs. Shri Atal Bihari Vajpayee* etc. The press was in full attendance. When I told Chief Justice Ray that I was asked to pay court fees in four appeals arising out of *habeas corpus* Petition, he just passed an order to refund ₹ 64 to me.

In these Special Leave Petitions, in the Supreme Court against this interlocutory order, the Attorney General, pleading for grant of special leave and stay, cited a similar case in which the Madhya Pradesh High Court in *Shiv Kant Shukla Vs. A.D.M. Jabalpur* had decided the *Habeas Corpus* Petitions as maintainable, and had admitted the appeal and granted stay of the hearing of that petition.

Appearing for the petitioners, Shanti Bhushan replied that the validity of the Emergency was not challenged before the M.P. High Court since the Emergency was itself challenged in these writ petitions from Karnataka. The validity of Presidential Order suspending the fundamental rights had to be decided before taking up the question of the maintainability of the petitions.

The Supreme Court Bench presided over by the Chief Justice A.N. Ray remanded the case of the High Court with the following order:

> Before entering into the merits of these cases on other ground, the High Court on hearing the parties will deliver judgment on the preliminary objection raised by the Government including the question whether the objections raised by the Government are preliminary.

Although the Supreme Court did not grant a stay to the Government, it prevented the High Court from hearing the *Habeas Corpus* petitions on merits without first deciding the preliminary of the objection. The Government thus got an opportunity to prolong the detention without facing the cases on merits. The Supreme Court, being the guardian of Fundamental Rights, should not have ordered the High Court to pass an interlocutory order in *habeas corpus* proceedings involving personal liberty.

When the High Court resumed the hearing of the *Habeas Corpus* petition, the Attorney General, Niren De, submitted that in terms of the Supreme Court Order, the High Court should first pass an order on the maintainability of the writ petitions and only then decide on the question of the validity of the Emergency.

This contention was opposed on behalf of the detenues, stating that in accordance with the Supreme Court order, the basic question of the validity of Emergency had to be decided simultaneously because the Attorney General's objections also rested upon the presumptions that the declaration of Emergency and the Presidential Order suspending Fundamental Rights under Articles 14, 21 and 22 was valid.

The High Court rejected the contention of the Attorney General; the Government again filed a special leave application against this decision before the Supreme Court. On October 25, the case came up before the Supreme Court presided over by Chief Justice Ray. Both the sides reiterated their contentions. The Supreme Court "disposed of" the petitions in terms of its earlier order.

Again the scene shifted to the Karnataka High Court. On hearing of the arguments of the counsels for the petitioners led by Shanti Bhushan and the Additional Solicitor General,

V.P. Raman, for the Government, the High Court formulated the following five issues:

(i) Can this court go into the question whether the Proclamation of Emergency by the President under Article 352 of the Constitution in view of the requirement of Clause (2) of Article 74 of the Constitution?
(ii) Can the Court go into the question whether the Proclamation of Emergency or continuance of Emergency is *mala fide*?
(iii) Whether the 38th Amendment of the Constitution by which clause (5) was inserted in Article 352 of the Constitution, is valid on the ground that it alters the basic features of the Constitution?
(iv) In spite of the Presidential Order suspending the enforcement of the Fundamental Rights conferred by Articles 21 and 22 of the Constitution, can this court examine whether an order of detention:
  (a) is in accordance with the provisions of the Maintenance of Internal Security Act?
  (b) was made *mala fide*? Or
  (c) was made on the basis of the relevant materials by which the detaining authority could have been satisfied that Order was necessary?
(v) Whether, in spite of the suspension of enforcement of the Fundamental Rights conferred by Articles 21 and 22 of the Constitution, can a person's right to freedom from arrest and detention except in accordance with law, be enforced?

The High Court on November 10, 1975, delivered its judgment on these preliminary issues. On the question of maintainability of the *habeas corpus* petition, the High Court held that in spite of the suspension of Articles 21 and 22 the *mala fide* and illegality of detentions could be challenged before a High Court following the rational of *Makhan Singh's case*.

On the question of validity of the continuance of the Emergency of 1971 and proclamation of the Emergency of 1975, the High Court held that it did not have the jurisdiction to decide on this matter.

As regards the question whether the Proclamation of Emergency of 1975 was signed on the advice of the Council of Ministers, the Court did notice the factual averment of the detenues that it was signed without any advice from the Council of Ministers was not controverted by the Government. But here again the Court considered that it had no jurisdiction to decide this question in view of the bar created by Clause 2 of Article 74 of the Constitution which states, "The question if any, and if so what advice was tendered by the Ministers to the President shall not be inquired into in any Court."

Thus while the detenues won on the question of maintainability of the *habeas corpus* petitions, they lost on the question of the emergency. Not wanting the petitions to be decided on merits, the Central Government moved the Supreme Court to set aside the interlocutory order of the Karnataka High Court on the question of maintainability of these petitions and prayed for stay of the hearing of the *habeas corpus* petitions on merit, which was granted by the Supreme Court bench constituting of Chief Justice A.N. Ray and Justice M.H. Beg.

As many as nine other High Courts following *Makhan Singh's case* held against the Government on the question of maintainability of the *habeas corpus* petition, but the Supreme Court admitted all the appeals of the Government and stayed the hearing of these petitions on merits.[10] The fate of the detenues now lay in the hands of the Supreme Court, which directed that all the appeals would be heard together and posted them for hearing on December 15, 1975.

Meanwhile, the Judges of the High Court, who gave judgments against the Government, were victimized. The confirmed Judges, were transferred while additional judges were not confirmed, thus administering a clear warning about what might be in store for the judges of the Supreme Court.

The fear of Government's revengeful attitude even affected judges except very few. For instance, Justice O. Chinappa Reddy who was transferred from Chief Justice of Andhra Pradesh High Court to the Punjab and Haryana High Court for giving judgment against the Government. While he was in Chandigarh, one C.L. Lakhan Pal, who like P.N. Lekhi was elected the President of the Delhi Bar Association, while in jail under the MISA and was also elected the President of the Punjab and Haryana High Court Bar Association. He died while he was in jail. The Bar as usual represented to Chief Justice Reddy for Full Court Reference to which he readily agreed for the next day at 10.30 A.M. The Chief Justice's Court was crowded with members of the Bar but no judge came for one hour. At about 11.30, Chief Justice O. Chinappa Reddy came alone and said "My colleagues have declined to join the Reference. I will take the Reference."

It may be mentioned that in case of Kuldip Nayyar, a well-known journalist, the Delhi High Court and the Nagpur Bench of the Bombay High Court in a batch of petitions of R.S.S. and Jana Sangh members in *K.M. Ghatate's case* refused to pass *interlocutory* orders on the Government's preliminary objection as to the maintainability of petitions. Instead they passed final orders. Kuldip Nayyar's petition was allowed and he was released,[11] while the petitions before the Nagpur Bench were dismissed on merits. These two judgments deserve close examination. So also the subsequent judgment of the Nagpur Bench of the Bombay High Court in a group of cases *U.O.G. etc. Vs. Dr. Mrs. Rekha Avasthi etc.* better known as *Matka Gambler's case* wherein the High Court had called for the record of the case. This judgment came when the Supreme Court was hearing the famous *habeas corpus* appeals and granted leave to appeal and stay of the order of the High Court and tagged it along with the appeals which it was hearing.[12]

It was published that the *Habeas Corpus* case would be heard by the Constitution Bench which means a five judges Bench. But since C.J. Ray was hearing a case consisting of three junior judges that time, I was afraid he would add any one judge and hear this case.

When I told Atalji my anxiety he said, "I do not object to the operation but it should be done by the most experienced hands." I went to C.K. Daphtary, the doyen of the Bar and former Attorney General of India, and told him about my anxiety. He said that he would mention it to the Chief Justice and asked me to take an appointment. Next morning as I was going to Chief Justice A.N. Ray's chamber, I met Asok Sen who was then the President of Supreme Court Bar Association; he said he would also go to the Chief Justice along with Daphtary. I told Chief Justice Ray, "Mr. Daphtary and Mr. A.K. Sen want to meet you urgently." He asked me the reason to which I said that I had not asked them the reason. He told me that he would meet them during the lunch break.

At that meeting Daphtary told him that he should constitute the Bench of five seniormost judges as he had done in *Mrs. Indira Gandhi's Election Case*, so that there would be no criticism. Justice Ray asked, "Mr. Daftary you have been the Attorney General of India, have you ever made such a request?" He said that he had done earlier when Justice S.R. Das was the Chief Justice of India (I think it was a whitelie). A.K. Sen added, "When I came this morning to the Court, some Bar members were thinking of passing a similar resolution and I told them not to do it and I would tell the Chief Justice about the Bar's concern."

Chief Justice Ray had not forgotten the Bar Resolution calling for an All India Lawyers' strike when he was appointed the Chief Justice superseding three senior-most judges as they along with the majority had decided against the Government in the famous *Keshava Nanda Bharti's case*. He told A.K. Sen, "Your Bar always wants to dictate by resolutions." That time he did not commit. But he constituted the Constitution Bench consisting of five senior-most judges to hear the *Habeas Corpus* appeals consisting Chief Justice A.N. Ray, Justices H.R. Khanna, M.H. Beg, Y.V. Chandrachud and P.N. Bhagwati.

I had requested all the senior Advocates to appear in this historic case. N.A. Palkhiwala, who was then writing a book, informed me of his inability to come, but said, "Don't worry the majority will reject the government's appeal and if any one holds in favour of government, I will fail him in 1st year LL.B. examination." But as it happened, four judges, except Justice H.R. Khanna, held in favour of the government.

Before adverting to the issues, arguments and judgments some memorable events during the Emergency may be mentioned.

In the December vacation, 1975, I visited detenues in Gwalior Jail and since most of the Madhya Pradesh leaders like Kusha Bhau Thakre, N.K. Sejwalkar were detained in Begum Ganj Sub-Jail, I went to see them. I took a bus from Gwalior which reached Begum Ganj at about 3 A.M. There was no place to stay, so I went to the police station, and they told me that I could use the cot in the police station. Early morning when I went to the Sub-jail, one teenage girl was sitting in the garden. I told her, I would like to meet the Jailor as I wanted to meet the detenues there. I was surprised that she just knocked at the gate of the jail, when the guard opened it and I was asked to go inside. It was a very small Jail about the size of a tennis court with two residential barracks on two sides and one side was a kitchen and dining area and the other side were the bathrooms etc. There were hardly 20 detenues and I knew most of them. Many started asking questions about what was happening outside. At that time Kusha Bhau Thakre asked all of them to sit in the courtyard and told me to narate all the happenings outside. When I was speaking the Jailor quietly came and sat down to listen to the story. He asked me to have lunch there and brought sweets from outside. I rested there in the afternoon and I left in the evening for Nagpur.

As Indira Gandhi's election appeal was allowed by the Supreme Court on November 17, 1975, Atalji asked me to tell the underground leaders to hold the *Satyagrah* which was to start from December 20, 1975, for some time. When I told him that the communication system was so bad that they could not stop the *Satyagrah*, Atalji jocularly remarked, "So our car is without any brakes. Let it go."

During the Emergency many active opposition workers became inactive for fear of being detained, while many who were inactive bravely came in to help. One such incident was of the well established travel agent Shenoy. He had assisted me in getting travel documents etc. in 1959 when I first went to America for studies. My father was detained in Thane Jail. I had some work in Bombay so I went to Thane before going to Bombay. When I met my father I told him, "I have time today and have not met Shenoy for ages. Do you know where he is now?" To my surprise he said, "He is with me in Thane Jail." And we requested the Jailor to call him. It was a pleasure meeting him after over 15 years but, shocked, I asked, "Mr. Shenoy of all the elites in Bombay how come you are in the jail?" He said, "Shri Yadavrao Joshi who was then the Karnataka State Pracharak of RSS was underground and he was arrested from my residence, and so I am here."

There was an inspiring example of Madhu Limaye who was detained in the Begum Ganj Jail in Madhya Pradesh. When I visited him he said to me that he had a radio which could catch only local bands. Yet the Deputy Inspector General of Police (DIG) who visited the jail and ordered the Jailor to take it from Limaye although he told him that he could not listen to the BBC or the Voice of America but only the government propoganda. When the Jailor came to him to collect his radio, Limaye said, "I will not give it to you and instead I broke it." He also told me to ask all the opposition members to resign from the Lok Sabha on April 13, 1976, the day its five-year term was over "Because according to us emergency being illegal the extension of Lok Sabha under Article 83 of the Constitution is also illegal". Madhu Limaye not only resigned from Lok Sabha on that day but also vacated the M.P. accommodation.

For the 1976 Rajya Sabha elections, the Jana Sangh decided to field Advaniji from Gujarat. Makrand Desai, then the President of the Gujarat unit went to the Bangalore Jail to obtain his signature on the nomination form but he was denied permission to meet Advaniji. So he filed a writ petition in the High Court. When the Court was about to pass an order, authorities said that they had no objection. The Court noted this and issued orders permitting him to see Advaniji.

Advaniji wanted to exercise his right to be present at the time of scrutiny. By way of caution, he sought court's intervention. Both the Government of India and the State opposed his prayer but the High Court on March 8, 1976 passed an order which stated:

> The Advocate General did not dispute that the petitioner being a detenue will not take away his right to be a candidate for election to the Parliament or State Legislature. It follows that he should have all reasonable facilities to exercise his rights and opportunity not withstanding him being under detention. If he is taken under detention to be present before the Returning Officer on 10.3.76 (last date for the nomination and until scrutiny is completed which cannot be beyond 12.3.76), we cannot see what reasonable apprehension can be of any security risk.

Accordingly he was taken by plane to Ahmedabad on March 9, 1976, and brought back to the Bangalore Jail. (facsimile of the copy of the letter (Plate 4) dated March 23, 1976 is enclosed.) After he was elected to the Rajya Sabha, he wanted to exercise his right of taking his oath in the Rajya Sabha, as he could not exercise all the rights and privileges of a member until he had taken his oath. So he filed a second petition and the High Court again directed that he should be taken to Delhi and after taking his oath he was to be brought back under police escort. Next morning i.e. one day before he

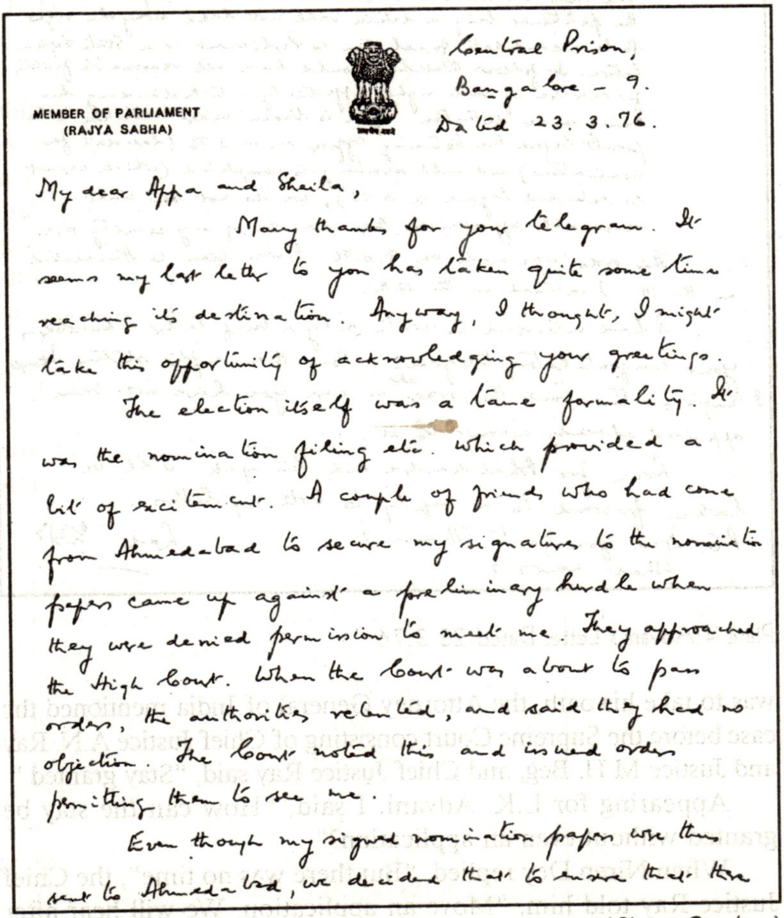

MEMBER OF PARLIAMENT
(RAJYA SABHA)

Central Prison,
Bangalore - 9.
Dated 23. 3. 76.

My dear Appa and Sheila,

Many thanks for your telegram. It seems my last letter to you has taken quite some time reaching its destination. Anyway, I thought, I might take this opportunity of acknowledging your greetings.

The election itself was a tame formality. It was the nomination filing etc. which provided a bit of excitement. A couple of friends who had come from Ahmedabad to secure my signature to the nomination papers came up against a preliminary hurdle when they were denied permission to meet me. They approached the High Court. When the Court was about to pass orders, the authorities relented, and said they had no objection. The Court noted this and issued orders permitting them to see me.

Even though my signed nomination papers were thus sent to Ahmedabad, we decided that to ensure that the

(*Plate 4 Contd. . . .*)

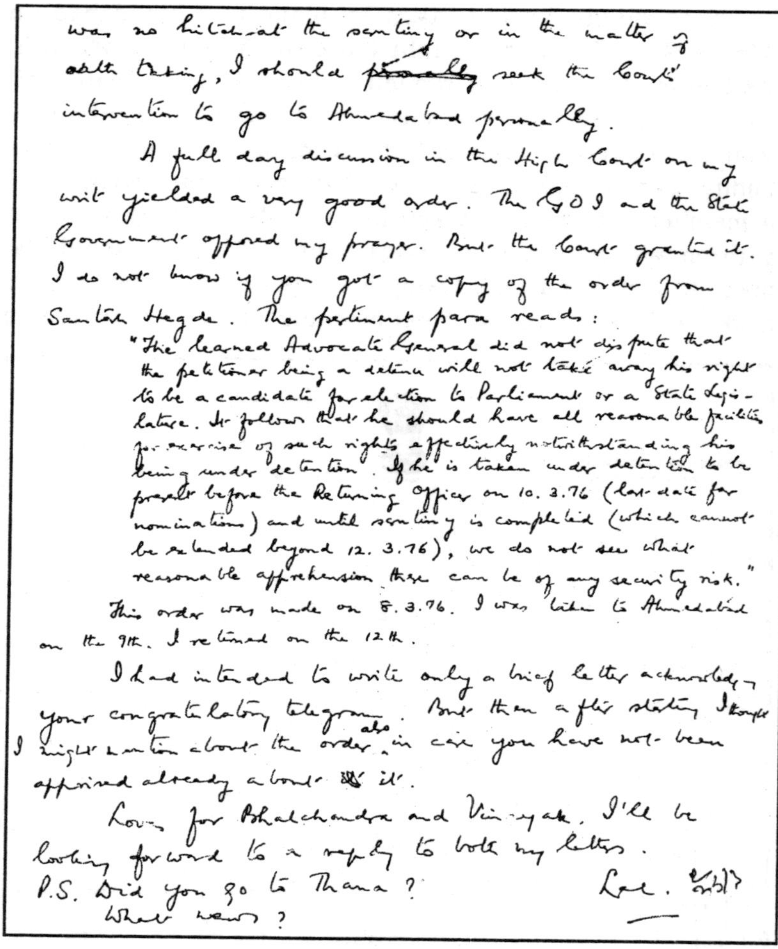

was no hitch at the scrutiny or in the matter of oath taking, I should ~~personally~~ seek the Court's intervention to go to Ahmedabad personally.

A full day discussion in the High Court on my writ yielded a very good order. The GOI and the State Government opposed my prayer. But the Court granted it. I do not know if you got a copy of the order from Santosh Hegde. The pertinent para reads:

"The learned Advocate General did not dispute that the petitioner being a detenu will not take away his right to be a candidate for election to Parliament or a State Legislature. It follows that he should have all reasonable facilities for exercise of such rights effectively notwithstanding his being under detention. If he is taken under detention to be present before the Returning Officer on 10.3.76 (last date for nominations) and until scrutiny is completed (which cannot be extended beyond 12.3.76), we do not see what reasonable apprehension there can be of any security risk."

This order was made on 8.3.76. I was taken to Ahmedabad on the 9th. I returned on the 12th.

I had intended to write only a brief letter acknowledging your congratulatory telegram. But then after starting I thought I might mention about the order also, in case you have not been apprised already about it.

Love for Bhalchandra and Vinayak. I'll be looking forward to a reply to both my letters.

Lal. 23/3

P.S. Did you go to Thana? What news?

Plate 4: Advani's Letter Dated 23.3.76

was to take his oath, the Attorney General of India mentioned the case before the Supreme Court consisting of Chief Justice A.N. Ray and Justice M.H. Beg, and Chief Justice Ray said, "Stay granted."

Appearing for L.K. Advani, I said, "How can the stay be granted without even an application?"

When Niren Dey replied, "But there was no time", the Chief Justice Ray told him, "Move an application. We will hear after lunch at 2 P.M." As expected, the stay was granted at 2 P.M.

But it is interesting to note that in the Bombay High Court some MISA detenues, who were Corporators, had filed an application to participate in the Bombay Mayoral election and their case had come for hearing before Justice V.D. Tulzapurkar on the same morning. That time the Government Advocate boldly told the Bombay High Court that the Supreme Court had stayed Advani from being taken to Delhi for taking his oath. This was about two hours before the Supreme Court had actually granted the stay. Justice Tulzapurkar, however, allowed the petition of Corporators and observed that the Government Advocate could approach the Supreme Court. Also, the airport authorities were told that a plane need not be sent to Bangalore to bring Shri Advani to Delhi as the Supreme Court had granted a stay. This too was before the stay was actually granted at 2 P.M.

The Government had formed the Swaran Singh Committee to give a report on exhaustive amendments of the Constitution and in April, 1976, allowed public debate of this report. This report made several drastic changes in the Constitution, such as in the Preamble, adding 'Socialist' and 'Secular' country, making the election of the Prime Minister, President and Vice-President beyond challenge on any ground in the Court, extending the normal life of Parliament from five years, to six years depriving the challenge to constitutional amendment on grounds of basic structure etc.

The Bar Association of India under the Chairmanship of C.K. Daphtary held a symposium on these amendments in 1976, which was widely attended by several advocates. There was a consensus among the member of the Bar that during the Emergency no drastic changes could by made to the Constitution and the Government should only attend to executive matters. Speaking at that seminar, I said that since this constitutional amendment was tabled in the Parliament after its normal life of five years had expired and was continuing because of the Emergency and the Emergency being a fraud on the Constitution, the extension of the life of the Lok Sabha under Article 83 was also unconstitutional. Therefore the entire amendment should be thrown out, lock stock and barrel. Furthermore, these amendments were not necessary as economic justice can be achieved only through socialism and thus there was no need to tie the country to the concept of socialism. It is not out of place to mention that for at least 15 years the concept of socialism had been so much eroded in India that it was now even despised and several economists look at it as a major cause of India's economic stagnation.

The Union of Civil Liberties also held a seminar on the proposed amendments. H.V. Kamath, a former ICS, reading out the banner of the seminar *Amending the Constitution* eloquently stated: "Take out A; it becomes *Mending the Constitution*. Take out M; it becomes *Ending the Constitution*." That is what the 42nd Amendment means." N.A. Palkhiwala later wrote a book on this infamous 42nd Constitutional Amendment, titled, *Constitution Defiled and Defaced*.

Once when Atalji, Shri Chandrasekhar and Shri Ram Dhan were at the AIIMS sitting on a bench near the lift and chanting, Shri Chandrasekhar asked, "We two M.P.s belong to the Congress. Why were we also arrested?" Atalji replied, "Because you were the ones who were persuading members of the Congress to step up pressure on Mrs. Indira Gandhi to resign."

Just at that time Mrs. Indira Gandi stepped out of the lift looked at them and went in towards the room of Shri H.R. Gokhale, who was also admitted there. I exclaimed, "You did not stand or even greet her!" Atalji said, "Why should we? We are her prisoners."

In all the *Habeas Corpus* appeals the main issues before the Supreme Court were: In view of the Presidential Order of 27 June 1975 under Article 359 suspending Fundamental Rights under Articles 14, 21 and 22 was a writ petition under Article 226 of the Constitution maintainable before the High Court on the ground that the order of detention was not in compliance with the provisions of MISA or that it was *mala fide*.

In the alternative, if such a petition was maintainable what was the scope of judicial scrutiny in view of the Presidential Order of 1975 and Section 16-A of MISA. But this Section was not challenged.

It is important to note that the Government was the appellant in all the appeals. The detenues before the Karnataka High Court had not preferred any cross appeal against the judgment of the

Karnataka High Court which held that it could not go into the justification of the Proclamation of Emergency or its continuance has been unconstitutional or *mala fide.*

Niren De, who led the argument on behalf of the Union of India, contended that Article 21 was the sole repository of the right to life and liberty and the judicial remedy to enforce this right being suspended, the detenue had no *locus standi* to enforce this right by evoking the jurisdiction of the High Court under Article 226, even if the order of detention was not in compliance with MISA or was *mala fide.* He further submitted that since the Presidential Order was "a bar at the threshold, the detenues could not evoke the jurisdiction of the Court under any other law ....because they were in fact indirectly trying to enforce their right to liberty which was suspended."

Referring to *Makhan Singh's case* decided by the bench of Seven Judges, Niren De contended that the Supreme Court's observation was *obiter dicta*, in which it had held that if detention was not in compliance with the law under which it was made, or if it was *mala fide*, the *habeas corpus* petitions were maintainable in spite of suspension of Articles 21 and 22 because these two grounds were outside the scope of Article 359. Secondly, according to Niren De, this case was not applicable because the Presidential Order of 1962 suspending enforcement of Articles 14, 21 and 22 was a conditional order, as it deprived a person of his right to liberty under the Defence of India Act or any other Rule made under the Act. On the other hand the Presidential Order of 1975 was a blanket order whereby his right to move the court and enforce his right under these articles to obtain his liberty was simply suspended without reference to any law or rules.

This argument was based on the different wordings of the Presidential Order of November 3, 1962, which according to him was a conditional order and read:

> In exercise of the powers conferred by clause (1) of Article 359 of the Constitution the President hereby declares that the right of any person to move any court for the enforcement of the rights conferred by Article 21 and Article 22 of the Constitution shall remain suspended for the period during which the Proclamation of Emergency

> issued under clause (1) of Article 352 thereof on the 26th October, 1962 is in force, *if such a person has been deprived of any such rights under the Defence of India Ordinance, 1962 (4 of 1962) or any rule or order made thereunder.*

On the other hand the Presidential Order of June 27, 1975 was a blanket order as it read:

> In exercise of the powers conferred by clause (1) of Article 359 of the Constitution, the President hereby declares that the right of any person (including a foreigner) to move any court for the enforcement of the rights conferred by Article 14, Article 21 and Article 22 of the Constitution and all proceedings pending in any court for the enforcement of the above mentioned rights shall remain suspended for the period during which the Proclamation of Emergency made under clause (1) of Article 352 of the Constitution on the 3rd December, 1971 and on the 25th June, 1975 are both in force...

The contention of Niren De that the 1975 Order was not a conditional but a blanket order as the 1962 Order was not correct because as H.M. Seervai correctly stated that if the Order of 1975 did not specify any law or order of detention it must follow that any law in force which violated the Fundamental Rights a person cannot be deprived of his life or liberty without any law. As such both the Orders were conditional. It may be mentioned that according to even International Law even during war the law of war operates and its violation as per the Nuremburg Principles, which were adopted by the U.N. in 1949, makes punishable to killing of unarmed persons or even soldiers as War Crimes.

It is submitted that the Seven Judges Bench in *Makhan Singh's case* did not deal with the Order suspending Fundamental Rights under Article 359 but the meaning of the Article 359 itself. The question for decision referred was "What is the true scope of the President's Order which has been issued under Articles 358 and 359?" and the Supreme Court held that detention not in compliance with law or *mala fide* was outside the scope of the bar imposed by the Presidential Order. It further held that under Article 359, laws in violation of Fundamental Rights could be passed but not if the legislature did not have legislative competence. Justice Subba Rao in his minority judgment in *Makhan Singh's case* held that Articles 358 and 359 did not allow passing any law in violation of Fundamental Rights. This seems to be a correct view. However, it has now become academic because these Articles were amended by the 38th Constitutional Amendment to make laws in violation of Fundamental Rights. This was done to meet one of the many challenges during the 1975 Emergency. But this amendment was retained by the 44th Amendment brought by the Janata government and is now a part of the Constitution.

To Justice Khanna's very pertinent query needs to be mentioned. Since the word *'life'* also figured along with the word *'liberty'* in Article 21 it would mean that the Government during the Emergency could take away even the life of a person without the authority of law or *mala fide*, and yet the courts would be powerless if this argument was accepted. Niren De replied in the affirmative. But added that if liberty or life was taken away illegally or *mala fide,* a suit could lie for damages after revocation of the Emergency. He agreed with Justice Khanna that even such a remedy could be thwarted by the Government by passing an Indemnity Act protecting authorities for their illegal action during the Emergency.

In fairness it must be mentioned that Niren De frankly told the court, "I am not happy arguing this case. But according to my interpretation, 'There is no half-way house. Either you are completely with me or completely with the other side.'

Niren De was always very crisp in his submission. In three days he concluded his arguments, and as usual he came out to smoke a cigarette. I happened to meet him in front of the Chief Justice's Court. That time he called me and told me, "I know you were instrumental in constituting this Bench, but the majority will be with me."

The Solicitor General, V.P. Raman, made an alternative argument that if the Attorney General's interpretation of Article 21 and the Presidential Order of 1975 was not accepted, then the production of a valid detention order by the detaining authority was a complete answer to the writ of *habeas corpus*. In view of Section 16A of MISA, the Court could not go behind the detention order to find out whether it was *mala fide* or not and in compliance with the law. He, therefore, contended that the Nagpur Bench of the Bombay High Court in the *Matka case* was not justified in directing the State to produce the material and the grounds of detention on which the satisfaction of the detaining authority was based.[11-12]

Shanti Bhushan who led the argument on behalf of the detenues submitted that writ petitions were maintainable and "the mandate of Parliament could not be ignored even in an emergency." *Mala fide* and illegal action was outside the scope of Article 359 as held by a Bench of Seven Judges of the Supreme Court in *Makhan Singh's case* and which was binding on the present bench of five judges, hearing the appeals. Giving absolute power to the executive to take away life and liberty and denying the right of *habeas corpus* amounted to depriving the judiciary of its pivotal role of protecting Fundamental Rights which violated the basic principles of the Constitution. Moreover, the High Court seeing the material on which the satisfaction of the detaining authority was based could not be said to be against "public interest".

Soli J. Sorabjee eloquently argued that the rule of law being one of the basic features of the Constitution, cannot be ignored not only in an emergency but even during actual war; individual liberty could not be interfered with unless supported by law. Therefore, the argument that a person can be deprived of his liberty or life in violation of law whatever be the nature of the Presidential Order is to be stated only to be rejected in view of the interpretation of the Presidential Order under Article 359, as held in *Makhan Singh's case*.

V.M. Tarukunde contended that once the *habeas corpus* petition was filed, the onus shifted on the detaining authority to prove the legality of the detention order.

Anil Diwan, arguing for Mrinal Gore, submitted that Indians would be worse than slaves under the Roman Law if they were denied access to courts in case of grievous bodily harm or inhuman treatment by interpreting Article 21 as the sole repository of the right to life and liberty. It is relevant to note that he also brought to the notice of the Court that Mrinal Gore was lodged in a cell along with prisoners infected with leprosy. S.N. Trivedi showed the Court blank cyclostyled orders signed by the detaining authorities. Ram Jethmalani pointing out how the High Court judges, who decided against the Government, were victimized by either being transferred or by not having their appointments confirmed. Furthermore, even their judgments were censored. He concluded with the memorable words, "Democracy is in a coffin but it is still breathing. Please do not nail the lid with your judicial hands."

M.C. Chagla, C.K. Daphtary, and A.K. Sen, also appeared for the detenues.

It was submitted by the author that the fate of the detenues depended on the interpretation that the court gives to Article 21 and the Presidential Order of June 27, 1975. Whether Article 21 is or is not the sole repository of the right to life and liberty; or whether these rights are the inalienable rights of man, which are raised to the status of and conferred as fundamental rights? Secondly, whether under the Presidential Order, because it did not specify the law under which a person is detained could he be detained *mala fide* and in contravention of detention law.

It was also further submitted that when there is a conflict between a municipal law and international law, the municipal courts have to give effect to municipal law. But when the provision of municipal law is capable of more than one interpretation, courts should give that interpretation which is in conformity and not in conflict with international law and the country's international obligations.

Furthermore, in view of Article 51 of the Constitution, it is the duty of the Court to interpret Article 21 and the Presidential Order in harmony with the U.N. Charter, the Universal Declaration of Human Rights and India's obligations under international law. Therefore, international law must be read into read down the Presidential Order and Article 21 of the Constitution. It is a well settled principle of interpretation that a municipal court should lean in favour of international law as leading authorities like Charles Fenwick[13] and Oppenheim have observed that there was always a presumption against the existence of a conflict between municipal law and international law. "This was because the common consent being the basis of international law, it was improbable that an enlightened State would intentionally enact a rule conflicting with the law of nations."[14]

It was also submitted that besides U.N. Charter, India was a party to the Universal Declaration of Human Rights of 1948,[15] the Convention on Prevention of Commission of Crime of Genocide of 1948, The Nuremberg Principles of 1949, the International Covenant of Civil and Political Rights of 1966[17] and the International Convention of Elimination of Racial Discrimination of 1967, and several other conventions. Therefore, India is duty bound not to violate these rights of its own citizens. Thus Article 21 and the Presidential Order cannot be interpreted to empower the Executive to violate Human Rights. The Preamble of the Declaration of Human Rights specifically stated, "If a man is not to be compelled to have recourse as a last resort of rebellion against tyranny and oppression, then Human Rights should be protected by the rule of law."[15]

This general truth was recognized not only by liberal political thinkers like Aristotle, Jean-Jacques Rousseau and John Locke but also by political thinkers who advocated the State supreme power over individuals to maintain order in society like David Gothair, Friedrich Wilhelm Nietzsche, Immanuel Kant and Karl Marx. Even Thomas Hobbes, the proponent of the theory of Divine Right of King, who advocated absolute power for the State to preserve order, conceded the right of an individual to rebel, if his life and limb were threatened.[19]

It was pointed out that the inherent and inalienable right to life and liberty mentioned in the U.N.Charter is specifically elaborated in Articles 8 and 9 of the Declaration of Human Rights, which reads as follows:

Article 8: "Everyone has a right of effective remedy by the competent national tribunal for acts violating the fundamental rights granted to him by the Constitution or by the law.

Article 9: "No one shall be subjected to arbitrary arrest and detention."[15]

The International Convention on Political and Civil Rights in Article 4 specifically states: "Even in an emergency, rights to life could not be interfered with."[17]

The Nuremberg Principles have been unanimously accepted by all the members of the United Nations and have become part of International Law. Principle 6 (c) which defines crimes against humanity includes murder, enslavement; Principle 7 specifically states that crime against humanity is a crime under international law and Principle 3 states: the fact a person, who committed such a crime and acted as head of the State or responsible government official does not relieve him from responsibility under International Law. Principle 4 states that acting on the orders of superiors also did not relieve a person from responsibility provided "moral choice was available to him."[18]

Robert Woetzel, an authority on International Law, commenting on the Nuremberg Principles in his book *The Nuremberg Trial and International Law* said:

No Government any longer possesses an undisputed right to treat its subjects at it pleases... The officials of every nation must now be aware that they too may be condemned as international criminals if they offend against the law of the nations... if they apply laws that are to prosecute groups of persons whose rights are recognized by most civilized nations. This is the meaning of Nuremberg.[19]

In view of the well settled rule of interpretation, universally recognized principles of international law as well as India's international obligations, read with article 51 it was submitted that Article 21 and the Presidential Order cannot be interpreted to give the Executive an unlimited right over the life or liberty of an individual even during an Emergency.

More important, Article 359 only empowered the President to suspend enforcement of Fundamental Rights and not abrogate a Fundamental Right during the Emergency. Power of suspension implies power of restoration and since life once taken cannot be restored, suspension of right to the life is outside the scope of Article 359 as it amounts to destruction of this right. This can only be done through a constitutional amendment and not through interpretation of the Presidential Order under Article 359.

The right to move the Court was permitted to be suspended during emergency under Article 359 of the Constitution, because the challenge the of the legality of the emergency was itself possible from the inception of the Constitution until the 38th Constitutional Amendment. But by the 38th Constitutional Amendment the Emergency had been rendered non-justiciable even if it were unconstitutional or *mala fide*. It was, therefore, the added duty of the Court to read down the Presidential Order and provisions of the MISA to protect the citizens from arbitrary and *mala fide* abuse of power.

The arguments were concluded on February 25, 1976. It is a well settled practice the world over to deliver the judgment in *habeas corpus* petitions as early as possible. But the judgment was not delivered for more than two months.

Shri Vajpayee asked me when the judgment would come as the fate of hundreds of detenues was at stake. I told him, "I shall file an application for early delivery of the judgment with your affidavit." When I filed the application, the Registrar of the Supreme Court called me and said, "Such an application has never been filed." I told him to place the application before the Court. He might have mentioned it to the Chief Justice A.N. Ray because he told me later that the application would come up for hearing on May 29, 1976. I went and told Atalji the judgment would most probably come before that date and it did on May 28, 1976. After the judgment was delivered, I told the Court that I would like to withdraw my application as it had become infractuous.

It is significant that after the judgment was delivered, Madhu Limaye's *Habeas Corpus* petition sent from the jail was "Dismissed as Withdrawn" by Bench presided by Chief Justice A.N. Ray. When Madhu Limaye received copy of the order, he wrote to the Chief Justice that he was not justified in passing that order as he had not withdrawn the petition and asked V.M. Tarkunde to mention the matter. On mentioning the case, Justice Chandrachud, who was a member of that Bench, objected to such an order and the petition was restored and as expected the Court passed an order dismissing it.

It may be mentioned that Madhu Limaye had a premonition about the verdict. On April 3, 1976, nearly months before the judgment from Narsinghpur Sub-Jail in Madhya Pradesh where he was detained he wrote to me. "Suddenly I have lost all interest in the Court proceedings." [Facsimile of the letter is enclosed (Plate 5)].

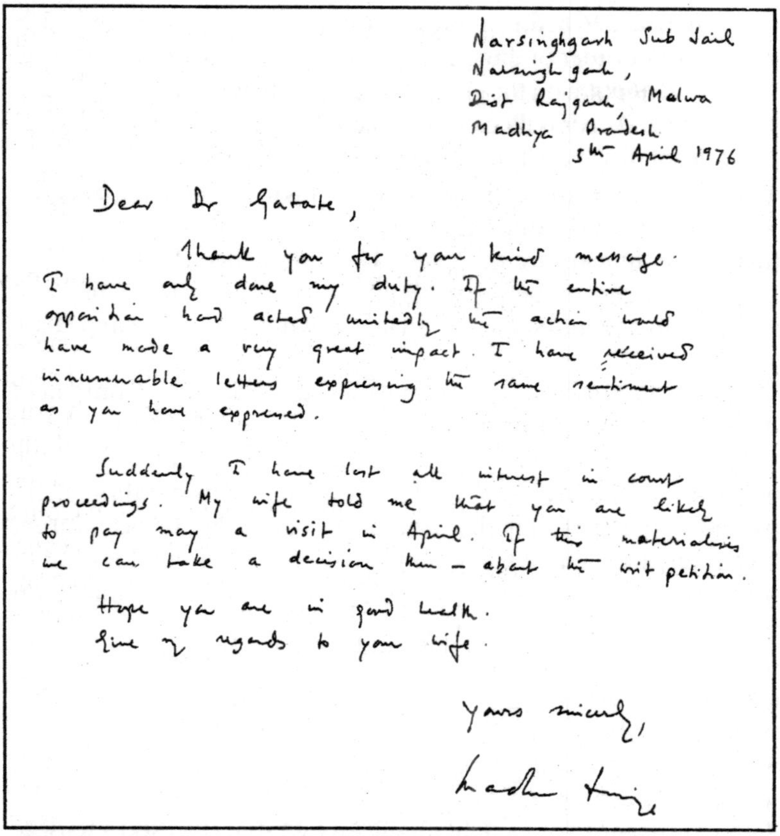

Narsinghgarh Sub Jail
Narsinghgarh,
Dist Rajgarh, Malwa
Madhya Pradesh
5th April 1976

Dear Dr Gatate,

Thank you for your kind message. I have only done my duty. If the entire opposition had acted unitedly the action would have made a very great impact. I have received innumerable letters expressing the same sentiment as you have expressed.

Suddenly I have lost all interest in court proceedings. My wife told me that you are likely to pay me a visit in April. If this materialises we can take a decision then – about the writ petition.

Hope you are in good health.
Give my regards to your wife.

Yours sincerely,
Madhu Limaye

Plate 5: Madhu Limaye's Letter Dated 5.4.76.

The arguments on behalf of the detenues were censored. But I have a singular distinction of my arguments being reported in the prestigious *The Times* of London (see Appendix II).

THE JUDGMENT

All the five judges wrote separate judgments, with Justice Khanna dissenting, giving elaborate reasons for their conclusion extending over 260 printed pages. The operative order by majority which laid down the law reads as under:

(i) In view of the Presidential Order dated June 27, 1975, no person has any *locus standi* to move any writ petition under

Article 226 before a High Court or *habeas corpus* or any other writ or order or direction to challenge the legality of an order of detention on the ground that the order is not in compliance, or the Act or is illegal, or is vitiated by *mala fides*, the factual or legal or is based on extraneous consideration;

(ii) Section 16A(9) of the Maintenance of Internal Security Act is constitutionally valid;

(iii) The appeals are accepted. The judgments are set aside;

(iv) The petitions before the High Court are now to be disposed of in accordance with the law laid down in these appeals.[20]

According to this operative order, the Supreme Court held that the detenue had no right to obtain release whatsoever. Even if detention was *mala fide* or was not in accordance with the provisions of the MISA or was for extraneous consideration, there was no opportunity for the detenue to obtain his release during the Emergency. There being no provision to limit the duration of the Emergency, the detenues could be detained indefinitely, on the sweet will of the government.

This pronouncement of the highest court of the land came as a shock. The preliminary objection of the Government as to the maintainability of the *habeas corpus* petitions, which was rejected by the nine High Courts was upheld by Chief Justice Ray, Justices Beg, Chandrachud and Bhagwati. Twenty-five Judges of various High Courts and Justice Khanna were told that they were wrong.

After the judgment, all newspapers wrote editorials but none in India praised the majority judgment, perhaps for fear of inviting the government's wrath. It may be recalled that Advani commenting on the behaviour of the press as a Minister for Information and Broadcasting after the Janata Government came to power, said; "When Indira Gandhi asked you to bend, you started crawling."

But P.L. Lakhanpal, a bold journalist, had been editor and publisher of his small weekly *Evening View* and had been publishing news about Court proceedings throughout the Emergency undaunted by censorship orders and threatened criminal action which were issued every week. After the judgment he carried the front page edition on May 2, 1976 issue of the *Evening View* with a headline *Sovereign Becomes Slave, Servant the Master. Bar and People*

Rudely Shaken by Judgment in Habeas Corpus Matters". He quoted Justice Khanna's famous or dissent and reaction of the several leading Members of the Bar. V.M. Tarkunde described it as "The Blackest Judgment ever delivered by the Supreme Court." M.C. Chagla commented, "Justice Khanna's judgment will shine for ever." And he compared the majority judgment, "The fire brigade which ran away at the first spark of fire." Shanti Bhushan said that the review of this judgment was imperative. H.M. Seervai stated that the High Courts rose to the occasion, but, "the Supreme Court shrank," while Jai Prakash Narain's reaction to the judgement was, "[It] has put out the last flickering candle of liberty."

One of the finest tributes to Justice Khanna was in the editorial of the *New York Times* two days after the verdict. In its April 30, 1976, issue it wrote:

> If India ever finds its way back to the freedom and democracy that were proud hallmarks of its first 18 years as an independent nation, someone will surely erect a monument to Justice H.R. Khanna of the Supreme Court. It was Mr. Justice Khanna who spoke fearlessly and eloquently for freedom this week in dissenting from the Court's decision upholding the right of Prime Minister Indira Gandhi's Government to imprison political opponents at will and without court hearings.
>
> Indian democrats are likely to remember only in infamy the four judges who obediently overturned the decisions of a half-dozen lower courts scattered across India, which had ruled in defiance of the Government that the right of habeas corpus could not be suspended, even during the emergency that Mrs. Gandhi declared last June. But they will long cherish the lonely judge who said, in words reminiscent of other enduring declarations for freedom. ..."[21]

As expected like other judges who were victimized for giving judgments against the Government, Justice Khanna who was the seniormost Judge in the Supreme Court was superseded from becoming the Chief Justice of India. Commenting on his supersession, Soli Sorabjee said, "He might have been superseded by the Government but he has superseded all the Judges in our heart."

When I went to see Atalji in AIIMS, he said, "In a situation like this, political battle cannot be won by legal means."

I informed Advaniji who was in the Bangalore Jail about Atalji's remarks. He in his letter of May 3, 1976 wrote, "Atalji is very right when he points to the limitation of legal battle in a situation of this kind. On the basis of what was reported about the judgment, Advaniji's reaction is rather illuminating. He wrote:

> The Supreme Court has decided not against the detenues but against itself. After all, no detenue was expecting to be released because of the Court judgment. If the verdict had been favourable, it would have only hastened the amendment of Article 226. Of course, that amendment too might have been challenged. But it only means that the Court battle would have gone on for another few months. Now so far as this confrontation is concerned, the curtain may be regarded to have been dropped. In a way it is good... whatever mileage could be derived from this battle, I think has been derived—Thanks to your efforts personally and the contribution of others. For nearly 8 months we have been able, through these writ petitions to mobilize wide support in Sections concerned with Courts in support of the cause of liberty. The only regret is that after the valiant battle put up by the High Courts, we should have to witness this kind of judicial abdication at the level of the highest Tribunal. It is certainly an anti-climax in this reversal of eight High Court judgments.
>
> You have asked if we should go in appeal on the issue of the Emergency. Well, my first reaction is no. The Detention issue was far simpler. H.C. decisions were entirely in conformity with the law of preventive detention laid down by the Supeme Court. When even on such an issue, the Supreme Court has preferred a volt face, I see not an iota of possibility of the Court taking a different view on such issue. We do not have full judgment with us; we would love to have it with us. But from the press reports it seems J. Chandrachud has commented even on the non-maintainability of Emergency and commended the High Courts for holding that the Emergency Proclamation was

not justiciable. Even so as you say we shall decide finally when the High Court dismisses our petitions [when] High Court reopens on May 24, not in June.

It was gratifying to see your argument about International Law had made the mark with J. Khanna and that he has in his dissenting judgment, specifically upheld it. That is a well deserved plaudit for you personally. [(Plate 6)]

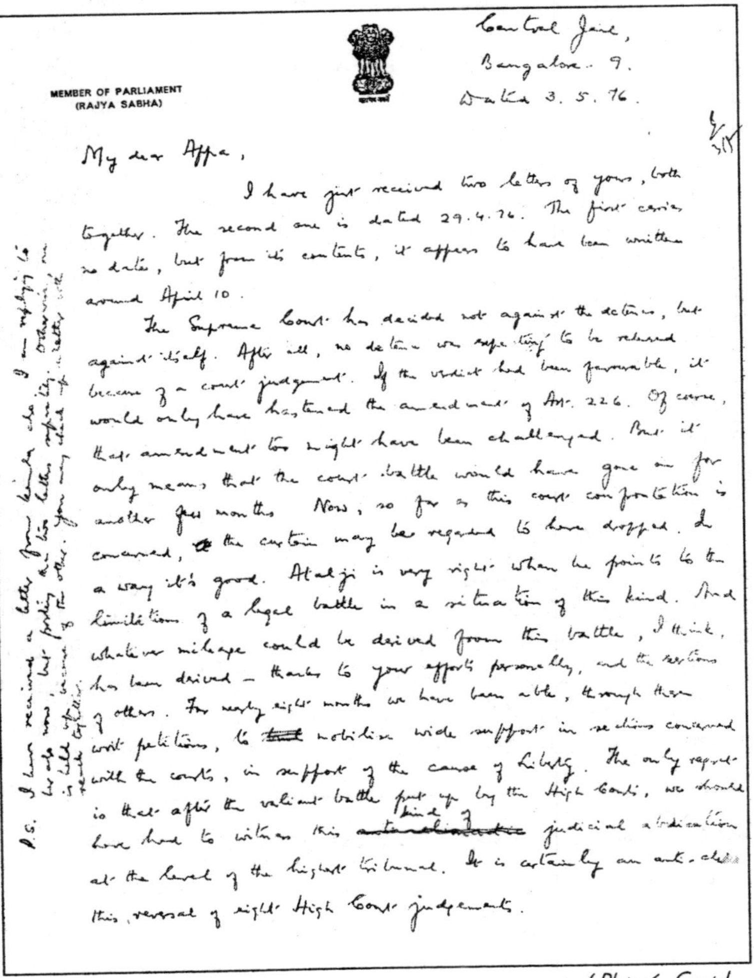

MEMBER OF PARLIAMENT
(RAJYA SABHA)

Central Jail,
Bangalore - 9.
Dated 3. 5. 76.

My dear Appa,

I have just received two letters of yours, both together. The second one is dated 29.4.76. The first carries no date, but from its contents, it appears to have been written around April 10.

The Supreme Court has decided not against the detenus, but against itself. After all, no detenu was expecting to be released because of a court judgment. If the verdict had been favourable, it would only have hastened the amendment of Art. 226. Of course, that amendment too might have been challenged. But it only means that the court battle would have gone on for another few months. Now, so far as this court confrontation is concerned, the curtain may be regarded to have dropped. In a way it's good. Atalji is very right when he points to the limitations of a legal battle in a situation of this kind. And whatever mileage could be derived from this battle, I think, has been derived – thanks to your efforts personally, and the sections of others. For nearly eight months we have been able, through these writ petitions, to mobilise wide support in sections concerned with the courts, in support of the cause of Liberty. The only regret is that after the valiant battle put up by the High Courts, we should have had to witness this ~~[illegible]~~ kind of judicial abdication at the level of the highest tribunal. It is certainly an anti-climax this reversal of eight High Court judgements.

P.S. I have received a letter from Kamla also. I am replying to her also now, but posting the two letters separately. Otherwise, one is held up because of the other. You may check up whether both reach together.

(*Plate 6, Contd. …*)

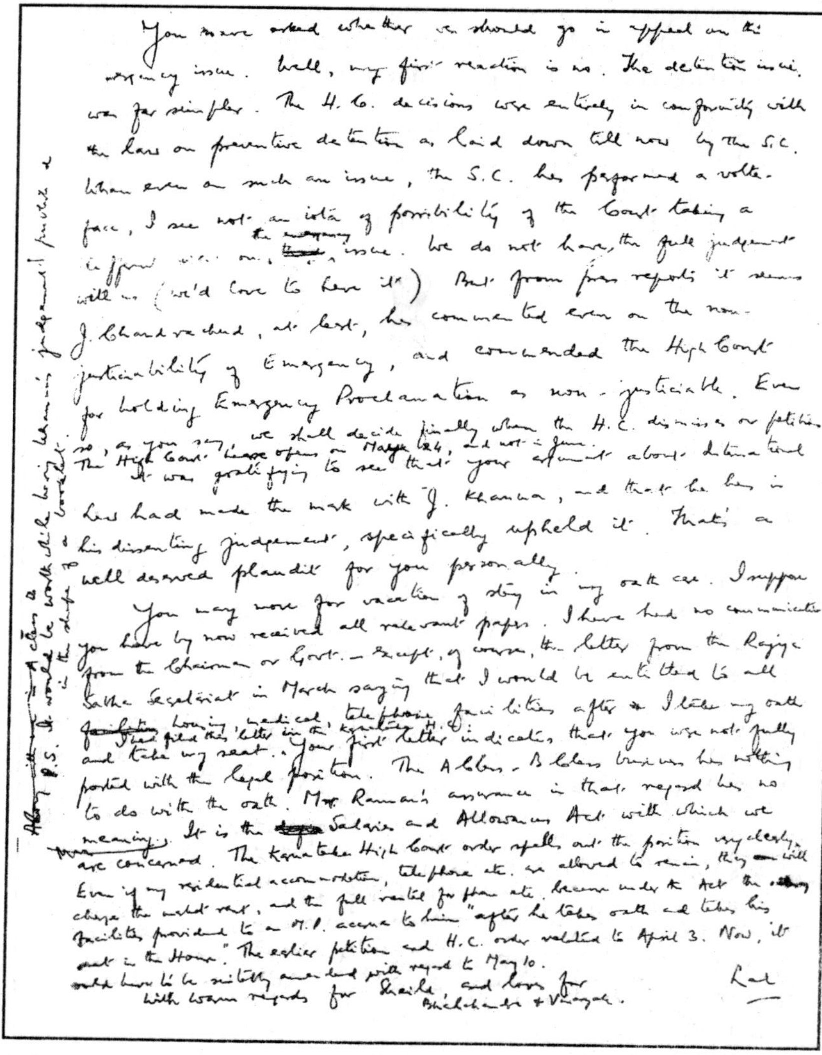

You have asked whether we should go in appeal on the emergency issue. Well, my first reaction is no. The detention issue was far simpler. The H.C. decisions were entirely in conformity with the law on preventive detention as laid down till now by the S.C. When even on such an issue, the S.C. has performed a volte-face, I see not an iota of possibility of the Court taking a different view on the emergency issue. We do not have the full judgement with us (we'd love to have it) But from press reports it seems J. Chandrachud, at last, has commented even on the non-justiciability of Emergency, and commended the High Court for holding Emergency Proclamation as non-justiciable. Even so, as you say, we shall decide finally when the H.C. dismisses our petition. The High Court leave opens on May 24, and not in June. It was gratifying to see that your argument about detention have had made the mark with J. Khanna, and that he has in his dissenting judgement, specifically upheld it. That's a well deserved plaudit for you personally.

You may move for vacation of stay in my oath case. I suppose you have by now received all relevant papers. I have had no communication from the Chairman or Govt. – except, of course, the letter from the Rajya Sabha Secretariat in March saying that I would be entitled to all facilities housing, medical, telephone facilities after I take my oath and take my seat. I had filed this letter in the Karnataka H.C. Your first letter indicates that you were not fully posted with the legal position. The Ablers-Bladers business has nothing to do with the oath. Mr. Raman's assurance in that regard has no meaning. It is the Salaries and Allowances Act with which we are concerned. The Karnataka High Court order spells out the position very clearly. Even if my residential accommodation, telephone etc. are allowed to remain, they will charge the market rent, and the full rental for phone etc. because under the Act the facilities provided to an M.P. accrue to him "after he takes oath and takes his seat in the House." The earlier petition and H.C. order related to April 3. Now, it would have to be suitably amended with regard to May 10.

With warm regards for Shaila, and love for Bhishmaks & Vinayak.

Lal

P.S. It would be worth while having Khanna's judgement printed & circulated in the shape of booklet. Along with it = a clear & [illegible]

Plate 6: Advani's Letter Dated 3.5.76 (see typed version on next page)

L.K. Advani
Member of Parliament
(Rajya Sabha)

Emblem

Central Jail
Bangalore-9
Dated 3.5.76

My dear Appa,

I have just received two letters of yours, both together. The second one is dated 29.4.76. The first carries no date, but from its contents, it appears to have been written around April 10.

The Supreme Court has decided not against the detenue, but against itself. After all, no detenue was expecting to be released because of a court judgement. If the verdict had been favourable, it would only have hastened the amendment of Art. 226. Of course, that amendment too might have been challenged. But it only means that the court battle would have gone on for another few months. Now, so far as this court confrontation is concerned, the curtain may be regarded to have dropped. In a way it's good. Atalji is very right when he points to the limitations of a legal battle in a situation of this kind. And whatever mileage could be derived from this battle, I think, has been derived - thanks to your efforts personally, through these writ petitions, to mobilise wide support in sections concerned with the courts, in support of the cause of Liberty. The only regret is that after the valiant battle put up by the High Courts, we should have had to witness this kind of judicial abdication at the level of the highest tribunal. It is certainly an anti-climax this reversal of eight High Court judgements.

You have asked whether we should go in appeal on this emergency issue. Well, my first reaction is no. The detention issue was far simpler. The H.C. decisions were entirely in conformity with the law on preventive detention as laid down till now by the S.C. When even on such an issue, the S.C. has performed a volte-face, I see not an iota of possibility of the Court taking a different view on the emergency issue.

We do not have the full judgement with us (we'd love to have it). But from press reports it seems J. Chandrachud, at least, has commented even on the non-justiciability of Emergency,

(*Contd.*)

and commended the High Court for holding Emergency Proclamation as non-justiciable. Even so, as you say, we shall decide finally when the H.C. dismisses our petitions. The High Court here opens on May 24, and not in June.

It was gratifying to see that your argument about International Law had made the mark with J. Khanna, and that he has in his dissenting judgement, specifically upheld it. That's a well deserved plandit for you personally. You may move for vacation of stay in my oath case. I suppose you have by now received all relevant papers. I have had no communication from the Chairman or Govt. – except, of course, the letter from the Rajya Sabha Secretariat in March saying that I would be entitled to all housing, medical, telephone facilities after I take my oath and take my seat. I had filed this letter in the Karnataka H.C. Your first letter indicates that you were not fully posted with the legal position. The A Class – B Class business has nothing to do with the oath. Mr. Raman's assurance in that regard has no meaning. It is the Salaries and Allowances Act with which we are concerned. The Karnataka High Court order spells out the position very clearly. Even if my residential accommodation, telephone, etc. are allowed to remain, they will charge the market rent, and the full rental for phone etc. because under the orders and facilities provided to M.P. accrue to him "after he takes oath and takes his seat in the House." The earlier petition and H.C. order related to April 3. Now, It would have to be suitably amended with regard to May 10.

With warm regards for Sheila and loves for Bhalchandra & Vinayak.

Sd/-
(L.K. Advani)

P.S.: I have received a letter from Kamala also. I am replying to her also now, but posting the two letters separately. Otherwise, one is held up because of the other. You may check up whether both reach together.

It would be worthwhile bringing Khanna's judgement published in the shape of a booklet.

ANALYSIS OF THE JUDGMENT

First of all the operative part of the order that the detenue did not have any *locus standi* to move a petition to challenge the order of detention on any ground whatsoever was in fact contrary to the views expressed by judges in majority, while Justice Khanna rejected outright the Government's contention. According to the three judges in majority they held that once a valid order of detention *i.e.* signed by authority empowered to detain—was shown and that the purpose of detention was in accordance with the provisions of law in response to the notice to the *habeas corpus* petition the court could not go behind the order. Justice Beg stated that the fact of "illegality applied by courts is not entirely abrogated or abandoned in the current emergency." Justice Chandrachud stated that relief could also be given in case of the false identify of the detenue. While Justice Bhagwati gave two examples when detenues could obtain release in spite of the Presidential Order, if the person was detained before June 25, 1975, Section 16A was not applicable and when the order of detention was made after June 25, 1975, and declaration under Section 16A was not made, that detention was necessary for effectively marinating the Emergency. In both these cases the detenue was entitled to receive grounds of detention and make representation to the detaining authority and to the Advisory Board. In such cases if the Government did not abide by the statutory obligations, the bar of the Presidential Order would not come in the way. He added that whenever a *habeas corpus* petition came to court, "It must not be rejected straightaway... the court would have to consider whether the Presidential bar is attracted. The operative order was in accordance with only one judge *i.e.* Chief Justice A.N. Ray who accepted "the sole repository theory" propounded by Niren De. .....with a logic that these rights were "the gift of law and could be forfeited by law" under the Constitution which was the supreme law of the land and the concept of the rule of law above the constitutional law was untenable.

Justice H.R. Khanna in his famous dissenting judgment tore this argument to pieces when he observed:

> .... Suspending the right of a person to move any court for the enforcement of the right to life and personal liberty is done under a constitutional provision and therefore it cannot be said that the resulting situation would mean the absence of the rule of law. This argument, in my opinion, cannot stand close scrutiny for it tries to equate illusion of the rule of law with the reality of the rule of law. Supposing a law is made in the matter of the protection of life and liberty, the administrative officers would not be governed by any law and that it would be permissible for them to deprive a person of life and liberty without any authority of law. In one sense, it might in that event be argued that even if lives of hundreds of persons are taken capriciously and maliciously without the authority of law, it is enforcement of the above enacted law [it is] in a purely formal sense, any system of norm based on a hierarchy of orders, even the organized mass murders of the Nazi regime qualify as law. The argument cannot, however, disguise the reality of the matter that hundreds of innocent lives have been taken because of the absence of the rule of law. A state of negation of the rule of law would not cease to be such a state because of the fact that such a state of negation of the rule of law has been brought about by statute.[20]

Nevertheless, the operative order was binding on the High Courts. The result was that all *habeas corpus* petitions pending in High Courts were dismissed. As a consequence, detenues could be detained as long as the Government wished during the Emergency, as there was then no limit on the duration of the Emergency, even if detention was *mala fide* and not in accordance with the provision of detention law.

Even if it is assumed, for the sake of argument, that the operative order was in accordance with the judgments of the majority of the judges and that the *locus standi* of the detenue to approach court was taken away, it was in respect of only challenging an order of detention, that is to say, for the purpose of obtaining release; nothing more, or nothing less.

There was nothing in the operative order to infer that there was no remedy if a detenue's right to life contained in Article 21 was infringed, if the detaining authority violated rules regarding conditions of detention, or subjected him to such condition by which detention became punitive or gave him inhuman treatment.

ARTICLE 21

As mentioned earlier, only Chief Justice Ray accepted the theory of Article 21 being a sole repository of the right to life and liberty and as such, no such rights existed outside Article 21. The other three judges in majority, however, confined their observation to personal liberty mentioned in the article. Justice Bhagwati, who held that the article covered *all attributes of personal freedom,* indirectly accepted the sole repository theory as far as personal liberty was concerned, while Justice Beg was of the view that even if Article 21 was not the sole repository of the right to personal freedom since Articles 19, 21 and 22 were suspended, every attribute of personal liberty was also suspended. Justice Chandrachud did not find it necessary to decide this question because according to him in view of Article 359 read with the Presidential Order, the detenue had "no legal capacity to move the High Court for release," while Justice Khanna totally rejected this theory.

If Article 21 was the sole repository to life and personal liberty as was held by Chief Justice Ray, one cannot understand what was the need to suspend Articles 19 and 22 which covered some aspects of personal liberty since they could also be traced to Article 21? The fact that these two articles were also suspended goes a long way in demolishing the sole repository theory. More importantly, it cannot be overlooked that Article 21 contains not only the right to personal liberty, but also the right to life. But by confining themselves to the question of liberty only Justices Beg, Chandrachud and Bhagwati, skirted the key issue whether the right to life can also be suspended.

This in turn raises some very fundamental questions. Can the President, who under Article 359 have the power only to suspend and not amend or abrogate a fundamental right, suspend a right which he cannot restore? Does not the power of suspension imply a duty of restoration? Since life once taken cannot be restored, does not suspension of the right to life amount to its destruction? Would it not then amount to constitutional amendment? Chief Justice Ray who accepted the sole repository even as regards to the right to life, ought to have answered these questions when they were specifically raised during the argument. In conforming its scrutiny of Article 21 to the right to personal liberty only, the other three majority judges should have also dealt with these questions because the subjects of interpretation the Article 21 itself in which the right to life also figures, along with liberty.

ARTICLE 359 AND THE PRESIDENTIAL ORDER OF 1975

The Presidential Order of 1975 was worded differently than that of 1962. While under the latter order the right to move for enforcement of Articles 19, 21 and 22 was suspended for persons detained under the Defence of India Act of 1962 or any rule made thereunder, the former did not make such qualifications. The majority judges accepted Niren De's contention that the 1975 Order was a blanket order and not a conditional order as in 1962 and came to the conclusion that even if a person was detained *mala fide* or without complying with the provisions of the law under which a person was detained no *Habeas Corpus* petition to obtain release was maintainable.

It is submitted that if no particular law was mentioned in the Presidential Order it followed that whichever law under which a person was detained had to be complied with, the State could deprive a person of his right only by the authority of that law, emergency or no emergency.

In the famous *Liversidege's case* which was decided in 1942 when England was fighting Germany with its back to the wall, Lord Parker, who spoke for the majority, observed:

"The fact that the nation is at war is no justification for any relaxation of the vigilance of the courts in seeing that the law is duly observed, especially in the matter so fundamental as liberty of the subject. Rather the contrary."[22]

Similarly, Lord Brickenhead in *O' Brien's case* stated:

> "It has through ages been jealously maintained by the courts of law as a check upon the illegal userping of power by the executive at the cost of liege."[23]

Dr. B.R. Ambedkar told the Constituent Assembly that it was expected that if the executive is honest in working the Constitution, then the Executive is bound to obey the Legislature without any kind of compulsory obligation being laid down in the Constitution. According to him the obligation to obey law was never found in any Constitution he knew of and had always to be presumed.

The presumption has been made explicit by the Supreme Court on several occasions, as mentioned earlier and that too in deciding *habeas corpus* cases of persons who were detained during the 1962 Emergency. In *Makhan Singh's case*, even the majority interpreting the scope of the Article 359 held that illegal or *mala fide* order of detention was not covered and could always be challenged despite the suspension of the remedy to enforce Fundamental Rights mentioned in the President's Order under Article 359 of the Constitution.

If the majority in this case felt that the judgment of the Seven Judge-Bench in *Makhan Singh's case* was wrong, they ought to have referred the case to a larger bench instead of explaining away the ratio of that case as *obiter* and impliedly overruling it which was impermissable.

SECTION 16A OF MISA

The majority held that Section 16-A of MISA, prevented the High Court from examining the grounds of detention or material and information on which the detention order was made, because they were matters of State and it was against public interest to disclose them and this provision was only as a rule evidence and the High Court could not examine the forbidden fruit. As the judiciary is one of the three limbs of the State, can such disclosure to the High Court be against public interest? It is submitted that Parliament was not empowered to encroach the jurisdiction of the High Court under Article 226 of the Constitution without the constitutional amendment in the guise of amending the provisions of MISA. Therefore, this provision should have either been read down as not restricting the High Court's constitutional power or struck down as violative of Article 226. Furthermore, the majority was not justified in making the declaration that Section 16A of MISA was valid because there was no appeal on this point by the detenues who were appellants. The Supreme Court, as Justice Khanna held, could not "enlarge the area of favourable decision *qua* the State and make its position worse compared to what it was before filing the appeal." It is submitted that Justice Khanna was right and the Supreme Court, by upholding the validity of this clause, short-circuited the procedure and bypassed the High Court.

HUMAN RIGHTS

If the majority erred in hastening to decide the question of validity of Section 16-A of MISA, when it was not put squarely before the court, it also erred in ignoring some important submissions. The judges, who were in majority, ought to have pronounced on the submission whether the right to life in Article 21 could be suspended under Article 359 without a constitutional amendment. Secondly, in view of Article 51 and India's international obligations in the field of Human Rights could Article 21 and the Presidential Order be interpreted to grant the Government unfettered powers to treat their subjects any way they pleased? When those points were specifically raised and argued, Justice Khanna, relying on the Declaration of Human Rights, upheld the arguments saying that if two constructions of the Presidential Order were permissible the Court should adopt that construction which would be in harmony and not in conflict with the country's international obligations.

But the three Judges, Chief Justice Ray, Justice Chandrachud and Justice Bhagwati did not even consider the argument which Justice Khanna thought to be "pre-eminently reasonable". Justice Beg did deal with the argument, but according to him nothing which was contrary to the provisions of the law could be enforced under any guise, and made an amazing observation:

> No lawyer can seriously question the correctness, in Public International Law, of the proposition that the operation and effect of such [emergency] provision are matters which are entirely the domestic concern of legally sovereign States and can brook no outside interference.

This observation is wholly incorrect. The sovereignty of the State to treat its citizens in any way it likes on the plea of domestic jurisdiction has long been rejected by the international community. In fact, India ever since independence, time and again, had raised the question of *Apartheid* and the racial laws of South Africa in the United Nations, and opposed the contention of South Africa that it was a domestic matter. The question of violation of Human Rights had become the question of international jurisdiction. The State cannot just at the will of those in governance, trample the Human Rights of any part of its populace because the rest of the civilized world stands behind them. To say the least, such a view as held by Justice Beg, could only encourage absolutism.

VALIDITY OF THE EMERGENCY

As pointed out earlier the question of justiciablity of the Emergency was not before the Supreme Court. Justice Chandrachud, however, observed that it was impossible to examine such questions of High State policy in courts of law. This should have been avoided as even the *obiter* is binding on the High Courts.

But Justice Beg went further. He said, "I am sure that the current Emergency has to be justified not only by the rapid improvements due to it in the seriously dislocated national economy and discipline but also by grave dangers of tomorrow, apparent to those who have eyes to see them."

Commenting on the statement made at the Bar about the plight of detenues, Justice Beg was harsh. He stated:

> I do not think that it is either responsible advocacy or performance of any patriotic or public duty to suggest that powers of preventive detention are being misused in

> the current emergency, when our attention could not be drawn to the allegation in a single case even by way of illustration of the alleged misuse instead of drawing upon one's own imagination to concur up phantoms. In fact I asked some learned counsels to indicate the alleged facts of any particular case before us to enable us to appreciate how the powers of preventive detention had been misused.
>
> Mostly the answers given were that the facts to the case were not before us at this stage which is true. But it is significant to note that no cases of alleged *malice infact* could be even brought to our notice.

Justice Beg's remarks that Advocates appearing for the detenues were irresponsible and questioning their patriotism was totally uncalled for. Nor was he correct in saying that not a single case of abuse of emergency powers by way of illustration was brought to the notice of the court. During the arguments it was specifically pointed out by Anil Divan that Mrinal Gore was being imprisoned with lepers and S.N. Dwivedi had produced blank detention orders signed by the authorities.

But as regards Government's treatment of the detenues was concerned, Justice Beg spoke with a different tone and stated without any facts before him:

> Furthermore, *we understand* that the care and concern bestowed by the State authorities upon the welfare of detenues who are wellhoused, well fed and well treated is almost maternal.

Justice Beg's observations about detenues receiving maternal treatment was a classic example of judicial forgetfulness for they were contrary to the facts of which he had personal knowledge from the proceedings before him. Before this judgment was delivered he was a member of the Bench presided over by Chief Justice Ray before whom the Government appealed against several orders of the Karnataka and Bombay High Courts allowing students to be taken in police custody so that they did not loose their academic year and to allow Shri L.K. Advani to perform his constitutional right to take the oath in the Rajya Sabha. Similarly, against the order of the Bombay High Court which allowed detenues getting food from home or from getting private medical treatment at the detenue's own expenses or allowing interviews to the family members as guaranteed by the Conditions of Detention Order of 1974. One had only to glance at the petitions regarding conditions of detention which were filed in the various High Courts and which are examined subsequently to know the type of treatment meted out to the detenues.

Justice Chandrachud, also was hopeful that the emergency would not tarnish India's image. In the conclusion of his judgment he stated:

> Counsel after counsel expressed the fear that during the Emergency, the Executive may whip and strip and starve the detenue and if this be our judgment, even shoot him down. Such misdeeds have not furnished the record of free India and I have *diamond-bright, diamond-hard hope* that such things will never come to pass.

How this fond hope was misplaced is found in the dockets of the Supreme Court in *Rajan's case*, which came before the Supreme Court.[25]

Rajan, an engineering student studying in Regional Engineering College, Calicut, in Kerala, was whisked away by the police on March 1, 1977. The affidavit filed before the Kerala High Court by K. Karunakaran, who was Home Minister during the emergency, stated that Rajan:

> ...happened to be tortured while in police custody at the Kottayam camp as a result of which he breathed his last while in such custody at the camp on the evening of 2.3.1976.

And Karunakaran, who had earlier denied that Rajan was taken into police custody, was forced to resign as the Chief Minister because of public indignation at the brutalities committed during this Emergency.

It is not out of place to mention here that my father who was detained in Thane Jail and was suspected of having cancer; I went to Bombay to request the then Chief Minister S.B. Chavan to release him on parole for a check-up to which he agreed. At that time Niren De was arguing a sugar license case in the Bombay High Court. I met him in the Court and he invited me in the evening at the Express Towers where he was staying.

He asked me, "What brings you to Bombay?" I replied, "Your argument that the detenue has no right to liberty or life being accepted in the *A.D.M., Jabalpur's case.* I am left only with a begging bowl." He told me, "After this case was over I went to the Prime Minister Mrs. Indira Gandhi and told her after the Emergency is lifted all the detenues will file cases for damages if their detention was *mala fide* or illegal. So please give me the files and I will examine them and advise as to who should be released. Om Mehta, who was then the Minister of State for Home, was also present. He said that there were thousands of files. I told the Prime Minister, I will take leave for three months and give a report as to who should be released and who should be detained," but Mrs. Indira Gandhi replied to me, "I can't show them to you for political reasons. So I was helpless." This he told me in private in September, 1976, when there was no inkling of the lifting of the Emergency.

In November, 1976, some leaders like Ashok Mehta, Charan Singh were released and there was speculation that the elections might be held soon. H.V. Kamath, who was not imprisoned, was one of the organisers for providing a joint opposition to the Congress. He told me to ask Vajpayee what his conditions for joining the front were. When I asked Atalji about this, he said "We have no conditions. We would agree to any name of the front, any symbol, or any flag." When I told this to H.V. Kamath, he said, "So Vajpayeeji has given *carte blanche*". I said, "Yes". The elections were announced on January 17, and on January 20, 1977, several political leaders were released and at the coordination meeting of the opposition leaders several points of dispute were raised, including by the Jana Sangha leaders. During that meeting Shri Kamath told Atalji, "Ghatate told me you had given a blank cheque. But now I find that this cheque has no date, no amount, not even a signature."*

Since all leading political leaders were released, Prime Minister Mrs. Gandhi invited them for a discussion. In that meeting, Atalji told her that all the opposition political workers should be released immediately in order to fight the elections. She replied it would take some time. Atalji countered "*Jis chaturai se aapne do din mey hazaron ko giraftar kiya, aap unko chhod bhi sakti hai*" (The shrewdness you showed in arresting thousands of people in two days, can also be used to release them).*

There was one very interesting case of Tikam Chand Khetri, Advocate from Guwahati, who was arrested under MISA. Surprisingly unlike other detenues, who were detained after the declaration of Internal Emergency were not entitled to receive grounds of detention because of the insertion of 16A of the MISA to prevent them from challenging their detention. Mr. Khetri, advocate of Assam High Court, was given grounds of detention. One of his charges was that he had criticized Indira Gandhi for declaring an Emergency, in the High Court Bar Association. He filed the *Habeas Corpus* Petition but the High Court dismissed it in view of the Supreme Court's operative order in *A.D.M. Jabalpur's case.* I filed a Special Leave Petition in the Supreme Court stating that this ground of detention was irrelevant and detention order deserved to be struck down as held by several judgments of the Supreme Court and pointed out that even in *A.D.M. Jabalpur's case*, Justice P.N. Bhagwati had held that, in an unlikely event if grounds of detention are given then petition could not be thrown out as not maintainable. And Courts could adjudicate on the validity of the detention. The petition came for hearing before a Bench of the Supreme Court presided over by Justice V.R. Krishna Iyer. He told me that he was transferring the petition to Chief Justice A.N. Ray's Bench. When I protested, he said, "I give you a choice, either it will be dismissed or I will transfer the petition." It was hardly a choice so I agreed that it may be transferred. But the Registry again happened to post it before Justice Krishna Iyer, as by that time elections were declared and the rigour of Emergency had been considerably reduced. When this petition came for hearing, the same Justice Krishna Iyer admitted the petition without any arguments. However when the appeal came up for hearing before Justice Murtaza Fazal Ali, the Janata Government had come to power and the emergency was withdrawn and my clients had been released. Justice Fazal Ali, therefore, disposed off this petition as it had become infructuous.

During the Emergency, neither of the constitutional wings *viz.*, the Legislature or the Judiciary came to the rescue of democracy. In the historic elections of 1977, it was the people who re-established democracy by decisively defeating the Congress including Indira Gandhi and sweeping the Janata Party to power. All the constituents of the Janata Party decided to merge and dissolve their separate parties.

Moving a resolution dissolving the Jana Sangha, Vajpayee's emotive words are memorable. He said: *"Attank-kal ke ghor andhere me Jana Sangha ka Deepak roushni deta tha. Ab suryodaya ho gaya hai, Deepak bujhane ka samay aa gaya hai."* (In the dark days of Emergency, our Deepak—symbol of Jana Sangha—was the only ray of hope. But now there is sun rise and time has come to snuff the flame).

That was the Emergency that was.

The Supreme Court Bar however embarrassed the Judges in majority for years for their judgment in the *A.D.M. Jabalpur's case.* To cite one instance, five years later when the Constitution Bench of the Supreme Court in the *Waman Rao's case* was presided over by Chief Justice Y.V. Chandrachud and consisted of Justice P.N. Bhagwati and three other Judges who were hearing the case, one of the challenges to the Agricultural Land Ceiling Amendment of 1976 was that of the Constitution Amendment placing this Act in the 9th Schedule to protect it from being challenged on the grounds of violation of Fundamental Rights was passed during the extended life of the Lok Sabha by one year permissible when the Emergency was in operation. Since the imposition of the Emergency itself was *mala fide* this extension of the Lok Sabha was also unconstitutional. Therefore, this Constitution Amendment Act was also invalid.

During the arguments, Chief Justice Y.V. Chandrachud observed, "After all, the Emergency is challenged by agricultural land holders." Mr. R.K. Garg, a Senior Advocate immediately got up and said. "We all know what you did when suspension of the right to life and liberty under the Emergency was challenged by the detenues".[25]

After over 28 years of the judgment in the *A.D.M. Jabalpur's case*, in 1994, the Nine-Judges Bench of the Supreme Court, Justice B.P. Jeevan Reddy speaking for the Nine-Judges Bench of the Supreme Court in the *Attorney General for India Vs. Amritlal*

Prajivandas case cited earlier that the Constitution Bench Judgment such at in the *Makhan Singh, K. Anand Nambiar* and *Jaya Chand Lall Sethia's cases* having held that the validity of the detention order can be challenged on the ground of non-compliance with the law or *mala fide* as these were not covered by the Presidential Order issued under Articles 358 and 359, correctly observed: "The majority opinion in the *A.D.M. Jabalpur's case*, however appears to have taken a contrary view." Having said so, it is submitted with great respect that he was not correct in holding, "It is not necessary to go into the correctness of the reasoning in the *A.D.M. Jabalpur case*, since it has not been debated before us." It is submitted that during the hearing, no such suggestion was made. Even so, Justice Jeevan Reddy should have noticed that in that very case Justice H.R. Khanna in his famous dissent concluded, "A dissent in a court of last resort, to use [Chief Justice Hughes words,] is an appeal to the brooding spirit of the law, to the intelligence of a future day, when a later decision may possibly correct the error into which the dissenting judge believes the court to have been betrayed," and ought to have overruled this case.

However, Justice Jeevan Reddy aptly observed:

> "The requirement of Emergency constitutes both the foundation as well as inplied limitation upon the power. What is warranted is what is necessary for effective implementation of the emergency."[26]

ENDNOTES

1. *Makhan Singh Tarsikka Vs. State of Punjab*, 1964 (4) S.C.R. 932.
2. *P.L. Lakhanpal Vs. U.O.I.* 1966 Supl. S.C.R. 209; *Gulam Sarvar Vs. U.O.I.*, A.I.R. 1967 S.C. 1334.
3. *Bhutnath Methe Vs. State of West Bengal*, 1974(1) SCC 645.
4. *S. Sadanand Vs. State of Kerala*, A.I.R. 1966.
5. For various Constitutional Amendments and of the MISA during the Emergency are given in the chart. See *Appendix-I*.
6. M. Rama Joice, who retired as Chief Justice of the Punjab and Haryana High Court, was acting in defending the detenues in the Karnataka High Court. He has given the details of events in his

book *The Great Legal Battle* for which I stand indebted for narrating the events in this Chapter.

7. By the 39th Constitutional Amendment Act *w.e.f.* 1975, August 10, 1975. See also Appendix I put in the 9th Schedule in one day including the Representation of the Peoples Act of 1951. To safeguard any challenge to pre-censorship of the press, the Prevention of Publication of Objectionable Matters Act was also passed and included in the 9th Schedule on May 27, 1976, by the Constitutional Amendment Act of 1976. Also see Appendix I.
8. By the 39th and 40th Constitutional Amendment; 49 Acts were put in the 9th Schedule in one stroke.
9. *Makhan Singh, loc. cit. Jaichand Lall Sethia Vs. State of West Bengal*, 1966 (Supp.) S.C.R. 464 and *K. Anand Nambiar Vs. Chief Secretary, Govt. of Madras*, 1966(2) S.C.R. 406.
10. *Makhan Singh Vs. State of Punjab, loc.cit.*
11. *K.M. Ghatate Vs. U.O.I.*, A.I.R. 1975 Bombay 324; *Bharti Nayyar Vs. UOI.* This judgment was censored and not published.
12. The analysis of these three judgments are given in Appendix III.
13. Charles G. Fenwick, *International Law*, 3rd edition, (Bombay, Allied Private Ltd. 1962) p. 90.
14. *Ibid.*, H. Lanferpacth, Ed. *Oppenheim's International Law,* 8th edition (London; Longman's 1961) pp. 45-46.
15. The U.N. General Assembly unanimously passed a resolution on the Universal Declaration of Human Rights, on December 10, 1948.
16. The U.N. General Assembly passed a resolution on the International Convention on Political and Civil Rights on December 16, 1966.
17. Sir William Holesworth, *A History of English Law*, Vol. 6 London: Mathun & Co. Ltd., 1969, 297.
18. The U.N. General Assembly passed a Convention on the Prevention and Punishment of the Crime of Genocide in 1948.
19. Robert K. Wotezel, *The Nuremberg Trial and Internal Law.*
20. *Additional District Magistrate, Jabalpur etc. Vs. S.S. Shukla etc.* 1976 (2) SCC 521.
21. For full text see *Appendix*-II.
22. *Liversidge Vs. Anderson*, 1942 A.C. 172.
23. *Secretary of State for Home Affairs Vs. O'Brien*, 1923 A.C. 603.
24. *Attorney General of India Vs. Amritlal Prajiwandas*, 1994(5) S.C.C. 54.
25. *K. Karunakaran Vs. T.V. Eachara Warrier* 1978(2) S.C.R., 20.
26. *Waman Rao & Ors. Etc. Vs. UOI & Ors. Etc.* 1981(2) SCC 362.
27. *Attorney General of India Vs. Amritlal Prajiwandas, loc.cit.*

CHAPTER FOUR

Conditions of Detention

"Whenever Fundamental Rights are flouted or legislative protection ignored to prisoner's prejudice the writ of this court will pierce... breaking through stone walls and iron bars to right the wrong and restore rule of law."

—*Justice V.R. Krishna Iyer*

While the *Habeas Corpus* cases were important from the view of liberty of the individual, there was another class of cases involving living conditions of the detenues. The detenues demanded to be kept in a reasonable state akin to their normal living style or as near it as possible, for preventive detention should only be an instrument of restraint and under no circumstances of slightest punishment.

Since a person is detained on the subjective satisfaction of the authorities and not as a punishment for a crime committed but as a preventive measure, the Supreme Court has held that restrictions placed must be minimum[1] and consistent with the effectiveness of detention because the jurisprudence of preventive detention is "qualitatively different from punitive detention".[2]

In view of this law laid down by the Supreme Court a plethora of cases and its warning that the detaining authority sometimes lost "distinction between preventive and punitive detention".[3] High Courts would grant relief to redress the grievances of the detenues, such as allowing them medical facilities, or food at their own cost or appearing for examination, or performing obsequious ceremonies of their kith and kin or allowing them to perform their statutory or constitutional rights such, as the right to go to a corporation for Mayoral elections, or to the Assembly to elect Standing Committees.

Whenever the detenue was required to be temporarily removed from jail, the High Courts would direct that he be taken out under police escort. As such, these reliefs would be granted without either releasing him or granting bail which was not permissible under preventive detention laws like MISA or COFEPOSA.[4]

In mark contrast the Chief Justice of India A.N. Ray, before whom all such cases were placed, during the Internal Emergency would not only admit Government's appeal but would also grant stay of the High Court order which often amounted to allowing the appeal. For example, in cases where the High Court had ordered the detenue to be taken for examination or to attend obsequious ceremonies, the grant of stay defeated the very purpose of relief asked by the detenue.

Once a stay order was granted on the Government's oral request, without there being even an application for stay or petition of appeal, as required by the Supreme Court Rules. This was in the case as mentioned earlier, wherein the Karnataka High Court had directed to produce L.K. Advani under police custody in the Rajya Sabha to perform his constitutional duty of taking the oath, under Article 99 of the Constitution as he was elected to the Rajya Sabha. When it was pointed out to the Court that it had no jurisdiction to pass such an order in the absence of there not being even an application for stay, Chief Justice Ray directed the Government to file necessary applications and then 'officially' granted stay. Though the stay was officially granted after the lunch break, at 2.00 p.m. The Government, knowing the courts' mind, had already cancelled the arrangements for Advani's flight from Bangalore to Delhi, before the High Court's order was actually stayed.

This, however, was not a general practice of the Supreme Court. Justice A.C. Gupta on April 18, 1976, refused to stay the order of the Nagpur High Court directing the Government to take the detenue Gurunath Kulkarni then in police custody to perform the last religious rites of his father. He, however, admitted the special leave petition as the Chief Justice's Bench had granted leave to appeal in similar cases. When the Government counsel later in the day asked for modification of the order on the ground that he had received instruction from the Government that the security of India was at stake, Justice Gupta tersely asked, "Are the Heavens going to fall, if a detenue is taken under police escort to perform last rites of his deceased father? Is the security of India so fragile?" and refused to change his order. This was a solitary case of a detenue which had not come before the Bench presided over by Chief Justice Ray as the Supreme Court was then on summer vacation.[4]

After the judgment in the A.D.M. Jabalpur's *case*, a batch of conditions regarding detention appeals, were posted for final hearing before Justices P.N. Bhagwati, Justice V.R. Krishna Iyer and Justice Murtza Fazal Ali. They were shown as Item No. 2 and No. 3 on the daily Board. The Solicitor General V.P. Raman prayed for one day's adjournment. I was the advocate for petitioners and suspecting some interior motive to take these cases before the Bench presided over by Chief Justice A.N. Ray, I said, "I don't mind adjournment but they should retain their position on this Board." Justice Bhagwati passed a specific order that this batch of appeals would retain their position. But they were not only transferred to the Bench consisting of Justice Beg and Justice Jaswant Singh but shown much lower in the list. I told C.K. Daphatary what had happened and requested him to mention this to Justice Bhagwati the next day which he readily agreed to. He read out the order of Justice Bhagwati and told Justice Bhagwati that his court's order was not complied with and asked "Are you not concerned with non-compliance of your own order?" All that Justice Bhagwati said was that it was for the Chief Justice to decide the board and he was not in a position to pass any order regarding the cases before other Benches.

It was highly improper for the Chief Justice to alter the judicial order of another judge by an administrative order. These batches of cases were shown lower in the list so that there was no chance of them being taken for hearing for a week during which Chief Justice Ray was on leave. As Justice Beg and Justice Jaswant Singh were to join him and hear undisposed cases before Justice Beg's Bench would be taken over for hearing by the bench presided over by the Chief Justice, all such appeals regarding conditions of detention finally came for hearing before this Bench.

There were thirty-five appeals against the orders of the High Courts of Bombay and Karnataka. The types of grievances of the detenues, which were before the Supreme Court were telling.[7] Allow us to have ₹200/- instead of ₹30/- per month from our family or friends to purchase toilet articles; food etc; allow us to have food or bedding from home subject to checking by Jail authorities; allow us to take examinations so that our academic careers did not suffer and allow one interview with family members per month as permitted by the Maharashtra Conditions of Detention Order of 1974. Allow us to attend the marriage ceremony or funeral of the kith and kin, and some detenues wanted to be treated as civil prisoners as they were neither under trial nor convicted prisoners.

One sick detenue wanted that he should be examined at least once a week and not be removed from Bombay jail where he was lodged without at least 24 hours notice. While one lady detenue wanted that she should be detained in such prison where she could have the benefit of other female detenues as also other facilities permitted under rules, other detenues who were elected representatives, wanted to be taken for a limited purpose to the Corporation for mayoral elections or to the Assembly for electing Standing Committees or to Municipalities for election of its President or as pointed out earlier to be taken to the Rajya Sabha to take an oath. High Courts had allowed their petitions.

As mentioned earlier whenever a detenue was required to be taken out of jail, High Courts directed that he be taken under police custody and police were allowed to keep a watch on the detenue and his house. It is relevant to note that the Bombay High Court had allowed the petitions and struck down clauses of the Maharashtra Condition of Detention Order of 1974 which did not permit detenue to be treated as civil prisoners and had also struck down several clauses of that order as punitive and unreasonable, such as a detenue would be supplied with neem stick for cleaning teeth, one soap cake per month, prohibition from keeping shaving kit and shaving by jail barber only once a week and restriction on playing indoor games like cards, carrom and chess. The Court also struck down the clause which gave arbitrary power to the government to withhold any facility or concession provided to detenue under this Order.[5]

A three-Judge Bench presided over by Chief Justice A.N. Ray who heard these appeals upheld the Government's contention that the detenue had *no locus standi* to evoke the jurisdiction of the High

Court for any relief regarding conditions of detention and allowed the appeals. According to the Supreme Court, writ petitions were not maintainable in view of the suspension of Articles 14, 19, 21 and 22 and in view of the majority decision of the Constitution Bench of the Supreme Court in the *A.D.M. Jabalpur's case* where a 'blanket ban' over judicial enquiry not only the validity of the order of detention but also regarding the Government Order laying down conditions of detention. According to the Court, all aspects of personal liberty were covered by Articles 19, 21 and 22 and enforcement of these articles being suspended, the power of the High Court under Article 226 to give any relief to the detenues was suspended even if the Government's, action was in violation of the Conditions of Detention Order and amounted to punitive detention. It also held that the Bombay High Court had therefore no jurisdiction to strike down clauses of the Conditions of Detention Order of 1974 on any ground whatsoever. And High Courts had no jurisdiction to grant any relief to the detenues whatever their grievances, including those flowing from statutory or constitutional rights. During the Emergency the only remedy for the detenue for all their grievances was to approach the Government as High Courts could not enforce a right of personal freedom during the emergency.[6]

This three-Judge bench of the Supreme Court erred in interpreting the operative order of the *A.D.M. Jabalpur's case* because the operative order held that only petition for release was not maintainable. This bench was not justified in enlarging the scope of the operative order and held that the detenue had no *locus standi* for redress of grievances even though they affected the right to life or other fundamental rights like Article 25, the Right to Religious Freedom which were not suspended by the Presidential Order. This was a judicial contravention of the judgment of the larger bench by smaller bench.

Secondly the finding of the court was that all aspects of personal freedom of a person, compendiously described as liberty, found in Articles 19, 21 and 22 was erroneous. This was because it ignored that Right to Freedom of Religious Guarantees under Articles 25 and 26, or right not to be discriminated on grounds of religion etc. under Article 25. This was not covered by the Presidential Order when this contention was specifically advanced by HM Seervai, who led the arguments on behalf of the detenues, and the court should have dealt with it. By this interpretation the Supreme Court suspended enforcement of Fundamental Rights under Article 25 also, although the Presidential Order did not do so.

Thirdly, Seervai, having specifically pointed out from the passages of the *A.D.M. Jabalpur's Case* of the five-Judge Bench that the operative order was not in conformity with the reasoning in the judgment of the majority of the Judges, this bench erred in holding that it was bound by the operative order in that case.

It is submitted that the Court is bound not by the conclusion but by the *ratio decidenti* i.e. the ratio of judgment which has to be deducted from its reasoning. This well established principle has been recognized by the Supreme Court in *Sham Rao case*.[6] When there are more than one judgments and along with the minority judgment it is the duty of the court to discover the reasoning on which the majority judgement based its decision; but if the reasoning does not support the decision, the court is not bound by it.[7] Therefore, this Bench should have either ignored the operative order of the *A.D.M. Jabalpur's Case* or should have referred these cases to a larger bench as the reasoning of the majority could not support the operative order.

As a result of this judgement, the detenue had not any right to obtain release against illegal and *mala fide* detention orders, and the doors of the court were closed to obtain relief even if they were ill treated, starved or even tortured. The Supreme Court left detenue with a begging bowl making not only their liberty but even their life dependant on the mercy of the Government. This judgment in fact had reduced the detenues to a status lower than that of persons who were imprisoned for committing crimes and virtually to the status of slaves by depriving them of all their Fundamental Rights.

However, the devastating psychological impact of this monstrous judgment got muffled because when the judgment was pronounced on January 27, 1977 i.e. after the elections were already declared, the rigour of the Emergency had reduced and the Government had released many political leaders and had promised to release other detenues.[8]

Justice B.P. Jeevan Reddy speaking for the nine-Judge Bench in the *Amritlal's Case* has criticized this judgment. He stated, "Indeed, this judgment has taken the extreme view, purported to follow A.D.M. Jabalpur, that even the restriction placed and facilities denied cannot be questioned in Court during the period [of the Emergency] the Order under Article 359(1) is in operation."[9]

ENDNOTES

1. *Sampati Prakash Vs. State of Jammu & Kashmir*, 1969 3 SCR 5.
2. *Hardhan Singh and Ors. Vs. State of West Bengal* 1975 (3) SCC 198. *Khudiram Das Vs. State of West Bengal* 1975 (2) SCC 81.
3. The Bombay High Court also struck down certain provisions of the Maharashtra Conditions of Detention Order imposing unreasonable hardship on the detenues as violative of Section 5 of the COFEPOSA Act.
4. *State of Maharashtra Vs. Gurunath Kulkarni* Case came up for admission and stay on 18th June, 1976, before the vacation Judge.
5. The type of grievance of the detenues and summary of orders passed by the High Court and catalogued by the Supreme Court in its judgement in the *Union of India and others Vs. Bhanudas Krishna Gawde, and others* 1977(1) SCC 834.
6. *B. Sham Rao Vs. the Union Territory of Pondicherry*; 1967 (2) SCR.650.
7. *Great Western Railway Co. Vs. Owners of S.S. Mostryn*; 1928 A.C. 57.
8. Two judgments were delivered on 25th January, 1977, one by Justice Jaswant Singh for himself and Chief Justice Ray, and the other concurring judgement by Justice Beg; see *Union of India etc. Vs. Bhanudas Krishna Gowde and Others*, etc. *loc. cit.*
9. *Attorney General of India etc. Vs. Amritlal Parjiwandas etc.* 1995 (5) SCC 54.

CHAPTER FIVE

Martial Law

"Martial Law is neither more nor less than the will of the General... In fact, Martial Law is no law at all".

—Duke of Wellington

Justice P.N. Bhagwati in the *A.D.M. Jabalpur's Case* observed that in view of the suspension of Fundamental Rights under Articles 21 and 22 under the Order 359 when the Emergency proclaimed, the writ of *Habeas Corpus* to the detenues who are detained under the Preventive Detention Law is not maintainable and to buttress his finding he has relied on the concept of martial law under which also the writ of *Habeas Corpus* is not available even to those who are about to be deprived of their life or liberty. He has referred to Article 34 which is in Chapter-III dealing with Fundamental Rights. This Article empowers Parliament to make law to indemnify any person for acts done, or validate any sentence passed, punishment inflicted or other acts done when martial law is in operation and reads as under:

> Notwithstanding anything in the foregoing provisions of this Part, Parliament may by law indemnify any person in the service of the Union, or of a State, or any other person in respect of any act done by him in connection with the maintenance or restoration of order in any area within the territory of India where martial law was in force or validate any sentence passed, punishment inflicted, forfeiture ordered or other act done under martial law in such area.

The purpose of this Article is to indemnify certain acts which are normally illegal or unconstitutional but in the process it contemplates imposition of Martial Law in India. This Article, which could lead to potential abuse, was not in the original draft of the Constitution prepared by the Drafting Committee. It was subsequently added and it is surprising that the Constituent Assembly did not even discuss it[1]: Hence, neither the Draft Constitution nor the Constituent Assembly debates provide any guidelines as to what type of Martial Law the Constitution makers had in mind when incorporating this Article in the Constitution, except that it contemplates the use of Martial Law power for "the maintenance or restoration of order in any area within the territory of India". This power, however, is different from the mere use of armed forces to aid civilian authorities, as is referred to in Entry 1 of List II. According to this entry, the Central Government on its own, or at the request of a State Government, can post the armed forces to help civil authorities to quell local disturbances or maintain law and order. In such cases the armed forces function under the control of the civil authorities and the offenders are prosecuted under normal law before ordinary courts.

Secondly, the use of words like "validate any sentence passed", "punishment inflicted" and "forfeiture ordered" in Article 34, shows that under Martial Law, military tribunals can be created and the administration would pass into the hands of the military.

Since the Constitution is silent about the concept of Martial Law or its scope, or the authorities who are empowered to declare it or conditions for its declaration or its continuance, it becomes necessary to examine its definition and the constitutional position of martial law as obtained in other democratic countries. Martial Law is defined in *Worton's Law Lexicon* as "suspension of ordinary law and government of a country or parts of it by military tribunals".[2] That implies, when Martial Law is declared, the command and administration of the area is exclusively handed over to the military; power and the civil authorities as well as the courts are superseded by military law and procedure, and offenders are tried by military tribunals.[3] This power is used in extreme situations when the executive finds itself unable to restore order through the civilian machinery, and has to hand over the control to the military to restore order.

The term Martial Law is sometimes used to mean military law. But since Article 33 empowers the Parliament to curtail by law, application of legal rights to the military for proper discharge of their duties and maintenance of discipline, such laws are to be distinguished from the concept of Martial Law mentioned in Article 34. Similarly, the definition of martial law, as understood in international law includes laws which are administered by military authorities in occupied enemy territory during war time.

In USA the President, who is the chief executive and the Commander-in-Chief of the Armed Forces, is empowered to declare martial law. Under Article 4(4) of the U.S. Constitution, the President can employ the armed forces and take all actions including imposition of Martial Law. This power, however, is given to the President of America to quell armed rebellion and enforce obedience to federal laws if there is grave resistance or military necessity during war.[4]

In the last two eventualities, the President on his own can declare martial law to safeguard the integrity and sovereignty of the country. There is no provision in the American Constitution for the declaration of an emergency and the martial law powers in America are more or less similar to the emergency powers in India but they can be used by the President only in times of war, or in case of an armed rebellion.

In USA when martial law is declared for a particular area, the civil administration there is replaced by military administration.[5] The legislature, however, is not given the power to enact indemnity laws. As a result, only *bona fide* and reasonable exercise of power, during martial law, is protected and all other actions taken during the operation of martial law can be challenged in the court of law after the martial law is revoked.[6] It is equally well settled in the *Sterling Case* that whereas the executive can decide when martial law should be imposed, it is for the judiciary to determine "what are the allowable limits of military discretion and whether or not they have been overstepped in a particular case.[7]

The Supreme Court of America, in interpreting Martial Law powers, have also held that military tribunals can be established to try civilians but only for acts of a military character and secondly, they cannot be established in areas remote from threats of war or insurrections.[8] Furthermore, accepting the concept that martial law cannot exist when civilian courts are functioning, it has been held in *Miligan's Case* that it is for the courts to decide whether a State of War or insurrection exist or not.[9] In view of the above decisions in the *Duncan's Case* the Act of Congress declaring martial law in Hawai could not substitute military courts for civilian courts for trial of civilians. It is a settled law that the power of declaring martial law is vested not in the legislature but in the President, who is the chief executive. Secondly in America, there is no protection against *mala fide* use of martial law power to those who enforce it and the judiciary has curtailed the use of these vast powers through judicial pronouncements.[10]

In France, the Council of Ministers under Article 36 of the 1958 Constitution can declare martial law, but its extension beyond 12 days can be authorized only by the legislature. Furthermore, the legislature as of right is in session as long as the martial law is in operation. The power and the scope of the military administration as also its duration are determined by legislation. Thus there is rigorous legislative control over the executive in its exercise of Martial Law Powers.

In Britain, though in theory the Crown has the prerogative to declare martial law, no such power has been exercised since the days of Charles I. Even during World War II, martial law was not proclaimed through the Royal prerogative. The emergency Power Act of 1940 did authorize the creation of special war courts to act in place of ordinary courts in the event of actual invasion, but such courts were never established.

Thus, we find that in practice it is not the executive but Parliament which can bring about a martial law situation in Britain, meaning thereby the suspension of ordinary law and courts. Martial law, according *to Halsbury's Laws of England 'is no law at all'*.[11] It has not been proclaimed in England for centuries despite grave emergencies. Professor Dicey views this as "an unmistakable proof of permanent supremacy of law under our constitution", and he proudly comments that it is unknown to the laws of England.[12]

Nevertheless, the British did not hesitate to impose martial law to suppress threats to their hold over Ireland or their empire. It was imposed in Canada in 1838, Jamaica in 1869, South Africa in 1904, Natal in 1907, and in Sind province of India during the 1942 Quit India Movement, besides several times in Ireland.[13]

This in turn has 'contributed' to the development of British Constitutional Law on this subject. According to the decisions of the Privy Council, as regards British colonies and Ireland, imposition of martial law is the function of the executive and after its withdrawal the legislature by enacting the law of indemnity could validly protect officials for unlawful acts done during the operation of martial law.[14] The purpose of the indemnity law, seems primarily to restrict this jurisdiction of the Courts. In the absence of such indemnity legislation, the courts could determine whether a state of war or insurrection or rebellion amounting to war, existed or not, to warrant the imposition of martial law.[15] The courts could also examine whether the amount of force employed was necessary or justified.[16]

According to the English judicial pronouncements when Martial Law is validly declared, the courts cannot issue even a writ of *habeas corpus* or in any way interfere with the military authorities to protect not only the liberty, but even the life of an individual, even if illegal and *mala fide* action is taken or threatened to be taken by the military administrators.

In *John Albert's Case*[17] the military authorities in Ireland, where martial law was in force in 1921, ordered all persons to deposit their fire arms with them within 24 hours. One John Albert, who did not obey the orders, was arrested and sentenced to death by the military tribunal. When he moved the court on the ground that the sentence was invalid, it was held that when the martial law was validly declared the courts had no power to interfere and give any relief. In view of the fact that the British imposed martial law only in their colonies and not on their own soil, since the advent of democracy in that country, it is doubtful whether this decision will hold water in case martial law is imposed in Britain.

However, in *Wrights Case* decided in 1979, it was held that the Act of Indemnity "couched in the usual terms will not protect malicious act". Professor Dicey relying on the lead case of *King*

Vs. Kim regarding the responsibility of the military in using force to repel force, has observed that officers and soldiers did not enjoy special privileges and if they employed excessive or unnecessary measures, they were liable to be called before the court of law.[18] Although the British used indemnity laws as a "legal" device to protect otherwise illegal acts of their officials, in order to protect their empire, whether indemnity laws mentioned in Article 34 of the Constitution, can be used to protect the abuse of power by a democratic government against its own people, is extremely doubtful. Even the British courts' interpretation of martial law in subsequent years opined that the indemnity legislation did not protect persons using excessive force.

The above survey of foreign constitutions shows that the power to declare martial law is the preserve of the executive rather than that of the legislature. As the President of India under Article 53 is the executive head of the Union as well as the Commander-in-Chief of the Defence Forces of the Union, as in America, one can assume that the power to declare martial law is the prerogative of the President and the function of the legislature under Article 34 is to legalize the otherwise illegal act *ex-post facto* done by persons in the service of the government during martial law, by passing indemnity laws. According to Basu, Article 34 "recognizes the possibility of the executive proclaiming martial law without any legislative sanction", as was done in Sind in 1942-1943.[19] This, however, cannot be a very sound precedent. In 1942, Sind was part of British India, and the Viceroy was answerable to the Crown. As such he did not possess unchecked power in this sphere.

Though there is no specific entry relating to martial law in the Constitution, Parliament, if it chooses, may declare martial law by legislative enactment by using its Residuary Power under Entry 97 of List I. This method of enacting martial law as practised in Britain would be a more healthy and democratic method, than to have martial law through a declaration by the President.

However, if Martial Law is declared by the President, there are no parliamentary checks, as found when the Emergency was proclaimed under Articles 352, 356 or 360 of the Constitution.

Also, there is no provision in the Constitution for the approval of the declaration of the martial law by the Parliament, or any parliamentary control over its duration. Nor is there any provision by which Parliament can terminate it by resolution.

More important, since martial law is a law, it is the prerogative of Parliament as the supreme law making body in our Constitution, and India has adopted a parliamentary democracy in which the legislature controls the executive. Parliament alone can bring in martial law as it is the legislature. It is submitted that it would be unconstitutional on the part of the President to encroach upon the jurisdiction of the legislature if he declares martial law on his own.

Moreover, the Constitution does not prescribe conditions under which martial law can be declared. Absence of constitutional checks when the consequences of imposition of martial law are graver than the proclamation of Emergency under Article 352, weakens the edifice of our democratic Constitution. During an Emergency, power is exercised by the civil administration while in the case of martial law, civilian administration is handed over to the military authorities and civilians can be tried by military tribunals. The Constitution is also ominously silent regarding the scope and nature of military powers during the operation of martial law.

Since Martial Law has never been proclaimed in independent India, there are no judicial pronouncements determining the scope of martial law powers. The American courts, as mentioned earlier, have held that civilians cannot be prosecuted by military courts for ordinary offences which are of a non-military character or that military courts cannot be established in areas which are not affected by rebellion or war.

However, Justice P.N. Bhagwati when in the *A.D.M. Jabalpur's Case* in support of his conclusion stated that no *habeas corpus* can lie when Article 21 is suspended, relied on the *Maligan's Case* and has observed:

> It is the basic characteristic of martial law that during the time it is in force the individual cannot enforce his right to life or liberty by resorting to judicial process and courts

cannot issue the writ of *habeas corpus* or pass any similar orders.[20]

It is unfortunate that Justice Bhagwati took support from *Maligan's Case* decided in 1921, and ignored the subsequent *Wright's Case* of 1979, and the *Kim's Case.* He also ignored the fact that the British Judges had different standards when deciding the case of the life and liberty of colonial subjects *visa-vis* British citizens. It is well known that often the same judge took a contrary view when sitting in the Privy Council deciding appeals from colonies and while deciding appeals arising from judgments of local courts affecting British nationals.

Although this observation of Justice Bhagwati is *obiter dicta*, it is nonetheless binding on High Courts, and in the event of the declaration of martial law, those who want to abuse their power to usher authoritarianism would not hesitate to use this observation to oust the jurisdiction of the Courts when martial law is in operation.

A close study of Justice Bhagwati's observations in the context of martial law, however, shows that he has curtailed otherwise unfettered martial law powers to some extent. He has pointed out that the declaration of martial law, which is only impliedly provided in the Constitution, cannot override the express provisions of the Constitution. Enforcement of Fundamental Rights cannot be suspended except under Articles 358 and 359 and this power is available only when Emergency is in operation under Article 352 of the Constitution. Hence, the declaration of martial law in India will not automatically deprive the courts of their power to issue writs including the writ of *Habeas Corpus* for enforcement of Fundamental Rights expressly protected under Articles 32 and 226 of the Constitution of India, unless there is also a Proclamation of Emergency under Article 352.

As the Constitution guarantees Fundamental Rights and also empowers the courts to protect persons from infringement of their Fundamental Rights, a person aggrieved by the action of the military authorities would be able to approach courts even during the operation of martial law unless enforcement of Fundamental Rights is suspended which can be done only during an emergency under Article 352. Under the amended Constitution by the 44th Constitutional Amendment, Fundamental Rights can only be suspended when an emergency is proclaimed under Article 352 on grounds of war or external aggression and not on the ground of armed rebellion threatening the security of India. This follows that martial law in which military authorities and tribunal have unfettered powers, can only be declared in the case of an emergency on grounds of war and external aggression is in operation. But as the power to suspend Article 21, which guarantees protection against deprivation of the Right to Life and Personal Liberty without the procedure established by law is now deleted, it seems the writ of *habeas corpus* would be available even during the operation of martial law.

Furthermore, there is no provision in our Constitution, as in the American Constitution, to suspend the writ of *habeas corpus* during the operation of Martial Law. Therefore, even if martial law is declared during an 'external' emergency, the High Courts and Supreme Court would have the power to issue a writ of *habeas corpus* if a person is illegally or *mala fide* detained or if the right to life is threatened by martial law authorities.

In other words, the rational of the *John Albert's Case* that the courts will not interfere even if a person alleges that his detention is illegal or *mala fide* or he is going to be illegally executed during the operation of martial law, cannot be applied in India. Secondly, the concept of martial law as found in Anglo-American jurisprudence can no longer be said to be applicable in India as the power of civilian courts is not taken away by the military tribunals.

In some respects, however, the scope of martial law power seems to be wider in India than in America. Whereas in America it can only be declared during an actual war, in India it can be declared even before the actual commencement of hostilities when there is a grave threat of war or external aggression. Moreover, there is no prohibition on the military administration to prosecuting civilians for offences which are not of a military nature; nor is there any restriction stating that the jurisdiction of the military tribunals has to be confined to strategic and sensitive areas only.

Nevertheless, the limitations on martial law can be inferred from judicial reasoning and logic. The Constitution does not contain any specific provision to that effect. Nor is there any authoritative pronouncement of the Supreme Court on the scope and nature of Martial Law Powers. With this state of law, lack of concrete checks to prevent the abuse of this vast brute power by the President who is the Chief Executive as well as the Supreme Commander of the Armed Forces, our democratic constitution can be wrecked if unscrupulous and ambitious persons are saddled in the seat of the President. Such examples are not wanting in history. Martial Law, unless strictly controlled, has often resulted in military take overs and overthrow of the civilian government.

It is submitted that Article 34 which impliedly recognizes imposition of martial law without defining it or expressly mentioning who has the authority to proclaim it, or conditions under which it can be declared, or duration for which it can be continued, should not find a place in our Constitution. This Article smacks of the potential of ushering in military rule.

Moreover, when the executive is armed with Emergency Powers under Article 352 to protect the sovereignty and integrity of the country either from war or external aggression or armed rebellion, there is no need for Article 34. Since Parliament has the power to enact Defence of India Act and Rules during an Emergency, the question of enforcing Martial Law does not arise. It is, therefore, imperative that Article 34 deserves to be deleted from the Constitution.

ENDNOTES

1. Tabular statement showing Articles of the Constitution of India with its corresponding clause in the Draft Constitution and dates on which discussed and approved, see *Constitutional Assembly Debates Official Reports* Vol. 1 (New Delhi, Lok Sabha Secretariat) 1966 p. 1.
2. A.S. Wherton, *Law Leicon,* (London: Sweet of Maxwell Ltd., 1976) p. 641.
3. A.V. Dicey, *Introduction to the Study of the Constitution,* 10th Ed. (London: Macmillan & Co. Ltd. 1961) p. 287.

4. *In re: Debs* (1985) 158 U.S. 564: Kelly and Harbinson American Constitution, pp. 443-447.
5. *Ex parte Maligan* (1866) 4 Wall 2; also see Durgadas Basu, *Commentary on the Constitution of India* Vol. 2, Calcutta; S.C. Sarkar and Sons (P) Ltd., 1962, pp. 296-299.
6. *Ibid.*
7. *Sterling Vs. Constantine* (1932) 287 U.S. 301 *at* 378.
8. *Madisen Vs. Kinsella,* (1952) 343 U.S. 341.
9. Ex. *Pane Maligan,* supra.
10. *Duncans Vs. Kohanmeku*, 1945 (327 U.S. 304.
11. *Lord Hailsham, Ed.* Halsbury's Law of England, 4th Edition, Vol. 8, (London. Butter Worts 1974) p. .
12. Butterworth's, 1974, pp. 624-626.
13. Durgadas Basu *Commentary on the Constitution of India op. cit.*, pp. 297-98; *Halsbury's Law of England, op. cit Telinko Vs. A.G. Natal* 1907 A.C. p. 93.
14. *Ex parte Marias* 1902 A.C. 109, Hood and Philips, 1952 Constitutional Law p. 440, 441.
15. *R. (Grade) Vs. Strickland* 1921 Irish Reports p. 317.
16. *Higgins vs. Williams* 1921 (2) Irish Report p. 386.
17. *John Albert's Case* (1921) 2 Irish Reports p. 241.
18. Dicey, *op. cit.* pp. 288-289.
19. Durgadas Basu *op. cit.*
20. *ADM Jabalpur etc. vs. Shivkant Shukla etc.*, 1976 (2) SCC 521.

CHAPTER SIX

THE 44TH CONSTITUTIONAL AMENDMENT[1]

"It is a right step but not a full step in the right direction."

At the time of the historic general election of 1977, the Janata Party had made a solemn commitment to the people of India that the Constitution would be suitably amended so that a transient majority would not be in a position to play havoc with the life and liberty of people in India and destroy its democratic polity. To ensure the non-repetition of the traumatic experiences of the nineteen dark months of Internal Emergency during the 1975, and prevent abuse of the provision of the Constitution, the Janata Government on May 9, 1978, tabled the 42nd Constitutional Amendment Bill in Parliament. On April 30, 1979 the Constitution of India was substantially amended by what is known as the 44th Constitution Amendment Act. Since the Internal Emergency was unconstitutional and *mala fide* in the opinion of the Janata Party, the extension of the life of the Parliament was also unconstitutional and since the 42nd Amendment Act had been passed during the extended life of the Parliament it should have been repealed in its entirety instead of the retaining of certain and amending other provisions of that Constitution. The Emergency Powers contained in Part XVIII of the Constitution were curtailed while the rigour of preventive detention laws was trimmed to a great extent by amending provisions of Article 22 relating to preventive detention but these provisions were not brought into force as discussed later and they are not yet enforced.

EMERGENCY POWERS AND FREEDOM OF LIFE AND LIBERTY

Article 352, which empowers the President to proclaim emergency when the security of India is threatened, has been hedged with several safeguards against the abuse of these powers. Most important, the vague phrase 'internal disturbance' has been substituted by the precise expression 'armed rebellion' so that an emergency could no longer be declared in case of internal disturbance unless there is an organized violence on the scale of a civil war or rebellion. The other two grounds *viz.* war and external aggression, when an emergency can be proclaimed under this Article being specific, were not amended.

Second, the President is not empowered to proclaim an emergency unless the decision of the Cabinet that the proclamation of an emergency is necessary is communicated to him in writing.

Thirdly, the proclamation of an emergency is required to be approved within one month, instead of two months, by a resolution of both the Houses of Parliament.

Fourth, the Proclamation of an emergency has virtually the effect of amending the Constitution, as it enables the central executive to suspend the right to enforce Fundamental Rights; make laws on subjects in the State lists etc. Therefore, it has been provided that the resolution approving the Proclamation should be passed by a two-thirds majority of the total membership of each House, as is required to amend the Constitution, instead of by a simple majority of the members present and voting.

Fifth, the executive power to continue an emergency indefinitely is taken away and for the continuance of an emergency approval by resolution of both the Houses is required every six months.

Sixth, the Lok Sabha is also given the power to revoke the proclamation of an emergency by a simple majority of Lok Sabha members present and voting. Moreover, if ten per cent or more of the total membership of the Lok Sabha give notice to a requisition for the purpose of considering the continuance of an emergency, it has to be summoned for this purpose within 14 days of the receipt of such a notice.

The power to revoke an emergency or move a resolution for considering the continuance of an emergency should have been given to the Rajya Sabha also, because unlike the Lok Sabha, it is a continuous body with two-thirds of its members retiring every two years. If for example, an emergency is declared when the Lok Sabha is dissolved, and elections are not held, or it is not possible to hold them because of the emergency, the emergency power of the executive would be beyond parliamentary control in spite of the existence of the Rajya Sabha. To maintain the supremacy of the Lok Sabha's control over the exercise of emergency powers, it could have been provided that this check would not be available to the Rajya Sabha, unless the Lok Sabha stands dissolved. Secondly, to ensure effective legislative control over the executive in matters concerning an emergency, provision should have been made to prohibit issuance of the party whip and disqualification.

To ensured vigilant control over exercise of emergency powers, the Parliament should as of right assemble within forty—eight hours of the issuance of the proclamation as in the Italian Constitution and should continue to sit, till the emergency is over.

The 38th Constitutional Amendment, enacted during the Emergency by which the satisfaction of the President as to the existence of conditions for the Proclamation of an emergency was made final, and the jurisdiction of the law courts was completely ousted, has been deleted. As such, the earlier position that the power to proclaim an emergency is a conditional power and therefore justiciable in a court of law has been restored.

Article 358 which relates to the automatic suspension of the seven freedoms mentioned in Article 19 has been amended so that these freedoms can be suspended only when the security of India is threatened by war or external aggression and not by armed rebellion.

Furthermore, freedoms mentioned in this Article would not be automatically suspended under Article 358 but only in relation to any law or executive action contained in recital to the effect that such a law or executive action relates to the Proclamation of an emergency.

An important amendment has been made to Article 359 which empowers the President to suspend an enforcement of Fundamental Rights contained in Part-III during an emergency. The President can no longer suspend the Right to Life and Personal Liberty under Article 21, or protection guaranteed in respect of offences under Article 20 of the Constitution of India. As such even during an emergency persons can move the court for enforcement of their Fundamental Rights. Thus the majority judgement of the Supreme Court in the *A.D.M. Jabalpur's Case* that in view of the suspension of the right under Articles 19, 21 and 22, no person can move a court for his release even if his detention is not in compliance with the law of *mala fide,* has been corrected by this amendment, but not totally. Article 359 is further amended to the effect that the suspension of any other Fundamental Rights will not apply in relation to any law or executive action unless such law or action contained a recital in relation to the emergency.

This amendment recognizes the inherent and inalienable right of man to life and liberty and they are not conferred by the Constitution and thus it is in accordance with India's obligation to promote Human Rights. Under this amended Article, the President, however, continues to have the power to suspend all other Fundamental Rights contained in Part-III of the Constitution of India. Is it necessary to suspend the Right to Equality contained in Article 14 in which the Rule of Law is enshrined; or the Right not to be discriminated on grounds of caste, religion or sex under Article 15; or abolition of untouchability guaranteed under Article 17; or prohibition of traffic in human beings guaranteed under Article 28? And if Article 32 which guarantees the Right to Constitutional Remedies for the violation of Fundamental Rights can be suspended will not be enforcement of all Fundamental Rights including that of Articles 21 and 22 stand suspended as well? It is one thing to empower the President to suspend Fundamental Rights like the Right to Freedom of Speech and Expression, to Assemble Peacefully, to Form Associations and Unions or the Right of Movement or to Prevent Trade in Certain Spheres which can hamper the Government effort to protect the country in an emergency. But one cannot understand why the President should have the power to suspend those Fundamental Rights which do not have the remotest nexus with the country's security especially when Fundamental Rights mentioned above are a reflection of Human Rights to which this country is committed.

In fact, this Constitutional Amendment should have deleted the Article 359 because all freedoms which might come in the way of government's effort to ensure the security of the country in a time of external aggression or war are found in Article 19 and suspension or enforcement of these freedoms, is already provided for under Article 358. Even the retention of the Article 358 is not necessary because each freedom mentioned in Article 19 is not absolute but is subject to reasonable restrictions. Hence, during an emergency Parliament can always curtail the scope of these liberties. Moreover, the 16th Constitutional Amendment specifically empowers the Parliament and the State Legislatures to make laws to impose reasonable restrictions in the interest of "the sovereignty and the security of India" in respect of three categories of rights mentioned in Clauses (a), (b) and (c) of Article 19(1) *viz.* Right to Freedom of Speech and Expression; to Assemble Peacefully without Arms; and to Form Associations or Unions.

This phrase in the interest of "the sovereignty and the security of India" could have been added to other freedoms mentioned in Article 19. But this is also not required because the provisos to this freedom already provide for imposition of reasonable restrictions in the interest of the "general public". This phrase, it is submitted, is wide enough to cover the country's sovereignty and security.

In times of a real emergency the experience has been that the Parliament has always given the executive all powers it desired and there is no reason why Parliament in future would not pass laws necessary to protect the security of India during an emergency. The only conceivable objection to the deletion of Articles 358 and 359 seems to be that if an aggrieved person goes to court for infringement of his Fundamental Right, the Government would have to justify that its laws and actions curtailing the individual right are reasonable before the court. But if any curtailment of freedom is reasonable in the context of danger facing the country, the courts, I am sure, would never come in the way of Government's effort to protect the country. There is no need to distrust the judiciary when it is also one of the wings of the Constitution like the executive and the legislature.

The purpose of temporary constitutional dictatorship envisaged in the emergency provision of the Constitution is to safeguard the security of the country, so as to protect and preserve the values India stands for. Article 359, if it is to be at all retained, should have been amended to give the executive only those powers that are absolutely necessary for protecting the security of India and all Fundamental Rights which have nothing to do with the security of the country, should have been kept outside the purview of the President's powers. This suggestion is also in accordance with Article 4(1) of the International Convention on Political and Civil Rights of 1966, which India has ratified and which states that the suspension of only those Fundamental Rights, which are absolutely essential for the security of the country, should be suspended. Since Article 4(3) of this Covenant requires that a country suspending any of the human rights and fundamental freedoms in an emergency should communicate their suspension orders to the U.N. and the inclusion of such provision by way of constitutional amendment would have been a step in the right direction.

Article 356 by which President's Rule can be imposed in the State in case of failure of the constitutional machinery has been amended so that the Proclamation, after approval of both Houses of Parliament, shall continue for six months and it would continue for a further period of six months after it is approved by Parliament. As such, the Government is now required to seek Parliament's approval to continue President's Rule beyond six months. Furthermore, if the Election Commission certifies that the extension of President's Rule beyond the period is necessary, then it can be extended for one year, but not beyond three years in any case. This amendment increases Parliamentary control on the extension of President's Rule, and ensures that the democratic system is restored within a minimum period necessary for holding elections. The Parliament should also have been given the power to disapprove the Proclamation by a 2/3rd majority and 10 per cent of the members to move a representation to disapprove President's Rule. The session of Parliament should be called in 14 days as in case of an Emergency declaration under Article 352.

Article 360 which provides for Financial Emergency which was amended by the 38th Constitutional Amendment by which the satisfaction of the President regarding the financial stability or credit of India or any part thereof when threatened was made final and non-justiciable, has been deleted.

An important amendment is made by inserting Article 361-A in the Constitution by which constitutional protection to publish proceedings of Parliament and State Legislatures is guaranteed even during an emergency. It may be recalled that during the 1975 Emergency, the Government censored even the proceedings of Parliament and no criticism of policies by Members of Parliament was allowed to be published. Furthermore, this Act was put in the 9th Schedule during the Emergency to protect any changes of Fundamental Rights. Since this Article is not a part of Fundamental Rights, it seems that during the Emergency, this valuable guarantee was operative.

However, there might arise a doubt whether the freedom of speech and expression of an elected representative on the floor of the House guaranteed under this Article would be suspended because it can be contended that it is a reflection of the Fundamental Right of Freedom of Speech and Expression guaranteed in Article 19(1)(a) which automatically gets suspended when an emergency is declared under Article 352. It would have been, therefore, better if Article 361(A) would have clarified that it is not controlled by Article 19(1) (a).

During the 1975 Emergency, the publications of Court proceedings and judgments which were not favourable to the Government were also censored. The 44th Constitutional Amendment should have provided for constitutional protection in respect of publication of the judgement and proceedings of the Court as has been done in case of proceedings of Parliament and State Legislatures. More so because under Article 141 of the Constitution, the judgement of the Supreme Court is the law of the land.

In the sphere of the Right to Liberty, the rigour of the preventive detention law has been reduced by amending Article 22(4) and (5). They are no more than pious wishes as the Government on one pretext or the other has not issued notification to bring this Constitutional Amendment in force.

The right thing, for the Government, committed to personal liberty and democracy, would be to exclude Article 22 from the President's powers of suspension under Article 359, except 22(3) which deals with enemy elies; Further, an amendment of Article 22 so that the right of legal consultation could be available to persons under preventive detention should be made.

Article 22, besides containing constitutional safeguards necessary for a preventive detention law, also gives protection to persons arrested under criminal law and clause (1) and (2) which reads as under:

"(1) No person who is arrested shall be detained without being informed, as soon as for such arrest nor shall he be denied the right to consult, and to be defended by a legal practitioner of his choice.

(2) Every person who is arrested and detained in custody shall be produced before the nearest magistrate within a period of twenty-four hours of such arrest excluding the time necessary for the journey from the place of arrest to the court of the magistrate and no such person shall be detained in custody beyond the said period without the authority of a magistrate."

The mere reading of these clauses show, that they contain elementary principles of criminal law in any civilized country. These principles are also incorporated in the Universal Declaration of Human Rights 1948. Why should there be a power to suspend these valuable guarantees, which are a hallmark of civilization? When the security of India is threatened it does not mean that the Government should claim the power to make a mockery of criminal justice.

Furthermore, the 44th Constitutional Amendment should have amended Article 22 to ensure that the right of a prisoner to consult and to be defended by a legal practitioner of his choice should be available to a person detained under the preventive detention laws. At present the legal position is that though this valuable right is guaranteed to a person who has committed an offence and is facing a trial, it is not guaranteed to a person who is detained for committing any crime but on a mere suspicion of the executive that he is likely to commit an offence in future. It is submitted that amendment to this effect is most essential.

It is surprising that the source of this draconian power of preventive detention continues to remain in the part dealing with the Fundamental Rights of a democratic Constitution. Its actual place is in Part VIII containing emergency provisions. No democratic country worth its salt has retained this drastic power in normal times. In countries like Britain, France, U.S.A. and Germany, preventive detention is used only when the country's existence is threatened by actual war or rebellion. Furthermore, in Britain detention is ordered not by a bureaucrat as in India but by an important person like the Home Secretary, who is an elected member and responsible to Parliament and he has to inform the parliament every month of the number of persons detained. In India the 44th Constitutional Amendment should have provided for preventive detention only during the operation of the Proclamation of Emergency under Article 352 and since India is a much larger country, the power of detention should have been rested in the hands of the Home Minister of the Union and the States and they should also be obliged to inform the legislatures every month of the number of persons detained. To argue that preventive detention laws are necessary in normal times is an admission of the legislature's incompetence to make effective laws and the executive's inability or unwillingness to enforce them.

There is one more glaring lapse from which the 44th Constitutional Amendment suffers. During the operation of an emergency under Article 352, Parliament under proviso Article 83(2) can by law extend the life of the Lok Sabha and State Assemblies for a period of one year at a time beyond its normal duration of five years. But having inserted clause (5) in Article 352 declaring that the emergency can be declared for six months and extended by six months at a time, that too by a two-third majority of the membership of the Parliament, should have been amended so that the life of the Lok Sabha and Assemblies is extended for six months at a time. The emergency, under Article 352 being the basis of the extension of the life of the Lok Sabha and Assemblies cannot be for a period more than that which is contemplated for emergency.

It may be reasonable to give such power to Parliament, because it may not be possible to hold elections in case the country is involved in war, or plagued by an armed rebellion. However, since the Proclamation of Emergency has virtually the effect of amending the Constitution, as explained earlier, Article 83 should have been amended so that the law extending the life of the Lok Sabha or Assemblies is also passed by a two-thirds majority of the total membership as is required for approving or extending the proclamation of an emergency and not by a simple majority, as is the present position.

Furthermore, the powers of the Lok Sabha whose life is extended because of an emergency should also be curtailed. This is because it is an 'Emergency Parliament', not representing the will of the people, but which continues to govern the country because of an extraordinary situation. In these circumstances power of Parliament and the Government should be strictly curtailed to carry on only routine administration and take only such necessary steps, including legislative measures, which are necessary for dealing effectively with the emergency situation. If, however, it is considered that it may not be practical to divest Parliament of its power to amend the Constitution during the extended life of the Lok Sabha, then a provision should be made to the effect that such constitutional amendment will cease to be in force unless it is approved by the Parliament within two or three months after the general elections, so that it has the sanctity of being approved by the Lok Sabha which represent the people.

By this Constitutional Amendment the MISA, Prevention of Publication of Objectionable Material Act and the Representation of Peoples Act were deleted from the 9th Schedule and are no longer immune from the challenge on the grounds of Fundamental Rights but these acts should, however, be permanently insulated from the amending power, under Article 368.

The 44th Constitutional Amendment has introduced some safeguards to prevent the abuse of emergency powers and has tried to put the Right to Life and Liberty on a more secure footing than before, and has corrected distortions which were introduced in the Constitution during the period of Internal Emergency. Nevertheless if the emergency provisions and preventive detention laws are to have the sanction of the Constitution, much needs to be done to preserve the democratic fabric of this Constitution in which civil liberties will be protected by law, which means civilized law.

Thus the 44th Constitutional Amendment is a right step but not a full step in the right direction.

It is appropriate to add a caveat. The Right to Life and Liberty being an inalienable right and not a conferred right by the

Constitution, the 44th Constitutional Amendment deleted it from the Order under Article 359 which empowered the President to suspend Fundamental Rights when an Emergency was proclaimed under Article 352 to meet the threat to the security of India. However, this Right was suspended for the State of Punjab because of the violent situation there by the 59th Constitutional Amendment of 1988 by the Congress government of Rajiv Gandhi. This amendment added Article 359A by which Article 21 was suspended for a period of two years for the state of Punjab.[1] It was a retrogade step as it empowered the government to deprive a person of his life and liberty *mala fide* and even in non-compliance with any law as it was held by the majority by the Supreme Court in *ADM, Jabalpur's Case*. As a result, the ghost of *ADM, Jabalpur's Case* was far from burried as it was thought when the 44th Constitutional Amendment had been enacted. It is submitted that when stringent acts like the Terrorists and Disruptive Act (TADA) and others concerning preventive detention, like the National Security Act (NSA) were in force was it necessary to suspend Article 21? V.P. Singh on becoming the Prime Minister, promised to delete Article 359A and the 63rd Amendment of 1989[2] besides amending Article 356, which required that elections be held after three years be extended for a further three years. This was because the Chief Election Commissioner and all political parties preferred to defer the elections till normalcy was restored. Finally, elections were held in 1992, in Punjab.

To avoid suspension of Article 21 it should have been declared as one of the basic features of the Constitution and kept it beyond the amending power of the Parliament as in the *Amrit lal's Case*[3] when the Nine Judges Bench was dealing with the Conservation of Foreign Exchange and the Prevention of Smuggling Act, an anointer preventive detention act.

ENDNOTES

1. The 44th Constitutional Amendment came into force w.e.f. January 3, 1979, except Clause 3 which provided safe safeguards to under detention law under Article 22 (3) (2). See Appendix III.
2. For 59th and 63rd Constitutional Amendments, see Appendix-1
3. *Attorney General of India Vs. Armit Lal* 1994(5) SCC 54. Also see Chapter-III.

CHAPTER SEVEN

Preventive Detention

"Blind unquestioning obedience is the law of tyrants and of slaves: it does not yet flourish on English soil... The subject is entitled to know why he is deprived of his freedom if only in order that he may, without a moment's delay, take steps to regain it."

—Lord Simond

In the foregoing pages we have seen that absolute despotism was established during the Internal Emergency with preventive detention as its main weapon. This entails is detention without trial. A person is deprived of his liberty not because he is found guilty by a judicial process of committing an offence, but on an apprehension that he is likely to commit an offence. He is in prison not by an order of a judge, but by order of the executive. Preventive detention is a draconian power as it makes the executive the prosecutor as well as a judge. It runs counter to the rule of law and makes deep inroads into the sphere of basic freedoms.

However, those who are entrusted with running a government have another point of view. According to them, they are conscious of the value of human liberty but individual liberty itself depends upon security and freedom of the country and secondly, there cannot be freedom to destroy freedom.

To reconcile the heeds of liberty of the individual in society and the safety and security of the State is an eternal dilemma of democrative governments all over the world. To balance these conflicting viewpoints, the framers of the Indian Constitution, while making provisions for preventive detention, also inserted some safeguards to prevent the abuse of these drastic powers. But the matter did not rest with the adoption of the Constitution. Its various aspects come before the Supreme Court for interpretation and decision time and again. It is appropriate to examine the origin, scope, position and relevance of preventive detention in India's democratic polity.

HISTORY OF PREVENTIVE DETENTION

The concept of preventive detention is as old as history. One is familiar with tales about kings imprisoning claimants to the throne, including their blood relations. Nicholas II, the Czar of Russia, had imprisoned his own son. Nearer home, Aurangzeb had imprisoned his father and even jailed his brothers. But they were autocrats and not democrats, a law to themselves and alien to the rule of law.

Flickering glimpses of the law of preventive detention were seen in the East India Company Act of 1780 under which the Governor General of India could detain non-British subjects. By the East India Company Act 1784, the Governor-General was empowered to detain any person suspected of carrying on correspondence or activities prejudicial to the peace and safety of British settlements or its possessions in India. But the detenue was given the right to know the grounds of detention within five days of his arrest and make a representation against the order of detention to the Governor-General-in-Council. It is significant to note that the detenue was also allowed to produce evidence and cross examine the witnesses of the prosecution. And if the Governor-General refused to release him, the former was required either to send him to England for trial or put him on trial in India. But there was no time limit fixed for bringing him to trial. As such, the period of detention without trial was left wholly to the discretion of the Governor-General. Subsequently the Governors of all the three Presidencies of Bengal, Madras and Bombay, were empowered to detain a person without trial under various laws, such as, the Bengal Regulation of 1812, Bengal State Prisoners' Regulation of 1818, the Madras State Prisoners' Regulation of 1819, the Bombay State Prisoners' Regulation of 1827, and the State Prisoners Act of 1850.

During Company Rule, preventive detention was freely resorted to and there was no right of *habeas corpus*. But when Company Rule was replaced by the British Crown in 1858—a relatively more civilized government—they not only gave the right of *Habeas Corpus* in 1882 under Section 491 of the Criminal Procedure Code but also did not resort to preventive detention except during war. Rules made under the Defence of India Act 1915 and Defence of India Act 1939, which were enacted at the outbreak of World War I and World War II respectively, provided for preventive detention. That is why preventive detention is often described as a war time or an emergency legislation to be used only in exceptional circumstances when the security, sovereignty and freedom of the country is itself in danger. It is equally significant to note that preventive detention was used not to deal with ordinary criminals, but against spies, traitors and saboteurs, suspected of endangering the very existence of the country. During World War II, those detained in Britain under the Defence of Realm Act of 1939, were only those who were suspected of espionage or acts of treason. Similarly, the United States after the declaration of war on Japan in 1941, had detained all persons of Japanese origin. So also, under the Defence of India Rules of 1939, hundreds of political leaders were detained when in 1942 the Congress launched the 'Quit India Movement' and were kept in detention till the war was over.

It may not be out of place to mention that Rowlatt Act of 1918 which was a preventive detention law, and specially excluded the remedy of *habeas corpus* had triggered a nationwide demonstration. It was described as a Black Act, because it barred a detenue from engaging a legal practitioner or approaching the court to obtain release. The slogan was "*Na Vakil, Na Daleel, Na Appeal*". (No advocate, no argument and no appeal)

PREVENTIVE DETENTION AND THE CONSTITUTION

Just as we had freely incorporated many provisions of the Government of India Act 1935, which we criticized during the Freedom Movement, we provided for preventive detention in the Constitution. But under the Government of India Act of 1935, only the provincial governments were given the power to make laws for preventive detention, and that too, only for "reasons connected with maintenance of public order" as per Entry I to List-2-Provincial Legislative List. But ironically, the framers of the Constitution drastically enlarged the scope of preventive detention. Both the Parliament as well as State Legislatures were empowered to make laws for preventive detention. Entry 3 of the Union List enabled the Parliament to enact laws of preventive detention for reasons connected with the "defence, foreign affairs and security of India", and Entry 9 of the Concurrent list empowered both Parliament as well as State Legislatures to make such laws for reasons connected with the "security of state, maintenance of public order and services of essential supplies to life of the community." It is necessary to understand that each of these six phrases is incapable of precise definition.

In *A.K. Roy's Case* the Supreme Court observed:

> "The concepts, defence of India, 'Security of India' Security of State, relations of India with foreign powers ...... are not of great certainty or definiteness... However, since these concepts are not defined ... court must strive to give to these concepts a narrower construction than what the literal words suggest. While construing the laws of preventive detention like National Security Act, care must be taken to restrict their application to as few a situation as possible... [as such phrases] are fraught with grave consequences if construed liberally."[2]

The court also narrowed down the meaning of "maintenance of supplies and services essential to the community" saying that no person could be detained under this head unless they are by law or notification published describing which of the services and supplies are essential to the community. But in this interdependent world literally any service or supply can be declared essential.

The concept of 'public order' is equally nebulous. Whether an activity is prejudicial to law and order or public order has been anybody's guess despite numerous decisions of the Supreme Court. Activity prejudicial to public order is described as activity which harms the even tempo of life and creates fear in the public. It is considered to be something more serious than a law—and—order problem. But as observed by the Supreme Court in the *Ram Manohar Lohia's case* these two concepts are overlapping.[3] The distinction being blurred the scope of abuse of the power of detention to circumvent regular criminal processes is wide and this also has been the experience.

As such, power granted under the law of preventive detention to the executive is dependent on the sweet will of the executive exercising this power. Having granted blanket power to legislatures to enact legislation to deprive a person of his liberty without trial to mitigate the rigour and harshness of such a law, limitation on this power has been introduced in Clauses 3 to 7 of Article 22 of the Constitution. These provisions are more of a limitation on Fundamental Right to personal liberty and it is strange that such provisions, like Article 34, which deal with Martial Law, find place in Chapter III of the Constitution which confers Fundamental Rights. More so, even these safeguards contained in this Article can be taken away by the executive when emergency is proclaimed under Article 352 as has been done in the past.

CONSTITUENT ASSEMBLY DEBATES

The provisions of the Draft Constitution proposing grant of the power of preventive detention to the Parliament and State legislatures and limitations placed on this power, provoked bitter debate and several amendments were moved in the Constituent Assembly.

Dr. B.R. Ambedkar, who introduced the provisions for preventive detention felt that "in the present circumstances" it was necessary to empower the executive to detain a person without trial and clauses 3 to 7 of Article 15A of the Draft Constitution i.e. Article 22 of the Constitution limited the power of the legislature by providing constitutional safeguards to a person detained under a preventive law.[4]

But several members of the Constituent Assembly recalling how the power of preventive detention was abused under British rule questioned the retention of such power in our democratic Constitution. Prof. Shibban Lal Saxena felt that the Constitution should not be disfigured by such a denial of personal liberty even if its need was felt because "this power may be abused more than it is used in the interest of the country".[5] Pandit Thakur Das Bhargav reminded the Constituent Assembly that "there was a time when detention without trial was regarded as a very heinous offence itself, when everyone said no person should be detained without trial", and warned, "It is in the blood of every executive officer and much more in India to have as much power as possible.... Where is the guarantee that any other Government which is not manned at the Centre like the present Cabinet will not abuse their power?"[6] In similar vein Mrs. Purnima Banerjee said, "Any form of detention without trial is obnoxious to the whole idea of democracy and our way of thinking."[7]

Mr. H.V. Kamath vehemently opposed the grant of the power preventive detention because, "a coterie of few men in authority could use it not really in the interest of country but for their "lust for power," and he prophesied:

> "Has anybody considered how some other person totally opposed to our ideals, to our conception of democracy, coming into power might use this Constitution against us and suppress our rights and liberties? This Constitution, which we are framing, may boomerang may [and] recoil on us and it would then be too late for us to rue the day when we made such provisions in the Constitution. I hope Sir, and I pray to God, that we shall be guided by wisdom, and vision for a long-term Constitution and we will see to it that the Constitution we are framing will not last merely for a few years but will last at least our life time, if not a few generations. If unfortunately this outlook is not there, the old biblical saying will come true..."Where there is no vision, the people perish".[8]

Mr. Anantashyanam Ayyangar feared that the Government might "recklessly" put citizens in jail, and warned that if there was a political rival capable of challenging the Government "the possibility is that you will clap him in jail".[9] Dr. Punjabrao S. Deshmukh pointed out that instead of trimming the power of preventive detention given under the Government of India Act of 1935, more power was being given to the executive which was "absolutely unnecessary if not dangerous also."[10]

As enough power was given under the Entry 3 of the Union List and the emergency provision of the Constitution to safeguard the security of India, H.V. Kamath opposed the power of preventive detention in the Concurrent List and felt that in a democratic country preventive detention should not be used for reasons connected with maintenance of public order and services of essential supplies to the life of the community and the States. He vehemently criticized the proposed draft entry in the Concurrent List which enabled the State Legislature to enact a preventive detention law for reasons connected with the "stability of the Government established by law", and hoped that the Constituent Assembly would not be a party to arm the Union or State Legislature "to detain a person merely because men in power think that the stability of the Government is in danger. It would be a worst tyranny of modern times" and... "Such provision would lead to very serious consequences in the hands of unscrupulous persons," and [2]appealed for deletion of this entry [from the Concurrent List] altogether.[11]

Dr. Ambedkar accepted the amendment and agreed to replace it by the words 'security of state'. A similar phrase, *viz.* 'security of India' was used in the Entry in the Union List.[12]

ARTICLE 22

The draft Article 15A *i.e.*, Article 22 which limited the power of the legislature in enacting the law of preventive detention was hardly satisfactory. It did not even provide for communicating the grounds of detention to the detenue. It was also silent about the period for which a person could be detained on these points as also regarding the Constitution of the Advisory Board, the procedure before it and whether the opinion of the Advisory Board was, or was not, binding on the executive.[13]

The Drafting Committee came in for heavy criticism for incorporating this article in Fundamental Rights Chapter. When "a Charter of freedom" was being considered, Mahavir Tyagi asked, "Is this a proper place for providing for curtailment of that very freedom and liberty?.... This is an article which will enable future Governments to detain people and deprive them of their liberty rather than guaranteeing it."[14] Similarly, Jaspat Rai Kapoor commented that this article was another example of conservatism which characterized the chapter on Fundamental Rights. This chapter according to him should more appropriately be called 'Limitations on Fundamental Rights' or 'Fundamental Rights and

Limitations thereon', because "emphasis seems to be not so much on rights and liberty as on restrictions and limitations thereof', and those people who were detained for security reasons were given "no rights worth its name."[15]

Dr. Bakshi Tek Chand described this article as the "most reactionary" and pleaded for its outright rejection. It was nothing but "a cloak" to deny liberty to an individual. According to him instead of being a Fundamental Right it was 'charter' to the legislatures to go on enacting a legislation under which persons can be arrested without trial and detained for such period as they think since the draft Constitution did not provide any time limit for which a person could be detained. He also pointed out that no constitution provided for preventive detention during peace time.[16]

Pandit Thakur Das Bhargav emphasized that during the emergency these safe-guards had no meaning as this Article itself could be suspended. Earlier opening the debate on this Article he tried to trim down the vast power of preventive detention given in the Entries in the Union List by proposing that the Parliament should have the power of preventive detention only for subversive and dangerous activities affecting the security of the country, relations affecting harmony between different communities or persons who were members of organizations declared unlawful; and to buttress his submission he quoted the words from Dr. Ambedkar's letter to the Drafting Committee wherein he had proposed that the preventive detention law should only be used against "those who were believed to be engaged in dangerous and subversive activities."

GROUND OF DETENTION

One of the glaring and most serious lacunas in the Draft Article was that it did not provide for communication of the grounds of detention to the detenue. Unless he was informed of the reasons for which he was detained, he would not be in a position to make a representation or give his defence against the order of detention to the detaining authority or to the Advisory Board or challenge his detention in court by way of a *habeas corpus* petition. Dr. P. K. Sen emphasized that it was the "unquestionable right" of a detenue to know the reasons for which he was being detained and they must be communicated to him.[17]

According to R.K. Sidhava, disclosure of grounds was also necessary in the public interest so that people would know that the government was detaining a person because he was using his freedom to destroy the freedom of others.[18] Bakshi Tek Chand along with Pt. Hyridaynath Kunjru, Nazzir Ahmed, H.V. Pataskar and H.V. Kamath pressed for the inclusion of these valuable safeguards,[19] and Dr. Ambedkar agreed to amend the article to the effect that "the detaining authority making an order of detention shall, as soon as may, be communicated to him the grounds on which the order has been made and offer him the earliest opportunity of making representation against the order."[20]

But the phrase "as soon as may be" also came for pointed criticism from the members who were keen that it must be made a constitutional duty to communicate the grounds of detention without delay. Pt. Kunjru wanted the clause to be strengthened to the effect that the grounds should be communicated "as soon as possible after his arrest as possible." While Dr. Bakshi Tek Chand pressed that communication of grounds must be "at once" as in Article 34 of the Japanese Constitution, H.V. Kamath insisted that it must be done "immediately".[21]

Dr. Ambedkar justified the phrase that "as soon as possible", really meant immediately after arrest if not before arrest[22] H.V. Kamath appealed to him not to stand on prestige but make it clear in black and white in the Constitution. But this was not made clear, with disastrous consequences.

Taking advantage of this vague phraseology, Parliament and State Legislatures have been enacting preventive detention laws stating that the grounds of detention shall be communicated "as soon as possible within five days or in case of special circumstances communicated in writing to detenue within ten to fifteen days." This provision of the Constitution permits the legislature pass a law that grounds of detention shall be given "as soon as possible" after one year or ten years, and thus totally denies the opportunity to the detenue from obtaining his release. This is because he cannot make a representation against the order of detention or even file a *habeas corpus* petition unless he knows the grounds of detention.

It is submitted that this is an unwarranted, arbitrary and unreasonable power granted to the detaining authority, more so, when detention laws, like the *MISA, COFEPOSA* or *NSA* have provided that grounds of detention shall be communicated by the detaining authority to the Government "forthwith". If they have to be communicated to the Government immediately, and there can be no detention without the grounds being before the detaining authority, there seems to be absolutely no reason *whatsoever* why they should not be communicated to the detenue along with the order of detention. This question came directly for decision before the Supreme Court in *Ashok Kumar's Case* and the Supreme Court held that Section 8 or the National Security Act which provided for communication of grounds of detention in five days was *intra vires* because Article 22 contemplated "as soon as possible" did not mean "immediately".[23]

The draft article did not mention a period for which a person could be kept in detention without trial. All that it provided was that Parliament prescribe by law the maximum period of detention. Under this provision, as H.V. Kamath pointed out, the legislature could pass a law permitting detention for life.[24] Pt. Thakur Dass Bhargav wanted one year to be the maximum limit,[25] while Smt. Poornima Banerjee urged that a six-month detention was enough and after six months if there was sufficient reason the detenue should be put to trial or he must be released.[26]

Bakshi Tekchand recalled that the Provincial Legislature after detaining persons during the freedom struggle had extended the period from six months to one year and then to three years and one provision which had provided for indefinite detention.[27] Pt. Hirdaynath Kunjru wanted that period should be quantified in the Constitution itself because the procedure before the Advisory Board was not satisfactory. It did not provide for personal representation, and the detenue was debarred from engaging a lawyer, there would only be a police report and in this state of affairs the Advisory Board could come to a wrong conclusion.[28] Both Anantashyanam Ayyangar[29] and Jaspat Rai Kapoor[30] wanted the provision for a periodic review of the detenues case after every three or six months and the latter urged Dr. Amebedkar to "at least concede" this small safeguard as he was not prepared to fix a definite time limit for detention. Dr. Ambedkar, however, stated that Parliament could by law provide for periodic review.

No detention law except the Preventive Detention Act of 1950, has provided for a periodic review. As such, once the Advisory Board has come to a conclusion that there are sufficient reasons for detention, the detenue has to undergo detention for a period that the detaining authority orders. Although the detaining authority, depending on the circumstances of the case, is expected to order detention for a lesser period than the maximum prescribed by law, the experience has been to put a detenue in jail for the maximum permissible period.

Since no period for detention without trial is fixed, Parliament has given *carte blanch* orders, just as under the British rule Provincial legislature had increased the period of detention, the Preventive Detention Act of 1950 provided for six months. MISA of 1971 provides orders, for one year, and COFEPOSA 1971, provided in certain cases for two years. Similarly, the National Security Act (NSA) of 1980 initially provided for one year and then it was amended in 1985 to increase the period for up to two years in certain cases. And if the legislation makes a law providing for detention for ten, fifteen or fifty years, it is legally permissible. Hence there is pressing need to curb this power of legislation by Constitutional amendment as regards the maximum period for which a person can be detained because the detenue is denied his precious right of personal liberty without even a trial where he cannot prove his innocence and regain his freedom.

The Constitution of the Advisory Board and procedure before it was also not satisfactory. Although Dr. Ambedkar had stated that no detenue "shall be kept for a longer period than three months without the authority of impartial tribunal",[31] the draft Article 22 that he himself proposed was quite different. In the first place the Government was to appoint the Advisory Board. Secondly, it was to "consist of persons who are or have been or qualified to be appointed as judges of the High Court" that is any person of 10 years practice with no judicial training could be appointed as a member of the Board. Pandit Thakurdas Bhargav wanted impartial tribunal and not an Advisory Board.[32] H.V. Pataskar insisted that this Article might be abused by the unscrupulous Government which "may nominate their own men" on the Board.[33] He agreed with T.T. Krishnamachari and Alladi Krishna Sawami[34] that by his amendment eminent lawyers who could not be made judges would be excluded, but felt that the advantage to be gained by the proposed clause outweigh the disadvantage.

Shri Tekchand Bhargav, Smt. Purnima Banerjee and Smt. Durgabai wanted the provision for guaranteeing a personal hearing to the detenue before the Advisory Board so that he could meet the points made by the Government. Pt. Thakur Das Bhargav and Smt. Purnima Banerjee felt that the power to detain without the sanction of the Advisory Board for three months was too long and suggested two months and fifteen days respectively.[35] Bakshi Tekchand insisted that it should be made clear that the explanation given by the detenue to the detaining authority should be placed before the Advisory Board.[36] Pt. Kunjru wanted a provision to the effect that the detenue should be allowed to make a separate representation to the Advisory Board and if the Government chose not to give reply, the Advisory Board should have the power to release the detenue.[37] H.V. Kamath wanted to know specifically from Dr. Ambedkar whether a person detained under the Law of Preventive Detention would be able to file a writ of *habeas corpus* to the High Court and the Supreme Court.[38]

In reply, Dr. Ambedkar said that 15 days was too short a period and a three-month period was decided because administrative difficulties could arise if a large number of persons came to be detained. He gave the assurance that all papers, including the detenue's representation, would be placed before the Advisory Board, and that this was implicit. The members asked that the matter be made "explicit'. He said that he was prepared to provide for the Parliament to prescribe the procedure but was not prepared to make any further concession. This in fact was no concession at all as everything was left to the sweet will of the Parliament.

Even Dr. Ambedkar did not agree to provide for an impartial tribunal about which he himself had spoken earlier. Also, his contention that detention beyond three months without obtaining the approval of Advisory Board would be illegal was not correct. Parliament was empowered under Article 22 (7) "to prescribe the circumstances under which the class or classes of cases in which a person arrested under any law providing for preventing detention may be detained for a period longer than three months". As such, the Government could detain a person for more than three months without even referring the case of a detenue to the Advisory Board. Thus all that the Parliament had to do was to specify circumstances and make categories and deny such persons the right of their case being examined by the Advisory Board within three months.

Some members wanted that when a person is detained without trial his family should be given some compensation; more so if he was a sole bread-winner.[39] Dr. Ambedkar reiterated that Parliament may by law provide for it. But he felt that if a person was destroying the foundation of the country he had hardly any right to ask for maintenance though he could claim a right to be fed.[40] It is submitted that guilt by association is alien to civilized law and family members cannot be subjected to financial hardship if the bread-winner is detained. And why should compensation or damages not be paid by the Government if its order of detention is found illegal or *mala fide* by the Advisory Board, the High Court or the Supreme Court? During the Internal Emergency, hundreds of families were ruined and even starved when persons were arrested in a *mala fide* manner. Even a writ petition for the right to be fed or clothed made by detenues was held to be not maintainable on the spacious reasoning of the Supreme Court in the *Bhenudas Gawde's Case* because the Fundamental Right of *Liberty and Life* under Article 21 had been suspended during that time.[41]

In view of past experiences under British Rule, Pt. Thakurdas Bhargav and H.V. Kamath wanted that when a person is preventively detained, the restrictions imposed should be minimal and provisions of Jail Rules regarding hard labour should not be applied to him.[42] Dr. Ambedkar did not refer to this point but there have been scores of cases of detenues being deprived of facilities like interviews with family members and being permitted a lesser number of interviews than those given even to the convicted prisoners; and the Supreme Court had again and again reminded the executive that restrictions on a detenue must be "minimal", consistent with detention, because a detenue is imprisoned not for committing any offence but only on a suspicion that he will commit one, and as such he was on a higher pedestal than an under trial or a convicted prisoner.[43]

To seek redress against the abuse of the power Anantshyanam Ayyangar wanted that the detenue should have right to consult and be defended by a lawyer.[44] Some members thought that this was provided in Clause 1 of Draft Article 15-A, but Dr. Ambedkar made it clear that this clause was not applicable to a person detained under a Law of Preventive Detention as Clause 3 of this Article specifically provided that the safeguard mentioned in Clauses 1 and 2 of Article 22 will not be available to a person detained under the Preventive Detention Law.[45] It has however been a practice to allow the detenue to consult a lawyer in preparing his representation to the detaining authority and the Advisory Board and consult and engage a lawyer for filing a writ of *habeas corpus* in the High Court or the Supreme Court. But it needs to be emphasized that this is a concession by the Government and not a right and as such can be denied if the Government so chooses.

In *Francis Mullin's Case*[46] a two-judge bench of the Supreme Court held that the restriction placed on the detenue that he could have consultation with a lawyer and within hearing distance of authorities was unreasonable and void of Articles 14 and 21.[46] But in *A.K. Roy's Case* the Supreme Court distinguished this judgment and observed that in *Francis Mullin's Case* the Court was not called upon directly to decide whether the detenue had the right to engage or consult a lawyer to defend himself before the Advisory Board and preparing and filing of the *habeas corpus* petition or other proceedings for securing his release; and held "reluctantly though" that in view of Article 22(3)(b) the detenue had no right to be defended by legal practitioners before the Advisory Board, but added that if a lawyer or legal advisor was engaged by the detaining authority or the Government before the Advisory Board, then not allowing the detenue to be represented by a lawyer would be discriminatory and would violate equality before the law under Article 14.[47]

A specific question was asked by Mr. H.V. Kamath as to whether a person detained with a Law of Preventive Detention could file a writ of *habeas corpus* in the High Court or the Supreme

Court to obtain the release,[48] the reply given by Dr. Ambedkar was rather surprising. He said such a writ would lie to, but its scope would be "limited to find out by the court whether the man has been arrested under a law and whether he has been arrested by the executive. Once the court cames to the conclusion that he is arrested under some law *habeas corpus* must come to an end".[49]

This is contrary to the well-settled principle and law that when a person is detained under a preventive detention law, mere production of an order of detention passed by a competent authority is not a complete answer. The detaining authority has to discharge the burden that he has complied with each provision in the detention law and meet the challenge of colourable or *mala fide* exercise of power if alleged by the detenue; otherwise detention is illegal.

Dr. Ambedkar, while replying to the debate had expressed hope that provisions regarding preventive detention in Article 22 of the Constitution "may become a dead letter in course of time." It is unfortunate that this article has been one of the most active Articles of the Constitution.[49]

PREVENTIVE DETENTION ACT OF 1950

Within a month of the birth of the Republic on 25th February 1950, a Bill to enact the preventive detention law was tabled in the Parliament. However, Sardar Vallabhbhai Patel, the then Deputy Prime Minister of India, who piloted the Bill said that it was not a pleasant task to bring in such a legislation immediately after the adoption of the Constitution and he was doing so with a "heavy heart.... One has to take actions which are most distasable."[50] The urgency for such legislation was because the Communists in large numbers were engaged in "dangerous and subversive" activities such as removing rails, cutting communication lines and threatening the "existence and security of India". Secondly the State preventive detention, like the Local Public Safety Act of Bihar was already declared unconstitutional. The Calcutta High Court had reserved its Judgment and about 350 persons were about to be released. The petition challenging State's acts were pending in the High Courts of Bombay and Calcutta. Therefore Central Legislation in conformity with Article 22 was urgently required.[51]

He appealed to the Parliament to pass the Bill on the same day to prevent the release of persons about whose "dangerous and subversive activity" the State Governments had no doubt. Sardar Patel pointed out that the Act provided additional safeguards than those contemplated in Article 22 as it provided for a review of the detention case after six months.[52]

However there was a long-drawn debate and even the Attorney-General of India was invited to explain the provisions of the Bill to the Parliament. Dr. Punjabrao Deshmukh, who had taken active part in the Constituent Assembly debates when Article 22 was discussed, wanted to limit the application of the Act to affected areas only because the authorities "have a tendency to use short-cuts whenever they are available",[52] while R.K. Chaudhary described it as a "black Bill".[53]

H.V. Kamath wanted the act should be so amended and that the Advisory Board should consist of persons not less than a District Magistrate followed by a review by Judges of High Courts either sitting or retired.[54]

These amendments ought to have been accepted to prevent the abuse of vast power under the Act. Nevertheless the reply given by Sardar Patel is worth a special mention. He said:

> "I am also glad that the Bill has met with careful criticism because the liberty of any citizen is sought to be taken away by a Bill. I have carefully scrutinized and the necessity of it is proved beyond doubt...I have passed through sleepless nights when I was asked to take up this measure."[55]

But it is equally significant to mention that the object of enacting the Preventive Detention Act of 1950, which Sardar Patel had described as an "emergent and extraordinary law", was to check "dangerous and subversion activities threatening the existence and security of the State." Yet the executive was vested with all the power mentioned in the Union List and Concurrent List, which was totally unwarranted. The Government could detain any person not only for activities prejudicial to the security of India and security of the States, but also for activities prejudicial to the maintenance of public order and service of essential supplies to the community.

It is equally significant to mention that the Bill giving such a vast power and being passed the same day the Government was a rushed-through affair by the Parliament. It had been introduced, and was passed same day. The President gave his assent on the next day and it became the law of the land.

The Preventive Detention Act of 1950, which initially passed as a temporary measure, was to come to an end on 1st April, 1951. But this deadline was extended to October 1952, and the Act was successively amended several more times till the Act was allowed to lapse on 31-12-1969 because of strong public agitation that it was being abused to detain political leaders and union workers.

There was severe criticism of the repeated extension of this Act. For example, when the amendment for extending the Act by three years was moved in 1954, the opposition criticized its extension. It was described as a "lawless law" which should not remain in the statute book in normal times. They feared that it would be used by the ruling party to remain in power by detaining opposition members. A.K. Gopalan leading the attack said that the way people were being detained and the grounds for which detention was ordered proved conclusively that the Act was directed against the opponents of the ruling Congress party on the information supplied to it by petty police informers; and that High Courts and the Supreme Court had severely criticized the "flimsy grounds" of detention. He also reminded the House that Sardar Patel and Rajagopalachari had been apologetic and conceded at the time of its first implementation and that it was an extraordinary law. But Dr. K.N. Katju who was then the Home Minister seeking its extension had no such qualms of conscience and wanted to make the Law of Preventive Detention "a part of normal law of the land".

Mr. N.C. Chatterjee opposing the extension of the Act said it was being extended not for the security of India but protecting and petuating the Congress rule of India and it had made a mockery of democracy by repeated extension of the life of the Act. He further said:

> "This Act is a slander of self-rule and India's capacity to run democratic Government... we have all along

> maintained that it is a black act, which is really a lawless law. The Home Minister reminds us that it is not a lawless law, because of the wonderful provision in the Constitution. I do maintain that a law can be lawless even if it is passed by an authority which has got legislative competence to do so. It will be lawless if it infringes the cardinal principles of jurisprudence, on which society is based."

And he reminded the House of Chief Justice Mahajan's observation in the *A.K. Gopalan's Case* that "The preventive detention laws are repugnant to democratic constitutions and they cannot be found to exist in any of the democratic countries of the world", since no democracy had preventive detention as a peacetime legislation. N.C. Chatterjee criticized the Home Minister for describing it as an essential and necessary legislation and pleaded for withdrawing this "hated and iniquitous" law.

Opposition members also challenged the government's claim that the Act had not been used against political opponents and charged the government for dishonouring its assurance that it would detain only those persons who were indulging in subversive activities. They also pointed out that cases of such misuse were brought and proved before the courts.

MAINTENANCE OF INTERNAL SECURITY ACT OF 1971 (MISA)

Within one-and-a-half years of the lapse of the Preventive Detention Act of 1950, which was in force for nearly two decades, another detention law was enacted. In the early seventies the situation across the border of East Pakistan was becoming grim and on 7th May, 1971, Maintenance of Internal Security Ordinance was promulgated to be replaced by the Maintenance of Internal Security Act of 1971 (MISA). The stated reason for bringing this drastic legislation was:

> "In view of the prevailing situation in the country and the developments across the border there is need for urgent and effective preventive action in the interest of the national security. It is, therefore, considered essential to

have power of preventive detention to deal effectively with threats to the defence of India's security and from espionage activities of foreign agents. Since existing laws available to deal with the situation have not been found to be adequate, the Maintenance of Internal Security Ordinance of 1971 has been promulgated. It is now proposed to replace the Ordinance by an Act."

Thus the purpose of the legislation was to meet the threat regarding the defence and security of India, particularly to deal with espionage and subversive activities of foreign agents. Yet like the Preventive Detention Act of 1950, power was sought to detain persons for activities prejudicial not only to the defence of India, relations with the foreign powers and the security of India, but also for the security of the State, maintenance of public order and maintenance of supplies and services essential to the community.

MISA was qualitatively different from its predecessor. It was not a temporary legislation. It also did not contain provisions for the periodic review of detention cases. Thus detention without trial instead of being, to use Sardar Patel's words, "extraordinary emergent legislation", was made a normal law of the land.

During the debate in the Parliament the Members of the Opposition expressed their apprehension that this Act would be abused, as was its predecessor, for political and other reasons having no connection with threats to the defence and security of India. Soon this became a reality.

When the Emergency was declared on 3rd December, 1971, because of the Pakistani aggression, as has been noticed earlier, (a) Presidential Order was issued under Article 359 suspending enforcement of Articles 14, 21 and 22. As such Preventive Detention Law could be enacted in violation of safeguards contained in Article 22. On the very next day the Defence of India Act of 1971 was enacted and under Section 6 of this Act various provisions of MISA were amended. Important amendments were regarding the period of detention and the reference to the Advisory Board. Section 13 which provided that when the Advisory Boards confirmed the order of detention a person could be kept in detention for a maximum period of 12 months or till the expiry of the Defence of India Act, whichever was later. As such detention could be continued as long the emergency was in force and there being then no time limit to the duration of emergency, a person could be detained indefinitely.

Moreover, Section 17-A was added by which, during the Emergency, a person detained for activities prejudicial to any one of the reasons mentioned in the Act, except the maintenance of supplies and services essential to the community, could be detained beyond a period of three months without obtaining the opinion of the Advisory Board, for two years. As such, a person who was detained for reasons connected not only with the security of India but also for activities likely to affect public order could be detained for two long years without the approval of the Advisory Board. Another important amendment was when case of such a detenue was placed before the Advisory Board it came to the conclusion that his continued detention was warranted and the detaining authority could detain him for three years. These amendments gave drastic powers to the executive and the period between 1971 to 1975 saw its widescale abuse. MISA was freely used to curb peaceful agitations of students against corruption in government, of labour unions and of railway employees; and the Supreme Court was literally flooded with *habeas corpus* petitions.

It is relevant to mention that Section 17-A of MISA was declared invalid by the Constitution bench of the Supreme Court in the *Sambhu Nath Sarkar's Case*[57] because the Parliament which alone was empowered to prescribe exceptional circumstances the valuable safeguard of not referring the case to the Advisory Board had not done.

In *Fagu Shaw's Case* validity of the amendment to Section 13 of MISA was challenged as the maximum period of detention was not fixed. However, the Constitution Bench of the Supreme Court by a majority held that detention was made co-terminus with the expiry of the Defence of India Act, which in turn depended on the revocation of the Proclamation of Emergency. As such, it could not be said to be indefinite as emergency would be revoked one day.[58] However, Justice P.N. Bhagwati recorded his dissent.

It is submitted that the majority view in the *Fagu Shaw's Case* erred in ignoring the mandate of Article 22 that it was an obligation which fastened the legislature to fix the maximum period of detention. And the Parliament could not amend Section 13 by Section 6 of the Defence of India Act by which the maximum period was made co-extensive during the duration of the Emergency because it had no control whatsoever on the question of revoking emergency which was the sole discretion of the President. The observation of the majority that Parliament did not abdicate its function of fixing a maximum period of detention is not correct. Its presumption that the President will not act unreasonably and continue the emergency even after the emergency has ceased to exist has been proved wrong as seen earlier.

The Supreme Court noticed the widespread abuse of power under MISA. Quashing the order of detention in *Anil Dey's Case* the Supreme Court had observed:

> "The liberty to citizen is a priceless freedom, in compliance with the provisions of the Constitution the said freedom can be curtailed, but only with strict compliance with statutory formalities which are the vigilant concern of the Courts to enforce."[59]

And as MISA did not provide for a periodic review the Supreme Court observed:

> "It was appropriate for a democratic Government not merely to confine preventive detention to serious cases but also to review periodically the need for continuance of detention because no one should languish in prison for a day longer than is 'absolutely necessary."'[59]

Criticizing the use of MISA for curbing student agitations in the famous *Ram Bahadur Rai's Case* the Supreme Court admonished the executive in the following words:

> "It is necessary to administer a reminder and a warning to the Government: peaceful protests and the voicing of a contrary opinion are powerful and wholesome weapons

> in the democratic repertoire. It is therefore unconstitutional to pick up a peaceful protestant and put him behind the prison bars.[60]

On 17th July, 1974, MISA was amended by an Ordinance to include in its scope activities prejudicial to the conservation of foreign exchange and prevention of smuggling. Thus, for the first time the power of preventive detention was extended for economic offences and those who were detained for these reasons could be detained for two years instead of one year. Furthermore, these detenues could be detained without obtaining the opinion of the Advisory Board for one year, instead of three months.[61]

CONSERVATION OF FOREIGN EXCHANGE AND PREVENTION OF SMUGGLING ACTIVITIES ACT OF 1974 (COFEPOSA)

This Ordinance was replaced by an independent enactment called the Conservation of Foreign Exchange and Prevention of Smuggling Activities Act of 1974 (COFEPOSA). Both the State and Central Government, were empowered to order detention for prevention of activities connected with smuggling or prejudicial to conservation of foreign exchange.

But whereas detention order under MISA could be issued by the District or even Additional District Magistrate, under COFEPOSA no officer below the rank of Joint Secretary was empowered to issue the order of detention.

This Act, like MISA, was also not a temporary law and the Government was armed with two laws of preventive detention. Although the opposition was all for curbing increasing smuggling activity, they felt that economic offenders should be tried and convicted; and instead of being preventively detained they should be punitively imprisoned. It was also felt that violation of foreign exchange and smuggling activities organized on a scale stated by the Government could not be without the connivance of a corrupt bureaucracy and political patronage. Therefore, if there were a public trial the political-bureaucratic nexus would be exposed and that is why this law was being enacted. Another criticism of this law was that it might be used to detain political opponents as well as to slander their image proved to be not without foundation. During the Internal Emergency opposition leaders like Rajmata Vijaya Raje Scindia of Gwalior and Maharani Gayatri Devi of Jaipur were detained under the COFEPOSA.

During the Internal Emergency, just as provisions of the Constitution were amended time and again to prevent opposition leaders from seeking their release, MISA, under which most of the opposition workers were detained along with the COFEPOSA, were also drastically amended. Thousands of persons were detained under MISA all over the country on the night of 25-26 June, 1975, when the Internal Emergency was proclaimed. The detaining authorities all over the country, imprisoned political opponents on orders of the Indira Gandhi government and they had no grounds before them to base their satisfaction as required by MISA. To avoid giving them grounds of detention within five days as required under Section 8, Section 16-A "special provision dealing with the emergency" was inserted by promulgating the Ordinance on the fourth day of the Proclamation of Emergency, made applicable to those detained on, or after 25th June, 1975. Under this clause, if the person who passed the order of detention was "satisfied that it is necessary to detain such person for effectively dealing with the Emergency" he was to make a declaration to that effect and communicate it to the detenue. Such declarations were made against all MISA and COFEPOSA detenues during the Internal Emergency, except in the case of one Tikamchand Khetri as mentioned earlier.

Once such a declaration was made, vital safeguards under Sections 8 to 12 of MISA did not apply. That is, the detenue could be detained without informing him the grounds of detention thus depriving him of the opportunity of making a representation against the order of detention to the detaining authority, or to the Government who had to approve it. Nor could he challenge the order of detention in court on the grounds that it was irrelevant, vague or non-existent. Further, government was not obliged in this case to the Advisory Board and as such, detention could continue without the approval of the Advisory Board. Moreover as Section 13 was already amended by Section 6 of the Defence of India and Defence of Internal Security Acts detention could continue indefinitely as long as emergency was continued. This new section did provide that within fifteen days of detention, and thereafter every four months, the Government was required to review if detention was necessary for effectively dealing with the Emergency and revoke it in case it was not found necessary. But no opportunity was given to a detenue to make a representation before the reviewing authority and all material including the grounds of detention and orders of confirmation, rejection of review etc. were to be treated "as confidential shall be deemed to be matters of State against public interest to disclose including to a person detained." Thus the safeguard of periodic review was illusory. And the detenues used to receive communication mechanically after every four months that their case was reviewed and the detention was necessary for effectively dealing with the Emergency.

To ensure that under no circumstances could the person detained be allowed to obtain his release without the approval of the governments, Section 15 of MISA and Section 12 of COFEPOSA which dealt with the temporary release of detenues, were amended by inserting Clause 6 which provided that notwithstanding anything contained in any other law, no person detained under these laws "shall be released whether on bail or bail bond or otherwise". Afraid that some loophole might be left unplugged a new section was inserted to the effect that no person detained under MISA "shall have any right to personal liberty by virtue of natural law or common law if any."

A similar provision was not inserted in the COFEPOSA. Another drastic amendment to COFEPOSA, however, was the introduction of Section 5A according to which if the detention was based on two or more grounds and if one of the grounds is bad because it is vague, irrelevant, non-existent or invalid for whatever reason, the order shall be valid because the order shall be presumed to have been made on each of the grounds.

The Supreme Court and even during British rule the Federal Court had consistently held in scores of decisions that if any one of the grounds was bad the order of detention had to be quashed. The Federal Court in *Keshav Talpade's Case* and the Supreme Court in cases since *Sibanlal Saxena's Case* repelled the contention that the order of detention was valid as one of the grounds was a good ground. The sound reason of the court has been that since the order of detention is made on the subjective satisfaction of the detaining authority on the basis of grounds before him and it is not possible to assess in what manner and to what extent each of the grounds "influenced the detaining authority and contributed to the creation of satisfaction on the basis of which the detention order was made to accept the contention, that order should be sustained even if one of the grounds is good, is to substitute an objective judicial test for the subjective decision of the executive authority which is against the legislative policy underlying in the Statute".[62]

But by this amendment a well settled law, that if one of the grounds is bad an order of detention has to be held illegal, was over-ruled. It will be seen later that this amendment made during the operation of the Internal Emergency giving more drastic power to the Government has not only been retained in COFEPOSA after the withdrawal of the Proclamation of Emergencies in 1977 but also has been extended to other preventive detention laws as well.

During the Internal Emergency, the MISA because of its gross abuse by the Indira Gandhi Government to perpetuate its rule, had become a hated legislation. And one the first acts of the Janata Government was the promise of its repeal, in the Janata Party's election manifesto. But COFEPOSA, which enabled detention even if one of the grounds was good was retained in the statute book although when in opposition the Janata leaders had criticized it, when it was enacted in 1974.

The Janata Party as pointed out earlier also brought in the 44th Constitutional Amendment Act in 1979, to check misuse of the emergency provision and "put right to life and liberty on more secure grounds". It amended the emergency provisions, contained in Chapter XVIII and barred the suspension of Articles 20 and 21 altogether. The Right to Liberty was further strengthened by amending those provisions of Article 22 dealing with preventive detention under Section 3 of this Amendment Act. By this amendment the period of detention for obtaining the opinion of the Advisory Board was reduced from three months to two months, obtaining the opinion of Advisory Board was made mandatory in all cases without exception and the constitution of the Advisory Board was altered significantly. The Board was to be appointed on the recommendation of the Chief Justice of a concerned High Court and it was to consist of sitting or retired Judges as members. This was in contrast to its being constituted by the executive and could consist of sitting or retired Judges of the High Court or persons qualified to be High Court Judges.

These amendments as noted by the Supreme Court in *A.K. Roy's Case* gave the "detenue an assurance that his case will be considered fairly and objectively by an impartial tribunal. However, this Section 3 which provided for these amendments to Article 22 was not brought into force.

Nevertheless, it is important to note that these constitutional safeguards contained in amended Article 22 could be made meaningless as this article could be suspended during an emergency proclaimed under Article 352. It is submitted that this article which gave valuable safeguards not only to detenues but also persons arrested under ordinary criminal law, such as, the rights to be informed about charges, the right to engage and consult a legal practitioner of his choice or be produced before a Magistrate within twenty-four hours could be suspended, making a mockery of the Right to Life and Personal Liberty and the 44th Amendment should have also insulated Article 22 from being suspended as it was done in the case of Articles 20 and 21.

After the dissolution of the Lok Sabha in August 1979, the non-representative-caretaker-Charan-Singh-Government, on October 5, 1979, promulgated an Ordinance known as—Prevention of Black Marketing and Maintenance of Supplies of Essential Commodities Ordinance, 1979. Thus another preventive detention law to deal with economic offences was ushered in; and that too in spite of the fact that 22 out of 24 State Governments had told the Central Government that they could check malpractices like black marketing, hoarding, profiteering and rise in prices of essential commodities under ordinary laws without resorting to preventive detention.

NATIONAL SECURITY ACT OF 1980

When the Indira Gandhi Government returned to power in 1980, she readily replaced this Ordinance by an Act stating that the Essential Commodities Act of 1955 was not found adequate to cope with the situation although its penal provisions were made more stringent. Thus the Prevention of Black Marketing and Maintenance of Supplies of Essential Commodities Act which also was not a temporary law of preventive detention came to be part of the normal statute book, from February 12, 1980.

This was not all. Soon after, on 22nd September, 1980, the dreaded MISA was revived by the promulgation of the National Security Ordinance. It is significant to note that amendment to Article 22 introduced by the 44th Constitutional Amendment was not brought in force, however, the National Security Ordinance as also Prevention of Black Marketing and Maintenance of Essential Supplies Ordinance constituted the Advisory Board according to the amended Article 22.

However, when the Bill replacing the Ordinance was tabled in the Parliament it was not in accordance with the amended but the original Article 22. The treasury benches wanting to have as wide a power of detention as possible and contended that since the Government had not issued a notification to bring into force Section 3 of the 44th Amendment, they were not bound to enact a law according to it. The opposition on the other hand charged that the 44th Amendment having been enacted the Government could not thwart the constituent will for no rhyme or reason and the Government was under duty to issue a notification to bring in force Section 3 of the 44th Amendment and not to do so was a fraud commited against the Constitution.

A.K. ROY'S CASE[64]

The omission of the Government for over two years in not performing its constitutional obligation to bring in force the amendment which had already been passed, came up for decision in the famous *A.K. Roy's Case* before the Supreme Court. The whole controversy centred around Clause 2 of Section 1 of 44th Amendment which reads as under:

"1. **Short title and commencement**—(1) This Act may be called the Constitution (Forty-fourth Amendment) Act, 1979.

2. It shall come into force on such date as the Central Government may, by notification in the official Gazette, and different dates may be appointed for different provisions of the Act."

By this Clause 2 of Section 1, the Constituent body had given discretion to the Central Government as to when various provisions of this Amendment Act were to be brought in force without specifying time limits. Some of the provisions were brought to force on 20th June ,1979 and all except Section 3 which amended Article 22 were brought into force on 1st August, 1979. But since the Advisory Board was already constituted as per the amended Article 22 under the National Security Ordinance of 1971, there could be no reason whatever for not bringing into force this constitutional amendment. It is relevant to note that Chief Justice Y.V. Chandrachud, speaking for the majority in the *A.K. Roy's Case,* dealing with the contention that the Central Government was under obligation to bring Section 3 of the 44th Amendment into force within a reasonable time. Since it had failed to do so, this Court was under the obligation to issue *mandamus* directing the Central Government to issue notification under Section 1(2), to bring it into force this Amendment without any delay. However, he observed:

> Our decision on this question should not be construed as putting the seal of approval on the delay caused by the Central Government in bringing the provision of Section 3 of the 44th Amendment Act in force. We quite see that it is difficult to appreciate what practical difficulty can possibly prevent the Central Government from bringing into force the provisions of Section 3 of the 44th Amendment.
>
> We have said at the very outset of the discussion of this point that our decision on the question as to whether a *mandamus* should be issued as prayed for by the petitioners, should not be construed as any approval on our part of the long and unexplained failure on the part

> of the Central Government to bring Section 3 of the 44th Amendment Act into force. We have no doubt that in leaving it to the judgment of the Central Government to decide as to when the various provisions of the 44th Amendment should be brought into force, the Parliament could not have intended that the Central Government may exercise a kind of veto over its constituent will by not ever bringing the amendment or some of its provisions into force. The Parliament having seen the necessity of introducing into the Constitution a provision like Section 3 of the 44th Amendment it is not open to the Central Government to sit in judgment over the wisdom of the policy of that section.

Similarly, Justice A.C. Gupta delivering a minority judgment for himself and Justice V.D. Tulzapurkar also observed:

> It seems impossible that any such difficulty should still persist preventing the Government from giving effect to Section 3 of the Amendment Act…I do not think it can be seriously suggested that Provision like Section 1(2) of the Constitution (Fourty-fourth Amendment) Act empowered the Government to scotch an amendment of the Constitution passed by Parliament and assented to by the President.

Justices A.C. Gupta and V.D. Tulzpurkar correctly held that the writ of *mandamus* would lie and the Parliament's competence to take necessary steps if it thought that the Government has "betrayed the trust does not make the default lawful or relieve the court of its duty." Chief Justice Chandrachud speaking for the majority having rightly held that Section 1(2) imposed a duty on the Central Government and having noticed that there was no reason for delay in the performance of that duty, erred in not issuing the *mandamus*.

The reason given by majority that this clause contained "no objective standard" for exercise of that discretion, is amazing. It is submitted that discretion was given to the Central Government as regards the time as to when the provisions were to be brought into force. It is a settled law that when no time is stipulated for performance of a duty, the law implies that the duty must be performed within a reasonable time and what is a reasonable time will depend upon the facts and circumstances of the case. In this case when the majority having found that the Central Government had given no reason and no reason could be given for delay in the performance of its duty, ought to have issued a *mandamus* especially when the duty related to the performance of the constitutional obligation of bringing in force Section 3 of the Constitutional Amendment which gave valuable safeguards to detenue in the matter of personal liberty.

"That a Supreme Court should proclaim its helplessness to enforce a duty" as H.M. Seervai observed "is distressing, it is even more distressing because that duty is related to the performance of constitutional duty. Further more, the Supreme Court having held "The Parliament could not have visualized that without any acceptable reason the Central Government may fail to implement its will... we hope that the Central Government will without any further delay bring Section 3... in force". Seervai sarcastically observed, "Hope remains hope." Even now this amendment is not enforced.

It is disturbing if not ironical that Justices P.N. Bhagwati and D.A. Desai, who constituted the majority and who were known for their judicial activism, shrank from issuing a *mandamus* to the Central Government to perform its constitutional duty to strengthen the right to personal liberty.

Having abdicated its function in providing a remedy, the two remedies suggested by the majority were equally theoretical. First, since the executive is responsible to the Parliament, the Parliament could censure the Government. To expect the Parliament that approved the National Security Act when it was in breach of the amended Article 22 to censure the Central Government, showed either ignorance of the role of party discipline in the parliamentary system or a feeble attempt to throw the burden on the other organ of the State. The second remedy suggested was that since the Parliament had conferred upon the Central Government the power to bring into force the provisions of the 44th Amendment, and if the Parliament thought that the Central Government had failed to act, the Parliament could have deleted Section 1(2) of the Amendment Act. In suggesting this remedy the majority judgment ignored the difference between the Parliament's power to amend a law and its power to amend the Constitution. The 44th Amendment Act was passed by the Parliament as well as the majority of the States exercising their constituent power but under Article 368, Parliament could not delete this clause except with the approval of the majority of the States. It was therefore beyond the power of the Parliament to delete Clause (2) of Section 1 of the 44th Amendment Act, except by a Constitutional amendment.

The other important question which came for consideration was whether Clause 2 of Section 1 of the 44th Amendment was ultra-vires of the amending power conferred upon the constituent body by Article 368. It is submitted that the power to amend the Constitution is vested in the Parliament and it cannot be delegated to an outside agency, *i.e.* the Central Government. By delegating this power to the Central Government the power to bring into force the various provisions of the Amendment the Parliament would be creating a parallel constituent body, which is not impermissible under Article 368. As this clause vested uncontrolled power in the Central Government to amend the constitution of its own sweet will, it was violative of the basic structure of the Constitution.

The reasoning of the majority in upholding the constitutional validity of this clause was that the Parliament had often enacted conditional legislation for delegating its power of enforcement of law to the executive and it relied on various pronouncements of the Supreme Court when it had upheld such delegation to the government and therefore it held "what is permissible to the legislature by way of conditional legislation cannot be considered impermissible to the Parliament when in the exercise of its constituent power,...the question as regards time of enforcement of a constitutional... amendment should be left to the judgment of the executive."

It is submitted that the majority failed to appreciate the qualitative difference between legislative and constituent powers and erred in equating them. When a law is passed, except a Money Bill, the President under Article 111 cannot withhold his assent and return it for reconsideration. But the President under Article 111 can withhold his assent and return it for reconsideration. But when the Constitutional Amendment Bill is passed the President under Article 368(2) has no choice but to give his assent to the Bill and thereupon "the Constitution stands amended." When the President also has no power to withhold a Constitutional Amendment, it does not stand to reason that the executive can be permitted to withhold it at its discretion. Secondly, the President under Article 123 enjoys limited legislative powers to promulgate an ordinance when both the Houses of Parliament are not in session, but no such power is given to the President in the matter of amendment of the Constitution. Furthermore, in case of ordinary law, Parliament can appoint an outside agency and leave it to its judgment when it should be brought into force because Section 5 of the General Clause Act contemplates such a situation as it reads. "Where any Central Act is not expressed to come into operation on a particular date, then it shall come into operation on the day on which it receives the assent."

It is also relevant to note that when the Constitution of India was adopted no discretion was given to the Government in the matter of bringing into force the various provisions of the Constitution. By Articles 294 and 395 some Articles came into force at once and the remaining on 26th January, 1950. There are several constitutional amendments, where the constituent body felt that some time may be required due to administrative exigencies requiring arrangements to be made to bring into force the provisions of the Amendment, they stipulated a future date, but did not give unfettered discretion to the Government in the matter of bringing the amendment into force. This is only a later phenomena to insert Clause 2 of the section in the Constitutional Amendment Act giving unfettered powers to the Government to bring into force the amendment. It was for the first time that the Supreme Court was called upon to pronounce on the validity of such a blanket power given to the Government in the matter of bringing into force a constitutional amendment and the majority ought not to have upheld its validity by applying rulings applicable to ordinary legislation.

Another allied question which came up for decision was whether Section 1 of the 44th Amendment which is quoted earlier was, or was not, a part of the substantive Amendment. Clause 1 of this section which stated that it will be called the 44th Constitutional Amendment would go in a foot-note indicating the date by which the amendment of the Constitution was amended.

While Clause 2, which provided for bringing into force various provisions of the 44th Amendment, was the only a machinery by which various provisions of the amendment came in operation. And after all the provisions of the Amendment were brought in force, clause 2 would wither away. Secondly both the clauses of this section did not amend any of the Articles of the Constitution. As such, they were not part of the substantive amendment.

Since Article 13(2) provides that any law which violates Fundamental Right shall be void Clause 2 of Section 1 being a law would have to meet the challenge of Fundamental Rights mentioned in Chapter III of the Constitution. As mentioned earlier the majority declined to issue a *mandamus* to compel the Central Government to bring into force Section 3 of the Amendment Act because the Parliament did not "lay down an objective standard to guide and control the discretion of the Central Government in the matter of bringing the various provisions of the Act into force." It is submitted that on this very count the Supreme Court should have struck down Clause 2 of Section 1 as violative of Article 14 as it conferred arbitrary and unguided power on the executive. Moreover, there can be no limitation on the enjoyment of Fundamental Rights by an Act or a law but can be upheld if found in the provisions of the Constitution itself. It is because of the unguided power given to the Central Government by Clause 2 of Section 1 (which is a law) that it did not bring into force Section 3 of the 44th Amendment Act. Since this resulted in restricting the enjoyment of the Fundamental Right conferred under amended Article 22 which had a direct bearing on personal liberty, this clause should have been declared violative not only of Article 14-19 but also of 21 of

the Constitution. If the majority found it was unable to issue a *mandamus* to bring into force Section 3 of the 44th Amendment, because Clause 2 did not prescribe "objective standard to guide and control discretion", then on this very ground, or any of the grounds mentioned above, it ought to have struck down this clause. As a consequence the amended Article 22 would have become part of the Constitution. This is because in the absence of this clause the Constitution would stand amended from the date the President gave its assent.

It is submitted that the judgment of the majority does not stand to reason and is pregnant with grave consequences as it can enable and has in fact enabled the Central Government to defeat the will of the constituent body by obstinate and arbitrary refusal to do its constitutional duty for over thirty years. This is despite repeated attempts by the opposition to bring into force this important constitutional amendment. Normally constitutional amendment must amend this Constitution as soon as the President signs it. But in case it has to be delayed in order to make some procedural or organizational changes, the constituent body must incorporate a definite future date before which this amendment must be brought into force as was the practice during the Nehru government. To avoid any such mischief in future, constitutional amendments should not include such clauses which give unguided power to any body.

As more than fifteen years have passed and Section 3 has not been brought into force a detenue under N.S.A. filed a similar writ petition and the Division Bench of the Supreme Court consisting of Justice A.P. Sen and L.N. Sharma referred the case to the Constitution Bench for reconsidering *A.K. Roys's Case*. But when the case came for hearing before the Constitution Bench presided over by Chief Justice Venkatramaih, this case was dismissed on the ground that the *habeas corpus* petition itself had become infructuous as the detenue had been released. It is submitted that the Court erred in not deciding the constitutional point involved because the detenue was released. In fact, Dr. Vasant Kumar Pandit, who had raised this question was not a detenue when he filed the petition, and the Supreme Court had adjudicated this question in the *A.K. Roy's case*.[65]

In *Attorney General of India etc. Vs. Amrit Lal etc.* again the author raised this question to challenge the validity of COFEPOSA, consisting of a 9-Judge Bench but again this Bench did not decide the question stating that they had upheld the validity of COFEPOSA. It is submitted that it was the constitutional duty of the Supreme Court to reconsider the judgment in the *A.K. Roy's Case* when a citizen is deprived of his fundamental right in a matter of liberty because the executive is bound by the command of the constituent body.

A.K. Roy's Case is also important because in that case the validity of the Law of Preventive Detention that is the National Security Act was challenged on two grounds. First, no worthwhile democracy like the United States of America, Britain and France have preventive detention in peace time. It is an emergency legislation, as described by Dr. Ambedkar, the Chairman of the Drafting Committee of the Constitution, preventive detention is to be used when the very existence of the country is threatened. It is not a normal law to be used for depriving person of his liberty. Secondly in view of the expanded meaning given to Article 21 in the *Menaka Gandhi's Case* which laid down a proposition that the procedure established by law, by which a person is deprived of liberty, it must mean fair, just and reasonable and not any procedure. In *A.K. Roy's Case* the majority judgment delivered by the Chief Justice noticed that some countries like U.K. and U.S.A. did not have preventive detention during peace time. But since the framers of the Constitution were aware of this and yet they legitimized it by providing for preventive detention in Entry 9 of the Union List and Entry 3 of the Concurrent List, "We cannot declare it unconstitutional by imparting our notions of what is right and wrong." According to him:

> "The power 'to judge fairness and justness of the procedure established by a law for the purposes of Article 21 is one thing and the power to decide upon the justness of law itself is quite another thing: that power springs from a due process' such as found in the 5th and 14 Amendments of the American constitution by which no person can be deprived of life, liberty or property without the due process of law."

ENDNOTES

1. *A.K. Roy etc. Vs. U.O.I. etc.* 1982 (1) SCC 271.
2. *Ram Manohar Lohiya Vs. State of Bihar* 1966(1) SCR 709.
3. Dr. B.R. Ambdkar *Constituent Assembly Debates* Vol. 9 (New Delhi Printed by Lok Sabha Secretariat) pp. 1496-98. The Draft Article 15A (Article 22 was debated on September 15 and 16, 1949 pp. 1496-1588). Also see Entry 3 of the Concurrent List of the Schedule 6 of the Constitution of India.
4. *H.V. Kamath, op. cit.,* pp. 507-08.
5. Pandit Thakurdas Bhargav, *Ibid.,* pp. 1505-08.
6. Smt. Purnima Banerjee, *Ibid.*, pp. 1510-11.
7. H.V. Kamath, *Ibid.,* pp. 1518-19.
8. Anatashayanam Ayyangar, *Ibid.*, p. 1547.
9. Dr. P.S. Deshmukh, *Ibid.,* pp. 728-29.
10. H.V. Kamath, *Ibid.*, pp. 926-27.
11. Dr. Ambedkar, *Ibid.,* p. 929.
12. For Draft Article 15A as it was tabled before the Constituent Assembly see Appendix I. It was actually in two parts. The first two clauses dealt with limitation of deprivation of personal liberty for criminal offences and Clause 3 dealt with enemy alien and person detained under preventive detention laws and Clauses 4 to 7 dealt with safeguards to persons detained under the preventive detention clause.
13. Mahavir Tyagi, *Ibid.,* pp. 1547-48.
14. Jaspal Roy Kapoor, *Ibid.,* pp. 1541-42.
15. Bakshi Tek Chand, *Ibid.*, p. 1529 and 1534-35; Pandit Thakur Das Bhargav, *Ibid.,* pp. 1546 and 1500.
16. Dr. P.K. Sen, *Ibid.,* pp. 1550-51.
17. R.K. Sidhva, *Ibid.,* pp. 1525-26.
18. Bakshi Tekchand, *Ibid.,* p. 1527. Pt. Hridayanath Kunzru, *Ibid.,* pp. 1551-52; Naziruddin Ahmad, *Ibid.,* p. 1509; V.P. Patskar, *Ibid.,* p. 1524 and H.V. Kamath, *Ibid.,* pp. 15121-23.
19. Dr. Ambedkar, *Ibid.*, p. 1560.
20. It may be mentioned that Clause 1 of Article 22 which deals with arrest under Ordinary Criminal Law provides for grounds of arrest to be given as soon as possible. Pt. Hridayanath Kunzru, *Ibid.,* pp. 1551-52; Dr. Bakshi Tek Chand, *Ibid.,* p. 1527; H.V. Kamath, *Ibid.,* pp. 1521-23.
21. Dr. Ambedkar, *Ibid.,* p. 1545. Also see H.V. Kamath, *Ibid.,* p. 1535.
22. *Ashok Kumar Vs. Delhi Admn.* 1982 (2) SCC 403.
23. H.V. Kamath, *Ibid.,* p. 1519.
24. Pt. Thakurdas Bhargav, *Ibid.,* pp. 1500-1501.

25. Smt. Purnima Banerjee, *Ibid.*, p. 1511.
26. Bakshi Tek Chand, *Ibid.*, pp. 1534-35.
27. Pt. Hridaynath Kunjru, *Ibid.*, p. 1552.
28. Anatashayanam Ayyangar, *Ibid.*, p. 1546.
29. Jaspal Rai Kapoor, *Ibid.*, pp. 1541-43.
30. Dr. Ambedkar, *Ibid.*, pp. 1561-62.
31. Pt. Thakurdas Bhargav, *Ibid.*, p. 1508.
32. H.V. Pataskar, *Ibid.*, pp. 1523.
33. T.T. Krishnamachari, *Ibid.*, pp. 1523-24; Alladi Krishna Swamy Ayyar, *Ibid.*, pp. 1535-38.
34. Tek Chand Bhargav, *Ibid.*, p. 1500; Smt. Purnima Banerjee, *Ibid.*, pp. 1510-11; Smt. Durgabai, *Ibid.*, pp. 1554-56.
35. Bakshi Teckchand, *Ibid.*, pp. 1534-1535.
36. Pt. Hridaynath Kunzru, *Ibid.*, pp. 1511-52.
37. H.V. Kamath, *Ibid.*, p. 1554.
38. Purnima Banerjee, *Ibid.*, p. 1511; Smt. G. Durga Bai, p. 1555.
39. Dr. Ambedkar, *Ibid.*, p. 1563.
40. *Union of India etc. vs. Bhanudas Krishna Gawde etc,* 1977(1) SCC 834.
41. Pt. Thakurdas Bhargav, *Ibid.*, p. 1507; H.V. Kamath, *Ibid.*, p. 1517.
42. *Sampat Prakash,* 1969(3) SCR 574 = 1969 (1) SCC 562.
43. Anatashayanam Ayyangar, *Ibid.*, p. 1574.
44. Dr. Ambedkar, *Ibid.*, p. 1560.
45. *Francies Caroli Mullin vs. Delhi Administration*, 1981(1) SCC 270.
46. *A.K. Roy etc. Vs. U.O.I etc.* 1982 (1) SCC 271.
47. H.V. Kamath, *Ibid.*, pp. 1517-18.
48. Dr. Ambedkar, *Ibid.*, p. 1564.
49. *ADM, Jabalpur etc. vs. Shiv Kant Shukla etc.*, 1976 (2) SCC 521.
50. Vallabhbhai Patel, Lok Sabha Debates Vol. II Part II, dated 25.2.75, 874-76 and 909-910.?
51. *Ibid.,* Also see Reasons and Objects of the Bill.
52. Punjabrao Deshmukh, *Ibid.* p. 885.
53. R.K. Chaudhary, *Ibid.* p. 901.
54. H.V. Kamath, *Ibid.*, p. 882.
55. Vallabhbhai Patel, *Ibid.* pp. 883-84.
56. *Sambhu Nath Sirkar vs. State of West Bengal,* 1973(1) SCC 856.
57. *Ram Bahadur Rai vs. State of Bihar,* 1975(3) SCC 710.
58. *Anil De vs. State of West Bengal,* 1974(4) SCC 514.
59. *Fagushah Vs. State of West Bengal.*, Bhagwati however gave dissenting judgment—1974 (4) SCC 152.
60. This provision was to be operative as long as the 1971 and 1975 Proclamation of Emergency were in force.
61. *Keshav Talpade vs. King Empror,* 1943 F.C.R. 88; *Ram Krishna Bhardwaj*

vs. Sate of Delhi 1953, SCR 708; *Sibban Lal Saxena Vs. State of U.P.,* 1954 SCR 418.

62. These amendments incorporated many suggestions made by the members of the Constituent Assembly (See Chapter II).
63. *A.K. Roy etc. Vs. U.O.I. etc.*-1982 (1) SCC 271.
64. Dr. Vasant Kumar Pandit had filed a writ petition challenging the Bill seeking to replace the Ordinance as it was not in accordance with the amended Constitution. This writ petition was decided along with *A.K. Roy's case* who had challenged the ordinance making power under Article 73 affecting Right to Life and Liberty under Article 21 as violative of Article 21 and the basic structure of the Constitution.
65. In the judgment delivered in *Francies Caroli Mullin vs. Delhi Administration case* on 28.12.1981 and reported in the 1981(1) SCC 270 it was stated "we would, however, like to affirm our respectful agreement with the decision in this case to the effect that the detenue has a right to consult a lawyer of his choice for the purpose of preparing his representations, advising him as to how he should defend himself before the Advisory Board and preferring and filing a *habeas corpus* petition or other proceedings securing his release. "However, administrative directions were issued on the basis of which AIR 1982 SC 710 changed the phrase and stated 'we would however, like to say that by this judgment we are neither affirming nor disapproving of the decision in Francies Mullin to the effect that the detenue has a right to consult a lawyer of his choice for the purpose of preparing has representation...' No one had filed a Review or an application for direction yet the Court *suo motu* placed the case for direction and changed its decision and held. "We must therefore, hold, regretfully though that the detenue has no right to appear through a legal practitioner in the proceedings before the Advisory Board." 1982(2) SCR 272.
66. June 6, 1986, the National Security Act was amended for two years by an Ordinance to facilitate detention in Punjab for two years and for six months before obtaining the opinion of the Advisory Board. This period was again extended for two years by Ordinance.

CHAPTER EIGHT

CONCLUSION

Mass imprisonment under preventive detention laws like the Maintenance of Internal Security Act (MISA), Conservation of the Foreign Exchange Act (COFEPOSA) and the Defence of India Rules (DIR), the *habeas corpus* cases captivate the Internal Emergency of 1975 eminently; so also its totalitarian grip, brutality and occasional courtesy, courage of lawyers and Judges of the High Court and the abdication of duty and judicial consciousness by the highest court of the land. The country also witnessed Indira Gandhi's conversion from *defacto* to *dejure* dictatorship and domination of all constitutional institutions.

INTERPRETATION OF THE EMERGENCY PROVISIONS

The phrase 'If the President is satisfied' appears five times in the Constitution and every time to meet an emergent situation. It empowers the President to proclaim an Emergency if he is 'satisfied' that there is a threat to the integrity and sovereignty of the country—Article 352—if there is a breakdown of the constitutional machinery in the State—Article 356—and when a situation has arisen whereby the financial security or stability of the country is threatened—Article 360. Similarly, if the President or the Governor, as the case may be, is 'satisfied' that there is urgent need to legislate by Ordinance when the legislature is not in session under Articles 123 and 230. In other words, satisfaction of the President and or Governor is a pre condition for exercising these extraordinary powers and they could be challenged if they are unconstitutional or violative of the Fundamental Rights, as pointed out earlier, in the *Bank Nationalisation Case* in 1970, because this power is conditional and justiciable.

This satisfaction of the President was one of the grounds for challenging the continuance of the Emergency of 1971 and the proclamation of the Internal Emergency of 1975, before the judiciary in the *habeas corpus* cases in the High Courts. It is pertinent to note that the 42nd Constitutional Amendment stated that in all these cases that this "satisfaction" cannot be challenged in any court on any ground. But the 44th Amendment deleted all these provisions. It is, therefore, clear that this "satisfaction" is not final and is assailable.

These amendments together with the words *"if"* the President or the Governor of the State or the Administrator (now Lt. Governor) of the Union Territory of Pondicherry, as the case may be "is satisfied" in these emergent situations were retained even in the 42nd Amendment, lend support to the former Chief Justice K. Subba Rao's theory of presidential discretion in extraordinary situations. In his Presidential address, while inaugurating a seminar on "Emergency in the Constitution and Democracy" held in March, 1975, he distinguished between the President to act "with the aid and advice of the Council of Ministers" under Article 74 and his "satisfaction" to proclaim an Emergency under Part VIII of the Constitution. According to him, the phrase "act" is quite different from the phrase "if the President is satisfied". According to him, one can act without applying his mind but to reach a satisfaction "involves mental process" on the basis of material placed before him. And the President has to take emergent action if he thinks that material provided by the Council of Ministers requires it. This interpretation does not do any violence to the language of the Constitution. It is submitted that such discretion is designatedly vested with the President because he is the protector and defender of the federal Constitution, the sovereignty of India as he is the head of the armed forces and is the only person who is elected by the entire country, though indirectly. Above all, by declaring any of the emergencies he himself does not get any power.

According to Justice Subba Rao, the only snag in such interpretations is that in case of collusion between him and his Council of Ministers to wreck the democratic and federal fabric of the Constitution it is the duty of the Supreme Court to quash such a proclamation if there is a clear misuse of power. "The fact that President asserts that he is satisfied is no answer, if the abuse of power is established. It is then the case of presidential action becoming contrary to the provisions of the Constitution and the Supreme Court can step in to protect Fundamental Rights".

Furthermore, the Constitution should be amended regarding impeachment of the President. As the impeachment proceedings require the existence of both Houses of Parliament and when the President is the subject of impeachment he should not have the power to dissolve the Lok Sabha to abort the impeachment proceedings. Also the President should not have the power to dissolve the Lok Sabha after an emergency is proclaimed as the Parliament is required to approve or disapprove it. Furthermore, the Constitution should provide that as soon as the Emergency is proclaimed, the Parliament, as of right, will assemble as soon as possible within a week; and it should continue in session throughout the duration of the Emergency to scrutinize that the orders made and instructions issued for effective implementation of the Emergency. Also the President should have the power to suspend only those Fundamental Rights which the situation demands should be suspended. Besides the Proclamation of Emergency along with the conditions necessary for suspending democracy and enforcement of such Fundamental Rights, should be communicated to the UN forthwith. And above all, the power of the courts to uphold Fundamental Rights and to scrutinize all executive actions should not be touched.

In case, the President issues a Proclamation without the concurrence of the Council of Ministers, which generally he will not do, because by such action he does not get additional powers. But if he does it can be disapproved by the Parliament. However, if the effective power to issue a Proclamation is given to the Council of Ministers, placing it before the Parliament will be an empty formality in view of its majority, party discipline and anti-defection law. It is submitted that when the above mentioned emergent powers are exercised in such cases both these restrictions i.e. party whip and anti defection law when it comes to approval or disapproval of such a Proclamation of Emergency should be made non applicable by a Constitutional Amendment, if necessary. Furthermore this interpretation of the satisfaction of the President in imposing authoritarian power will satisfy the condition that the authority that creates the constitutional dictator should not be under the control of such a dictator.

JUDICIARY

Under the Constitutional scheme, the higher judiciary has the onerous responsibility to maintain the discipline of the Constitution and is endowed with the power to strike down any law, including the Constitutional amendment, if it is *ultra vires* of the Constitution.

The healthy convention of appointing the seniormost Judge as the Chief Justice of India was ignored in 1973. After the judgment in the famous *Keshvananda Bharti's Case* 1973(4) SCC 225, the three seniormost judges of the Supreme Court were superseded in the appointment of the Chief Justice of India, as they held against the government along with the majority in this case that democracy, judicial review, federalism and the rule of law amongst others, were basic features of the Constitution which were beyond the amending power of the Parliament. It created a tribe in the words of Chief Justice M. Hidayatulla, "Looking forward judges instead of forward looking judges."

It would not be inappropriate to mention here that Atal Bihari Vajpayee, then in the opposition, apprehended such an onslaught on the independence of the judiciary and had moved an amendment to Article 124, three years before the supersession that the seniormost judge should be appointed as the Chief Justice of India. This amendment after an acrimonious debate in the Lok Sabha was rejected.

Similarly in 1979, to further ensure the independence of the judiciary, he made several suggestions by way of a Constitutional Amendment Bill. He had proposed that the retirement age of High Court Judges should be increased to 65 years similar to that of the Supreme Court Judges as proposed recently by the Law Minister Verappan Moily. The former proposed it so that there is no race to go to the Supreme Court while the reason for the latter was to have enough experienced Judges to reduce the arrears. Furthermore, in that amendment Vajpayee proposed the adoption of the American system, "Once a Judge always a Judge." This would entitle the Judges to receive the same benefits after retirement so that they will not seek government favours such as grant of commissions etc. He also proposed that since the judiciary is expected to be impartial they should be debarred from seeking any job under any government after retirement, such as the Comptroller or Auditor General of India, as in Article 148(4). To add, I would suggest that the same criteria should be applied to the Members of the Election Commission who are also required to function impartially. We have seen a sorry spectacle of the Chief Election Commissioner becoming a Member of the Rajya Sabha and then the Minister of the ruling party. This has directly eroded the impartiality of the high office of the Election Commission in the public eye.

The Emergency of 1975 captures the darkest period of the judiciary as nothing else. Sixteen High Court Judges who gave judgments against the government were either transferred or not confirmed. It sent a clear message to the Judges that their fate was dependent on agreeing with the government. After the *ADM, Jabalpur's Case* 1976 (2) SCC 521, Justice H.R. Khanna, the senior-most Judge of the Supreme Court who gave the famous dissenting judgment, was also superseded. He told me later, "When I decided to give this judgment, I knew I would be superseded." However, the Attorney-General Niren De who argued for the government in this case, according to Granville Austin in his book *Working of the Democratic Constitution*, wrote that Justice Khanna told him that Niren De said to Justice Khanna, "May I congratulate you for your great judgment." It was said at that time amongst the lawyers that Justices M.H. Beg, Y.V. Chandrachud and P.N. Bhagwati agreed with the majority because they were in line for becoming Chief Justices and did not want to antagonize the government.

During the 1975 Emergency, the Parliament and the Judiciary abdicated their constitutional obligations and helped to make Indira Gandhi become an absolute autocrat. Democracy and peoples rights were not protected by persons who worked the Constitution but were rescued by ordinary people in the historic elections of 1977 by defeating the Indira Gandhi government including herself.

CONSTITUTIONAL AMENDMENT AND PREVENTIVE DETENTION

In analyzing the 44th Constitutional Amendment in Chapter VI, certain lacunas were pointed out and suggestions were made. In view of the experience in working the Constitution over the last six decades the following additional amendments are necessary.

The first and foremost is the amendment of Article 368 which deals with Constitutional amendment. Provision should be made that the Constitution should be amended as soon as it is assented to, by the President. In exceptional cases if some time is required to implement some provisions of the amendment, specific dates should be provided for their implementation as was done in the original Constitution of 1950. And the government should not be given unlimited discretion to implement the amendments and thus virtually vetc the constituent will as it has happened in implementing provisions regarding preventive detention, in Article 22 by the 44th Amendment. They are not implemented although more than 30 years have passed and for no rhyme or reason.

Secondly, as the Law of Preventive Detention is not an ordinary law but an emergency legislation to protect the county from subversive activities, it should be only enacted when an Emergency under Article 352 is declared as in other democracies such as U.K. and U.S.A. Moreover, such detention laws should lapse with the withdrawal of the emergency and secondly, the States should not have the power to pass Preventive Detention Laws and this should be removed from the Concurrent List and included only in the Union List of Schedule VII of the Constitution. Moreover, detention orders should be passed by the concerned Minister responsible to the Legislature as mentioned earlier.

Thirdly, like Article 20 and 21 provisions in Article 22 regarding the criminal justice system provided in Clauses 1 and 2 of this Article should be placed beyond the power of suspension placed under Article 359 along with Sub Clauses in Clause 3 dealing with preventive detention. Moreover, it should be specified that the grounds of detention should be given to the detenue immediately or as soon as possible within 24 hours, so that he can take steps to obtain his release, It may be remembered that Dr. Ambedkar while discussing the phrase had said "as soon as possible" implied within 24 hours. But we have seen that the Preventive Detention Act provides "as soon as possible" within five days, seven days and even fifteen days, to give grounds of detention.

Fourthly, it should provide for periodic review of detention as was done in the Preventive Detention Law of 1950.

Suggestions given by the Supreme Court from the *Sampath Kumar's Case* to the *A.K. Roy's Case* should be implemented, such as the detenues should be permitted to wear their own clothes, have their own food, and get medical facilities at their own expenses. Their families should be informed of the place of their detention, should not be removed from one place to another without proper notice, allowed interviews with members of their families at least once a week, allowed to read books and newspapers and last but not the least, have reading material, writing material according to their requirements to reduce the rigour of preventive detention and place detenues on a higher footing than persons who have committed offences. Moreover, Article 21 should be excluded from the ordinance making power as mentioned earlier because legislation by Ordinance is of a temporary nature and does not enjoy the approval of the legislature. Therefore, it is not "a law established to deprive a person of his life and liberty."

It is pertinent to note that Clause 3(a) of Article 22 gives no right to a person who is a "enemy alien" unlike persons who are imprisoned for criminal offences or under detention laws. This phrase "enemy alien" is not defined in the Constitution. When the Constitution was framed, the wars were followed by an official declaration and concluded by a peace treaty. However, since 1950 wars like the Korean War, Indo China War, the Vietnam War, Indo-Pak Wars of 1965 and 1971 or the recent Iraq War etc. are waged without any such declarations. Yet the Geneva Convention of 1899 regarding the rights of prisoners of war (POW) is followed. Only foreign persons whose country is at war are arrested without uniform for espionage or subversive activities and are given no rights under international law. The government has a right to detain them or exchange them as was done in the case of Gary Powers, an American pilot who was captured by the Soviet Union during the Cold War after his spy plane was shot down in Soviet Territory and was detained until he was exchanged for the Soviet spy Alex Able by U.K. through diplomatic negotiations.

The 9th Schedule of the Constitution introduced by the 1st Constitutional Amendment deserves to be deleted because any law included in the 9th Schedule cannot be challenged on the ground that it is violative of any of the Fundamental Rights. This makes a mockery of Fundamental Rights and violates the basic tenets of the Constitution that all laws have to comply with Fundamental Rights. Our experience has been that hundreds of laws have been placed in the 9th Schedule. Furthermore constitutionally all laws can be placed in the 9th Schedule, making Fundamental Rights, which are supposed to be the essence of the Constitution, only paper rights.

These are some of the suggestions made in the interest of the democratic functioning of the government.

APPENDIX-I

Relevant Provisions of the Constitutional Amendments and Preventive Detention Acts: MISA and COFEPOSA

GOVERNMENT OF INDIA ACT OF 1935

Section 102. Power of Federal Legislature to legislate if an emergency is proclaimed—(1) Notwithstanding anything in the preceding sections of this chapter, the Federal Legislature shall, if the Governor-General has in his discretion declared by Proclamation (in this Act referred to as a "Proclamation of Emergency") that a grave emergency exists whereby the security of India is threatened whether by war or internal disturbance, have power to make laws for a Province or any part thereof with respect to any of the matters enumerated in the Provincial Legislature List:

> Provided that no Bill or amendment for the purposes aforesaid shall be introduced or moved without the previous sanction of the Governor-General in his discretion, and the Governor-General shall not give his sanction unless it appears to him that the provision proposed to be made is a proper provision in view of the nature of the emergency.

(2) Nothing in this section shall restrict the power of a Provincial Legislature to make any law which under this Act it has power to make, but if any provision of a Provincial law is repugnant to any provision of a Federal Law which the Federal Legislature has under this section power to make, the Federal law, whether passed before or after the provincial law, shall prevail,

and the Provincial law shall to the extent of the repugnancy, but so long only as the Federal law continues to have effect, be void.

(3) A Proclamation of Emergency—

(a) may be revoked by a subsequent Proclamation;
(b) shall be communicated forthwith to the Secretary of State and shall be laid by him before each House of Parliament; and
(c) shall cease to operate at the expiration of six months, unless before the expiration of that period it has been approved by Resolutions of both Houses of Parliament.

(4) A law made by Federal Legislature which that Legislature would not but for the issue of a Proclamation of Emergency have been competent to make shall cease to have effect on the expiration of a period of six months after the Proclamation has ceased to operate, except as respects things done or omitted to be done before the expiration of the said period.

*[(5) A Proclamation of Emergency declaring that security of India is threatened by war or by internal disturbance may be made before the actual occurrence of war or of any such disturbance if the Governor-General in his discretion is satisfied that there is imminent danger thereof.]

DRAFT CONSTITUTION

275. Proclamation of Emergency—(1) If the President is satisfied that a grave emergency exists whereby the security of India or any part of the territory thereof is threatened, whether by war or external aggression or internal disturbance, he may, by Proclamation, make a declaration to that effect.

(2) A Proclamation issued under clause (1) of this article (in this Constitution referred to as 'a Proclamation of Emergency'—

(a) may be revoked by a subsequent Proclamation;

* Subsitution 5 was added by the Amendment with effect from April 1, 1937.

(b) shall be laid before each House of Parliament;
(c) shall cease to operate at the expiration of two months unless before the expiration of that period it has been approved by resolutions of both House of Parliament;

make such incidental and consequential provisions as appear to the President to be necessary or desirable for giving effect to the objects of the Proclamation, including provisions for suspending in whole or in part the operation of any provisions of this Constitution relating to any body or authority in the State:

Provided that nothing in this clause shall authorize the President to assume to himself any of the powers vested in or exercisable by a High Court or to suspend in whole or in part the operation of any provisions of this Constitution relating to High Courts.

(2) Any such Proclamation may be revoked or varied by a subsequent Proclamation.

(3) Every Proclamation under this article shall be laid before each House of Parliament and shall, except where it is a Proclamation revoking a previous Proclamation, cease to operate at the expiration of two months unless before the expiring of that period it has been approved by resolution of both House of Parliament:

> Provided that if any such Proclamation is issued at a time when the House of the People is dissolved or if the dissolution of the House of the People takes place during the period of two months referred to in this clause and the Proclamation has not been approved by a resolution passed by the House of the People before the expiration of that period, the Proclamation shall cease to operate at the expiration of thirty days from the date on which the House of the People first sits after its reconstitution unless before the expiration of that period resolutions approving the Proclamation have been passed by both Houses of Parliament.

(4) A Proclamation so approved shall, unless revoked, cease to operate on the expiration of a period of six months from the

date of the passing of the second of the resolution approving the Proclamation under clause (3) of this article:

Provided that if and so often as a resolution approving the continuance in force of such a Proclamation is passed by both Houses of Parliament the Proclamation shall, unless revoked, continue in force for a further period of six months from the date on which under this clause it would otherwise have ceased to operate, but no such Proclamation shall in any case remain in force for more than three years:

Provided further that if the dissolution of the House of the People take place during any such period of six months and a resolution approving the continuance in force of such Proclamation has not been passed by the House of the People during the said period, the Proclamation shall cease to operate at the expiration of thirty days from the date on which the House of the People first sits after its reconstitution unless before the expiration of that period resolutions approving the Proclamation have been passed by both Houses of Parliament.

276. Effect of Proclamation of Emergency—Where a Proclamation of Emergency is in 25 operation, then, notwithstanding anything contained in this Constitution—

(a) the executive power of the Union shall extend to the giving of directions to any State as to the manner in which the executive power thereof is to be exercised;
(b) The power of Parliament to make laws with respect to any matter shall include power to make laws conferring powers and imposing duties or authorizing the conferring of powers and the imposition of duties upon the Government of India or officers and authorities of the Government of India as respect that matter.

277. The President may, while a Proclamation of Emergency is in operation, by order, direct that all or any of the provisions of articles 249 to 259 of this Constitution shall for such period, not extending in any case beyond the expiration of the financial year in which such proclamation ceases to operate, year in which such proclamation ceases to operate, as may be specified in the order, have effect subject to such exceptions or modifications as he thinks fit.

"The after article 277, the following new article be inserted:

> '**277A. Duty of the Union to protect States against external aggression and internal disturbance**—It shall be the duty of the Union to protect every State against external aggression and internal disturbance and to ensure that the government of every State is carried on in accordance with the provisions of this Constitution'."

"That article 277 be re-numbered as clause (1) of article 277, and to the said article as so re-numbered the following clause be added:

> '(2) Every order made under clause (1) of this article shall, as soon as may be after it is made, be laid before each House of Parliament'."

"That for article 278, the following articles be substituted:

Provision in case of Failure of Constitutional machinery in States.

278. Provision in case of Failure of Constitutional machinery in States—(1) If the President, on receipt of a report from the Governor or Ruler of a State or otherwise, is satisfied that the Government of the State cannot be carried on in accordance, with the provisions of the Constitution, the President may by Proclamation—

(a) assume to himself all or any of the functions of the Government of the State and all or any of the powers vested in or exercisable by the Governor or Ruler, as the case may be or any body or authority in the State other than the Legislature of the State;

(b) declare that the powers of the Legislature of the State shall exercisable by or under the authority of Parliament;

(c) make such incidental and consequential provisions as appear to the President to be necessary or desirable for giving effect to the objects of the Proclamation, including provisions for suspending in whole or in part the operation of any provisions of this Constitution relating to any body or authority in the State?

Provided that nothing in this clauses shall authorize the President to assume to himself any of the powers vested in or exercisable by a High Court or to suspend in whole or in part the operation of any provisions of this Constitution relating to High Court.

(2) Any such Proclamation may be revoked or varied by a subsequent Proclamation.

(3) Every Proclamation under this article shall be laid before each House of Parliament and shall except where it is a Proclamation revoking a previous Proclamation, cease to create at the expiration of two months unless before the expiration of that period it has been approved by resolution of both Houses of Parliament:

> Provided that if any such Proclamation is issued at a time when the House of the people dissolved or if the dissolution of the House of the people takes place during the period two months referred to in this clause and the Proclamation has not been approved by a solution passed by the House of the people before the expiration of that period, the proclamation shall cease to operate at the expiration of thirty days from the date on which the House of the people first sits after its reconstitution unless before the expiration of that period resolutions approving the proclamation has been passed by both House of parliament.

(4) A proclamation so approved shall, unless revoked, cease to operate on the expiration a period of six months from the date

of the passing of the second of the resolution approving the proclamation under clause (3) of this article:

> provided that if and so often as a resolution approving the continuance in force of such proclamation is passed by both Houses of parliament the proclamation shall, unless evoked, continue in force for a further period of six months, from the date on which under is clause it would otherwise have ceased to operate, but no such proclamation shall in case remain in fore for more than three years:

Provided further that if the dissolution of the House of the People takes place during such period of six months and a resolution approving the continuance in force of such proclamation has not been passed by the House of the people during the said period, the proclamation shall cease to operate at the expiration of thirty days from the date on which the house of the people first sits after its reconstitution unless before the expiration of that period resolutions approving the proclamation have been passed by both Houses of parliament.

278A. (1) where by a Proclamation issued under clause (1) of article 278 of this Constitution it has been declared that the powers of the Legislature of the State shall be exercisable by or under the authority of Parliament, it shall be competent—

(a) for Parliament to delegate the power to make laws for the State to the president or any other authority specified by him in that behaif;

(b) for Parliament or for the President or other authority to whom the power to make laws is delegated under sub-clause (a) of this clause to make laws conferring powers and imposing duties or authorizing the conferring of powers and the imposition of duties upon the Government of India or officers and authorities of the Government of India;

(c) Any Law made by or under the authority of Parliament which Parliament or the President or other authority referred to in sub-clause (a) of clause (1) of this article would not, but for the issue of a Proclamation under article 278 of this Constitution, have been competent to make shall to the extent of the incompetency cease to have effect on the expiration of a period of one year after the Proclamation has ceased to operate except as respects things done or omitted to be done before the expiration of the said period unless the provisions which shall so cease to have effect are sooner repealed or re-enacted with or without modification by an Act of the Legislature of the State."

279. While a Proclamation of Emergency is in operation, nothing in article 13 of Part III of this Constitution shall restrict the power of the State as 40 defined in that Part to make any law or to take any executive action which the State would otherwise be competent to make or to take.

280. Suspension of the rights guaranteed by article 15 of the Constitution during emergencies—(1) Where a Proclamation of Emergency is in operation, the President may by order declare that the right to move any court for the enforcement of such of the rights conferred by Part III of this Constitution as may be mentioned in the order and all proceedings pending in any court for the enforcement of the rights so mentioned shall remain suspended for the period during which the Proclamation is in force or for such shorter period as may be specified in the Order.

(2) An order made as aforesaid under clause (1) of this article shall as soon as may after it is made be laid before each House of Parliament.

280A. Provisions as to financial emergency—(1) If the President is satisfied that a situation has arisen whereby the financial stability or credit of India or of any part of the territory thereof is threatened, he may by a proclamation make a declaration to that effect.

(2) The provisions of clause (2) of article 275 of this Constitution shall apply in relation to a proclamation issued under clause (1) of this article as they apply in relation to a Proclamation of Emergency issued under clause (1) of the said article 275.

(3) During the period any such proclamation as is mentioned

in clause (1) of this article is in operation, the executive authority of the Union shall extend to the giving of directions to any State to observe such canons of financial propriety as may be specified in the directions, and to the giving such other directions as the president may deem necessary and adequate for the purpose.

(4) Notwithstanding anything contained in this Constitution—

(a) Any such direction include—

(i) a provision requiring the reduction of salaries and allowances of all or any class of persons serving in connection with the affairs of a State;

(ii) a provision requiring all Money Bills or other Bills to which the provisions of article 182 of this Constitution apply to be reserved for the consideration of the President after they are passed by the Legislature of the state;

(b) it shall be competent for the President during the period any proclamation issued under clause (1) of this article is in operation to issued directions for the reduction of salaries and allowances of all or any class of persons serving in connection with the affairs of the Union including the judges of the Supreme Court and the High Courts.

(5) Any failure to comply with any directions given under clause (3) of this article shall be deemed to be a failure to carry on the Government of the State in accordance with the provisions of this Constitutions.

1950 CONSTITUTION

14. Equality before law—The State shall not deny to any person equality before the law or the equal protection of the laws within the territory of India.

19. Protection of certain rights regarding freedom of speech, etc.—(1) All citizens shall have the right—

(a) to freedom of speech and expression;

(b) to assemble peaceably and without arms;
(c) to form associations or unions;
(d) to move freely throughout the territory of India;
(e) to reside and settle in any part of the territory of India; [and] 44th amendment
(f) to acquire hold and disposed of property;
(g) to practice any profession, or to carry on any occupation, trade or any business.

(2) Nothing in sub-clause (a) of clause (1) shall affect the operation of any existing law, in so far as it relates to, or prevent the State from making any law relating to libel, slander, defamation, contempt of Court or any matter which offends against decency or morality or which undermines the security of, or tends to overthrow, the State.

(3) Nothing in sub-clause (b) of the said clause shall affect the operation of any existing law in so far as it imposes, or prevent the State from making any law imposing, in the interests of public order, reasonable restrictions on the exercise of the right conferred by the said sub-clause.

(4) Nothing in sub-clause (c) of the said clause shall affect the operation of any existing law in so far as it imposes, or prevent the State from making any law imposing, in the interests of public order or morality, making any law in the interest of public order or morality, reasonable restrictions on the exercise of the right conferred by the said sub-clause.

(5) Nothing in sub-clauses (d), (e) and (f) of the said clauses shall affect the operation of any existing law in so far as it imposes, or prevent the State from making any law imposing, reasonable restriction on the exercise of any of the rights conferred by the said sub-clauses either in the interests of the general public or for the protection of the interests of any Scheduled Tribe.

(6) Nothing in sub-clause (g) of the said clause shall affect the operation of any existing law in so far as it imposes, or prevent the State from making any law imposing, in the interests of the general public, reasonable restrictions on the exercise of the right conferred by the said sub-clause, and, in particular, nothing in the said sub-clause shall affect the operation of any existing law

in so far as it prescribed or empowers any authority to prescribed or prevent the State from making any law prescribing or empowering any authority to prescribe, professional or technical qualifications necessary for practicing any profession or carrying on any occupation, trade or business.

20. Protection in respect of conviction for offences—(1) No person shall be convicted of any offence except for violation of a law in force at the time of the commission of the act charged as an offence, nor be subjected to a penalty greater than that which might have been inflicted under the law in force at the time of the commission of the offence.

(2) No person shall be prosecuted and punished for the same offence more than once.

(3) No person accused of any offence shall be compelled to be a witness against himself.

21. Protection of life and personal liberty—No person shall be deprived of his life or personal liberty except according to procedure established by law.

22. Protection against arrest and detention in certain cases—(1) No person who is arrested shall be detained in custody without being informed, as soon as may be, of the grounds for such arrest nor shall be denied the right to consult, and to be defended by, a legal practitioner of his choice.

(2) Every person who is arrested and detained in custody shall be produced before the nearest magistrate within a period of twenty-four hours of such arrest excluding the time necessary for the journey from the place of arrest to court of the magistrate and no such person shall be detained in custody beyond the said period without the authority of a magistrate.

(3) Nothing in clauses (1) and (2) shall apply—

(a) to any person who for the time being is an enemy alien; or

(b) to any person who is arrested or detained under any law providing for preventive detention.

(4) No law providing for preventive detention shall authorize the detention of a person for a longer period than three months unless—

(a) an Advisory Board consisting of persons who are, or have been, or are qualified to be appointed as, Judges of a High Court has reported before the expiration of the said period of three months that there is in its opinion sufficient cause for such detention.
(b) such person is detained in accordance with the provisions of any law made by Parliament under sub-clause (b) of clause (7).

(5) When any person is detained in pursuance of an order made under any law providing for preventive detention, the authority making the order shall, as soon as may be, communicate to such person the grounds on which the order has been made and shall afford him the earliest opportunity of making a representation against the order.

(6) Nothing in clause (5) shall require the authority making any such order as is referred to in the clause to disclose facts which such authority considers to be against the public interest to disclose.

(7) Parliament may by law prescribe—

(a) the circumstances under which, and the class or classes of cases in which, a person may be detained for a period longer than three months under any law providing for preventive detention without obtaining the opinion of an Advisory Board in accordance with the provisions of sub-clause (a) of clause (4);
(b) the maximum period for which any person may in any class or classes of cases be detained under any law providing for preventive detention; and
(c) the procedure to be allowed by an Advisory Board in an inquiry under sub-clause (a) of clause (4).

74. (1) There shall be a Council of Ministers with the Prime Minister at the head to aid and advice the President in the exercise of his functions.

(2) The question whether any, and if so what, advice was tendered by Ministers to the President shall not be inquired into in any Court.

83. (1) ...

(2) The House of the People, unless sooner dissolved, shall continue for five years from the date appointed for its first meeting and no longer and the expiration of the said period of five years shall operate as dissolution of the House:

Provided that the said period may, while a Proclamation of Emergency is in operation, be extended by Parliament by law for a period not exceeding one year at a time and not extending in any case beyond a period of six months after the Proclamation has ceased to operate.

123. Power of President to promulgate Ordinances during recess of Parliament—(1) If at any time, except when both Houses of Parliament are in session, the President is satisfied that circumstances exist which render it necessary for him to take immediate action, he may promulgate such Ordinances as the circumstances appear to him to require.

(2) An Ordinance promulgated under this article shall have the same force and effect as an Act of Parliament, but every such Ordinance—

(a) shall be laid before both Houses of Parliament and shall cease to operate at the expiration of six weeks from the reassembly of Parliament, or, if before the expiration of the period resolutions disapproving it are passed by both Houses, upon the passing of the second of those resolutions; and

(b) may be withdrawn at any time by the President.

Explanation—Where the Houses of Parliament are summoned to reassemble on different dates, the period of six weeks shall be reckoned from the later of those dates for the purposes of this clause.

(3) If and so far as an Ordinance under this article makes any provision which Parliament would not under this Constitution be competent to enact, it shall be void.

172. Duration of State Legislatures—(1) Every Legislative Assembly of every State, unless sooner dissolved, shall continue for five years from the date appointed for its first meeting and no longer and the expiration of the said period of five years shall operate as a dissolution of the Assembly.

Provided that the said period may, which a Proclamation of Emergency is in operation, be extended by Parliament by law for a period not exceeding one year at a time and not extending in any case beyond a period of six months after the Proclamation has ceased to operate.

(2) ...

213. Power of Governor to promulgate Ordinances during recess of Legislature—(1) If at any time, except when the Legislative Assembly of a State is in session, or where there is a Legislative Council in a State, except when both Houses of the Legislature are in session, the governor is satisfied that circumstances exist which render it necessary for him to take immediate action, he may promulgate such Ordinances as the circumstances appear to him to require.

Provided that the Governor shall not, without instructions from the President, promulgate any such Ordinance if—

(a) a Bill containing the same provisions would under this Constitution have required the previous sanction of the President for the introduction thereof into the Legislature; or

(b) he would have deemed it necessary to reserve a Bill containing the same provisions for the consideration of the President; or

(c) an Act of the Legislature of the State containing the same provisions would under this Constitution have been invalid unless, having been reserved for the consideration of the President, it had received the assent of the President.

(2) An Ordinance promulgated under this article shall have the same force and effect as an Act of the Legislature of the state assented to by the Governor, but every such Ordinance—

(a) shall be laid before the Legislative Assembly of the State, or where there is a Legislative Council in the State, before both the Houses, and shall cease to operate at the expiration of six weeks from the reassembly of the Legislature, or if before the expiration of that period a resolution disapproving it is passed by the legislative Assembly and agreed to by the Legislative Council, if any, upon the passing of the resolution or, as the case may be, on the resolution being agreed to by the Council; and

(b) may be withdrawn at any time by the Governor.

Explanation—Where the Houses of the Legislature of a State having a Legislative Council are summoned to reassemble on different dates, the period of six weeks shall be reckoned from the later of those dates for the purposes of this clause.

(3) If and so far as an Ordinance under this article makes any provision which would not be valid if enacted in an Act of the Legislature of the State assented to by the Governor, it shall be void.

Provided that, for the purposes of the provisions of this Constitution relating to the effect of an Act of the Legislature of a State which is repugnant to an Act of Parliament or an existing law with respect to a matter enumerated in the Concurrent List, an Ordinance promulgated under this article in pursuance of instructions from the President shall be deemed to be an Act of the Legislature of the State which has been reserved for the consideration of the President and assented to by him.

Article 239 (1) Subject to the other provisions of this Part a State specified in Part C of the First Schedule shall be administered by the President acting, to such extent as he thinks fit, through a Chief Commissioner or a Lieutenant-Governor to be Government of a neighboring State…

(2)…

352. Proclamation of Emergency—(1) If the President is satisfied that a grave emergency exists whereby the security of India or of any part of the territory thereof is threatened, whether by war or external aggression or internal disturbance, he may, by Proclamation, make a declaration to that effect.

(2) A proclamation issued under clause (1)—

(*a*) may be revoked by a subsequent Proclamation;

(*b*) shall be laid before each House of Parliament;

(*c*) shall cease to operate at the expiration of two months unless before the expiration of that period it has been approved by resolutions of both Houses of Parliament:

Provided that if any such Proclamation is issued at a time when the House of the People has been dissolved or the dissolution of the House of the People takes place during the period of two months referred to in sub-clause (*c*), and if a resolution approving the Proclamation has been passed by the Council of States but no resolution with respect to such Proclamation has been passed by the House of the People before the expiration of that period, the Proclamation shall cease to operate at the expiration of thirty days from the date on which the House of the People first sits after its reconstitution unless before the expiration of the said period of thirty days a resolution approving the Proclamation has been also passed by the House of the People.

(3) A Proclamation of Emergency declaring that the security of India or of any part of the territory thereof is threatened by war or by external aggression or by internal disturbance may be made before the actual occurrence of war or of any such aggression or disturbance if the President is satisfied that there is imminent danger thereof.

353. Effect of Proclamation of Emergency—While a Proclamation of Emergency is in operation, then—

(*a*) notwithstanding anything in this Constitution, the executive power of the Union shall extend to the giving of directions to any State as to the manner in which the executive power thereof is to be exercised;

(*b*) the power of Parliament to make laws with respect to any matter shall include power to make laws conferring powers and imposing duties, or authorising the conferring of powers and the imposition of duties, upon the Union or officers and authorities of the Union as respects that matter, notwithstanding that it is one which is not enumerated in the Union List:

354. Application of provisions relating to distribution of revenues while a Proclamation of Emergency is in operation—(1) The President may, while a Proclamation of Emergency is in operation, by order direct that all or any of the provisions of articles 268 to 279 shall for such period, not extending in any case beyond the expiration of the financial year in which such Proclamation ceases to operate, as may be specified in the order, have effect subject to such exceptions or modifications as he thinks fit.

(2) Every order made under clause (1) shall, as soon as may be after it is made, be laid before each House of Parliament.

355. Duty of the Union to protect States against external aggression and internal disturbance—It shall be the duty of the Union to protect every State against external aggression and internal disturbance and to ensure that the Government of every State is carried on in accordance with the provisions of this Constitution.

[**356. Provisions in case of failure of constitutional machinery in States**—(1) If the President, on receipt of a report from the Governor [1] of a State or otherwise, is satisfied that a situation has arisen in which the Government of the State cannot be carried on in accordance with the provisions of this Constitution, the President may by Proclamation—

(*a*) assume to himself all or any of the functions of the Government of the State and all or any of the powers vested in or exercisable by the Governor [2]*** or any body or authority in the State other than the Legislature of the State;

*** Reference to provisions or provision of this constitution shall in relation to the state of Jammu and Kashmir, be construed as including references to provisions or provision of the Constitution of Jammu and Kashmir.

1. The words "or Rajpramukh" omitted by the Constitution (Seventh Amendment) Act, 1956, s. 29 and Sch.
2. The words "or Rajpramukh, as the case may be" omitted by s. 29 and Sch., *ibid.*

(*b*) declare that the powers of the Legislature of the State shall be exercisable by or under the authority of Parliament;

(*c*) make such incidental and consequential provisions as appear to the President to be necessary or desirable for giving effect to the objects of the Proclamation, including provisions for suspending in whole or in part the operation of any provisions of this Constitution relating to any body or authority in the State:

> Provided that nothing in this clause shall authorise the President to assume to himself any of the powers vested in or exercisable by a High Court, or to suspend in whole or in part the operation of any provision of this Constitution relating to High Courts.

(2) Any such Proclamation may be revoked or varied by a subsequent Proclamation.

(3) Every Proclamation under this article shall be laid before each House of Parliament and shall, except where it is a Proclamation revoking a previous Proclamation, cease to operate at the expiration of two months unless before the expiration of that period it has been approved by resolutions of both Houses of Parliament:

> Provided that if any such Proclamation (not being a Proclamation revoking a previous Proclamation) is issued at a time when the House of the People is dissolved or the dissolution of the House of the People takes place during the period of two months referred to in this clause, and if a resolution approving the Proclamation has been passed by the Council of States, but no resolution with respect to such Proclamation has been passed by the House of the People before the expiration of that period, the Proclamation shall cease to operate at the expiration of thirty days from the date on which the House of the People first sits after its reconstitution unless before the expiration of the said period of thirty days a resolution approving the Proclamation has been also passed by the House of the People.

Provided also that in the case of Proclamation issued under clause (1) on the 18th day of July, 1990 with respect to the State of Jammu and Kashmir, the reference in the first proviso to this clause to "three years" shall be construed as a reference to "seven years".

(4) A Proclamation so approved shall, unless revoked, cease to operate on the expiration of a period of six months from the date of passing of the second of the insolution approving the proclamation under clause (3):

Provided that if and so often as a resolution approving the continuance in force of such a Proclamation is passed by both Houses of Parliament, the Proclamation shall, unless revoked, continue in force for a further period of six months from the date on which under this clause it would otherwise have ceased to operate, but no such Proclamation shall in any case remain in force for more than three years.

Provided further that if the dissolution of the House of the People takes place during any such period of six months and a resolution approving the continuance in force of such Proclamation has been passed by the Council of States, but no resolution with respect to the continuance in force of such Proclamation has been passed by the House of the People during the said period, the Proclamation shall cease to operate at the expiration of thirty days from the date on which the House of the People first sits after its reconstitution unless before the expiration of the said period of thirty days a resolution approving the continuance in force of the Proclamation has been also passed by the House of the People.

357. Exercise of legislative powers under Proclamation issued under article 356—(1) Where by a Proclamation issued under clause (1) of article 356, it has been declared that the powers of the Legislature of the State shall be exercisable by or under the authority of Parliament, it shall be competent—

(*a*) for Parliament to confer on the President the power of the Legislature of the State to make laws, and to authorise the President to delegate, subject to such conditions as he may think fit to impose, the power so conferred to any other authority to be specified by him in that behalf;

(*b*) for Parliament, or for the President or other authority in whom such power to make laws is vested under sub-clause (*a*), to make laws conferring powers and imposing duties, or authorising the conferring of powers and the imposition of duties, upon the Union or officers and authorities thereof;

(*c*) for the President to authorise when the House of the People is not in session expenditure from the Consolidated Fund of the State pending the sanction of such expenditure by Parliament.

358. Suspension of provisions of article 19 during emergencies—While a Proclamation of Emergency is in operation, nothing in article 19 shall restrict the power of the State as defined in Part III to make any law or to take any executive action which the State would but for the provisions contained in that Part be competent to make or to take, but any law so made shall, to the extent of the incompetency, cease to have effect as soon as the Proclamation ceases to operate, except as respects things done or omitted to be done before the law so ceases to have effect.".

359. Suspension of the enforcement of the rights conferred by Part III during emergencies—(1) Where a Proclamation of Emergency is in operation, the President may by order declare that the right to move any court for the enforcement of such of the rights conferred by Part III as may be mentioned in the order and all proceedings pending in any court for the enforcement of the rights so mentioned shall remain suspended for the period during which the Proclamation is in force or for such shorter period as may be specified in the order.

(2) An order made as aforesaid may extend to the whole or any part of the territory of India.

(3) Every order made under clause (1) shall, as soon as may be after it is made, be laid before each House of Parliament.

360. Provisions as to Financial emergency: (1) If the President is satisfied that a situation has arisen whereby the financial stability or credit of India or of any part of the territory thereof is threatened, he may by a Proclamation make a declaration to that effect.

(2) The provisions of clause (2) of article 352 shall apply in relation to a Proclamation issued under this article as they apply in relation to a Proclamation of Emergency issued under Article 352.

(3) During the period any such Proclamation as is mentioned in clause (1) is in operation, the executive authority of the Union shall extend to the giving of directions to any State to observe such canons of financial propriety as may be specified in the directions, and to the giving of such other directions as the President may deem necessary and adequate for the purpose.

(4) Notwithstanding anything in this Constitution—

(*a*) any such direction may include—

(*i*) a provision requiring the reduction of salaries and allowances of all or any class of persons serving in connection with the affairs of a State;

(*ii*) a provision requiring all Money Bills or other Bills to which the provisions of article 207 apply to be reserved for the consideration of the President after they are passed by the Legislature of the State;

(b) it shall be competent for the President during the period any Proclamation issued under this article is in operation to issue directions for the reduction of salaries and allowances of all or any class of persons serving in connection with the affairs of the Union including the Judges of the Supreme Court and the High Courts.

1st AMENDMENT
(With Effect From June 18, 1951)

Amendment of article 19—(2) Nothing in sub-clause (a) clause (1) shall affect the operation of any existing law, or prevent the State from making any law, in so far as such law imposes reasonable restrictions on the exercise of the right conferred by the said sub-clause in the interests of the security of the State, friendly relations with foreign States, public order, decency or morality, or in relation to contempt of court, defamation or incitement to an offence.

7TH AMENDMENT

(With Effect from November 7, 1956)

Amendment of Article 239 substitute following;

"(1) Save as otherwise provided by Parliament by law, every Union territory shall be administered by the President acting, to such extent as he thinks fit, through an administrator to be appointed by him with such designation as he may specify.

(2)...

16TH AMENDMENT

(With Effect from October 10, 1963)

Amendment of Article 19—(2) At the words "the sovereignty and integrity of India"

(3) At the words "the sovereignty and integrity of India or"

(4) At the words "the sovereignty and integrity of India or"

38TH AMENDMENT

(With Effect from August 1, 1975)

Amendment of Articles 123, 213, 229B and Clause 4 namely; Notwithstanding anything in this Constitution, the satisfaction of the Governor mentioned in clause (1) shall be final and conclusive and shall not be questioned in any court on any ground.

Amendment of article 352—In article 352 of the constitution, after clauses shall be inserted, and shall be deemed always to have been inserted, namely:

"(4) The power conferred on the President by this article shall include the power to issue different Proclamations on different grounds, being war or external aggression or internal disturbance or imminent danger of war or external aggression or internal disturbance, whether or not there is a Proclamation already issued by the President under clause (1) and such Proclamation is in operation.

(5) Notwithstanding anything in the Constitution,—

(*a*) the satisfaction of the President mentioned in clause (1) and clause (3) shall be final and conclusive and shall not be questioned in any court on any ground;

(*b*) subject to the provisions of clause (2), neither the Supreme Court nor any other Court shall have jurisdiction to entertain any question, on any ground, regarding the validity of —

(*i*) a declaration made by Proclamation by the President to the effect stated in clause (1); or

(*ii*) the continued operation of such Proclamation.

Amendment of article 356—In article 356 of the Constitution, after clause (4), the following clause shall be inserted, and shall be deemed always to have been inserted, namely:

(5) Notwithstanding anything in this Constitution, the satisfaction of President mentioned in clause (1) shall be final and conclusive and shall not be questioned in any court on any ground.".

Amendment of article 359—In article 359 of the Constitution, after clause (1), the following clause shall be inserted, and shall be deemed always to have been inserted, namely:

[1][(1A) While an order made under clause (1) mentioning any of the rights conferred by Part III is in operation, nothing in that Part conferring those rights shall restrict the power of the State as defined in the said Part to make any law or to take any executive action which the State would but for the provisions contained in that Part be competent to make or to take, but any law so made shall, to the extent of the incompetency, cease to have effect as soon as the order aforesaid ceases to operate, except as respects things done or omitted to be done before the law so ceases to have effect:]

1. Ins. by the Constitution (Thirty-eighth Amendment) Act, 1975, s. 7 (retrospectively).

8. Amendment of article 360—In article 360 of the Constitution, after clause (4), the following clause shall be inserted, and shall be deemed always to have been inserted namely:

42ND AMENDMENT
(With Effect from 3.1.1977)

Amendment of Article 74—(1) Add who shall, in the exercise of his functions, act in accordance with such advice.

Amendment of article 352—In article 352 of the Constitution—

(a) in clause (1), after the words "make a declaration to that effect", the following shall be inserted, namely:-

"in respect of the whole of India or of such part of the territory thereof as may be specified in the Proclamation";

(b) in clause (2), in sub-clause (a), after the word "revoked", the words "or varied" shall be inserted;

(c) after clause (2), the following clause shall be inserted, namely:

"(2A) Where a Proclamation issued under clause (1) is varied by a subsequent Proclamation, the provisions of clause (2) shall, so far as may be, apply in relation to such subsequent Proclamation as they apply in relation to a Proclamation issued under clause (1).".

Amendment of article 353—To article 353 of the Constitution, the following proviso shall be added, namely:

"Provided that where a Proclamation of Emergency is in operation only in any part of the territory of India,—

(i) the executive power of the Union to give directions under clause (a), and

(ii) the power of Parliament to make laws under clause (b), shall also extend to any State other than a State in which or in any part of which the Proclamation of Emergency is in operation if and in so far as the security of India or any part of the territory thereof is threatened by activities in or in relation to the part of the territory of India in which the Proclamation of Emergency is in operation.".

Amendment of article 356—In article 356 of the Constitution, in clause (4), for the words "six months", wherever they occur, the words "one year" shall be substituted.

Amendment of article 358—To article 358 of the Constitution, the following proviso shall be added, namely:

"Provided that where a Proclamation of Emergency is in operation only in any part of the territory of India, any such law may be made, or any such executive action may be taken, under this article in relation to or in any State or Union territory in which or in any part of which the Proclamation of Emergency is not in operation, if and in so far as the security of India or any part of the territory thereof is threatened by activities in or in relation to the part of the territory of India in which the Proclamation of Emergency is in operation.".

Amendment of article 359—In article 359 of the Constitution,—

(a) to clause (1A), the following proviso shall be added, namely:

"Provided that where a Proclamation of Emergency is in operation only in any part of the territory of India, any such law may be made, or any such executive action may be taken, under this article in relation to or in any State or Union territory in which or in any part of which the Proclamation of Emergency is not in operation, if and in so far as the security of India or any part of the territory thereof is threatened by activities in or in relation to the part of the territory of India in which the Proclamation of Emergency is in operation.";

(b) to clause (2), the following proviso shall be added, namely:

"Provided that where a Proclamation of Emergency is in operation only in a part of the territory of India, any such order shall not extend to any other part of the territory of India unless the President, being satisfied that the security of India or any part of the territory thereof is threatened by activities in or in relation to the part of the territory of India in which the Proclamation of Emergency is in operation, considers such extension to be necessary.".

Amendment of article 357—(1) In article 357 of the Constitution, for clause (2), the following clause shall be substituted, namely:

"(2) Any law made in exercise of the power of the Legislature of the State by Parliament or the President or other authority referred to in sub-clause (a) of clause (1) which Parliament or the President or such other authority would not, but for the issue of a Proclamation under article 356, have been competent to make shall, after the Proclamation has ceased to operate, continue in force until altered or repealed or amended by a competent Legislature or other authority.".

(2) The amendment made by sub-section (1) shall apply also to any law referred to in clause (2) of article 357 of the Constitution which is in force immediately before the coming into force of this section.

44TH AMENDMENT OF 1979

(44th Amendment Act was enacted on April 30, 1979 and came into force w.e.f. June 20, 1979 except amend. to Article 22.)

Amendment of Articles 20 and 21—Under the Order of the President Article 359, enforcement of Article 21 cannot be suspended.

Amendment of Article 22—In article 22 of the Constitution,—

(a) for clause (4), the following clause shall be substituted, namely:-

(4) No law providing for preventive detention shall authorize the detention of a person for a longer period than two months unless an Advisory Board constituted in accordance with the recommendations of the Chief Justice of the appropriate High Court has reported before the expiration of the said period of two months that there is in its opinion sufficient cause for such detention.

Provided that an Advisory Board shall consist of a Chairman and not less than two other members, and the Chairman shall be a serving Judge of the appropriate High Court and the other members shall be serving or retired judges of any High Court.

Provided further that nothing in this clause shall authorize the detention of any person beyond the maximum period prescribed by law made by Parliament under sub-clause (a) of clause (7).

Explanation—In this clause, "appropriate High Court" means,—

(i) in the case of the detention of a person in pursuance of an order of detention made by the Government of India or an officer or authority subordinate to that Government, the High Court for the Union territory of Delhi;

(ii) in the case of the detention of a person in pursuance of an order of detention made by the Government of any State (other than a Union territory), the High Court for that State; and

(iii) in the case of the detention of a person in pursuance of an order of detention made by the administrator of a Union territory or an officer or authority subordinate to such administrator, such High Court as may be specified by or under any law made by Parliament in this behalf;

(b) in clause (7),—

(i) sub-clause (a) shall be omitted;

(ii) sub-clause (b) shall be re-lettered as sub-clause (a); and

(iii) sub-clause (c) shall be re-lettered as sub-clause (b) and in the sub-clause as so re-lettered, for the words, brackets, letter and figure "sub-clause (a) of clause(4)", the word, brackets and figure "clause(4)" shall be substituted. (This amendment is not enforced)

Amendment of Article 74—After Clause-1, the following is inserted; "Provided that the President may require the Council of Ministers to reconsider such advice, either generally or otherwise, and the President shall act in accordance with the advice tendered after such reconsideration.

Amendment of Articles 123, 213 and 129B delete Clause 4.

Amendment of article 352—In article 352 of the Constitution,—

(a) in clause (1)—

(i) for the words "internal disturbance", the words "armed rebellion" shall be substituted;

(ii) the following Explanation shall be inserted at the end, namely:-

"Explanation—A Proclamation of Emergency declaring that the security of India or any part of the territory thereof is threatened by war or by external aggression or by armed rebellion may be made before the actual occurrence of war or of any such aggression or rebellion, if the President is satisfied that there is imminent danger thereof.";

(b) for clauses (2), (2A) and (3), the following clauses shall be substituted, namely:-

"(2) A Proclamation issued under clause (1) may be varied or revoked by a subsequent Proclamation.

(3) The President shall not issue a Proclamation under clause (1) or a Proclamation varying such Proclamation unless the decision of the Union Cabinet (that is to say, the Council consisting of the Prime Minister and other Ministers of Cabinet rank appointed under article 75) that such a Proclamation may be issued has been communicated to him in writing.

(4) Every Proclamation issued under this article shall be laid before each House of Parliament and shall, except where it is a Proclamation revoking a previous Proclamation, cease to operate at the expiration of one month unless before the expiration of

that period it has been approved by resolutions of both Houses of Parliament:

> Provided that if any such Proclamation (not being a Proclamation revoking a previous Proclamation) is issued at a time when the House of the People has been dissolved, or the dissolution of the House of the People takes place during the period of one month referred to in this clause, and if a resolution approving the Proclamation has been passed by the Council of States, but no resolution with respect to such Proclamation has been passed by the House of the People before the expiration of that period, the Proclamation shall cease to operate at the expiration of thirty days from the date on which the House of the People first sits after its reconstitution, unless before the expiration of the said period of thirty days a resolution approving the Proclamation has been also passed by the House of the People.

(5) A Proclamation so approved shall, unless revoked, cease to operate on the expiration of a period of six months from the date of the passing of the second of the resolutions approving the Proclamation under clause (4):

> Provided that if and so often as a resolution approving the continuance in force of such a Proclamation is passed by both Houses of Parliament the Proclamation shall, unless revoked, continue in force for a further period of six months from the date on which it would otherwise have ceased to operate under this clause:

> Provided further that if the dissolution of the House of the People takes place during any such period of six months and a resolution approving the continuance in force of such Proclamation has been passed by the Council of States but no resolution with respect to the continuance in force of such Proclamation has been passed by the House of the People during the said period, the Proclamation shall cease to operate at the expiration of thirty days from the date on which the House of the People

first sits after its reconstitution unless before the expiration of the said period of thirty days, a resolution approving the continuance in force of the Proclamation has been also passed by the House of the People.

(6) For the purposes of clauses (4) and (5), a resolution may be passed by either House of Parliament only by a majority of the total membership of that House and by a majority of not less than two-thirds of the members of that House present and voting.

(7) Notwithstanding anything contained in the foregoing clauses, the President shall revoke a Proclamation issued under clause (1) or a Proclamation varying such Proclamation if the House of the People passes a resolution disapproving, or, as the case may be, disapproving the continuance in force of, such Proclamation.

(8) Where a notice in writing signed by not less than one-tenth of the total number of members of the House of the People has been given, of their intention to move a resolution for disapproving, or, as the case may be, for disapproving the continuance in force of, a Proclamation issued under clause (1) or a Proclamation varying such Proclamation,—

(a) to the Speaker, if the House is in session; or
(b) to the President, if the House is not in session, a special sitting of the House shall be held within fourteen days from the date on which such notice is received by the Speaker, or, as the case may be, by the President, for the purpose of considering such resolution.";
(c) clause (4) shall be renumbered as clause (9) and in the clause as so renumbered, for the words "internal disturbance" in both the places where they occur, the words "armed rebellion" shall be substituted;
(d) clause (5) shall be omitted.

Amendment of article 356—In article 356 of the Constitution,—

(a) in clause (4),—
    (i) for the words, brackets and figure "one year from the date of the passing of the second of the

resolutions approving the Proclamation under clause (3)", the words "six months from the date of issue of the Proclamation" shall be substituted;

(ii) in the first proviso, for the words "one year", the words "six months" shall be substituted;

(iii) in the second proviso, for the words "one year", the words "six months" shall be substituted;

(b) for clause (5), the following clause shall be substituted, namely:

"(5) Notwithstanding anything contained in clause (4), a resolution with respect to the continuance in force of a Proclamation approved under clause (3) for any period beyond the expiration of one year from the date of issue of such Proclamation shall not be passed by either House of Parliament unless—

(a) a Proclamation of Emergency is in operation, in the whole of India or, as the case may be, in the whole or any part of the State, at the time of the passing of such resolution, and

(b) the Election Commission certifies that the continuance in force of the Proclamation approved under clause (3) during the period specified in such resolution is necessary on account of difficulties in holding general elections to the Legislative Assembly of the State concerned.".

39. Amendment of article 358—Article 358 of the Constitution shall be renumbered as clause (1) of that article, and—

(a) in clause (1) as so renumbered,—

(i) in the opening portion, for the words "while a Proclamation of Emergency is in operation", the words "While a Proclamation of Emergency declaring that the security of India or any part of the territory thereof is treatened by war or by external aggression is in operation" shall be substituted;

(ii) in the proviso, for the words "where a Proclamation of Emergency", the words "where such Proclamation of Emergency" shall be substituted;

(b) after clause (1) as so renumbered, the following clause shall be inserted, namely:-

"(2) Nothing in clause (1) shall apply—

(a) to any law which does not contain a recital to the effect that such law is in relation to the Proclamation of Emergency in operation when it is made; or

(b) to any executive action taken otherwise than under a law containing such a recital.".

40. Amendment of article 359—In article 359 of the Constitution,—

(a) in clauses (1) and (1A), for the words and figures "the rights conferred by Part III", the words, figures and brackets "the rights conferred by Part III (except articles 20 and 21)" shall be substituted;

(b) after clause (1A), the following clause shall be inserted, namely:

"(1B) Nothing in clause (1A) shall apply—

(a) to any law which does not contain a recital to the effect that such law is in relation to the Proclamation of Emergency in operation when it is made; or

(b) to any executive action taken otherwise than under a law containing such a recital.".

59TH AMENDMENT ACT, 1981
(With Effect from March 30, 1988)

Amendment of article 356—In article 356 of the Constitution, in clause (5), for the proviso, the following proviso shall be substituted, namely:

"Provided that nothing in this clause shall apply to the Proclamation issued under clause (1) on the 11th day of May, 1987 with respect to the State of Punjab.".

Insertion of new article 359A.—(1) After article 359 of the Constitution, the following article shall be inserted, namely:

"359A. Application of this Part to the State of Punjab— Notwithstanding anything in this Constitution, this Part shall, in relation to the State of Punjab, be subject to the following modifications, namely:

(a) in article 352,—

(i) in clause (1)—

(A) for the opening portion, the following shall be substituted, namely:-"If the President is satisfied that a grave emergency exists whereby—

(a) the security of India or of any part of the territory thereof is threatened, whether by war or external aggression or armed rebellion; or

(b) the integrity of India is threatened by internal disturbance in the whole or any part of the territory of Punjab,

he may, by Proclamation, make a declaration to that effect in respect of the whole Punjab or of such part of the territory thereof as may be specified in the Proclamation.". Came into force on 30.3.1988.

64TH AMENDMENT ACT, 1990
(With Effect from April 16, 1990)

Amendment of article 356—In article 356 of the Constitution,—

(a) in clause (4), after the second proviso, the following proviso shall be inserted, namely:
"Provided also that in the case of the Proclamation issued under clause (1) on the 11th day of May, 1987 with respect to the State of Punjab, the reference in the first proviso to this clause to "three years" shall be construed as a reference to "three years and six months".';

(b) In clause (5), the following proviso shall be inserted at the end, namely:
"Provided that nothing in this clause shall apply to the Proclamation issued under clause (1) on the 11th day of

May, 1987 with respect to the State of Punjab.".

Came into force w.e.f. 16.4.1990.

'THE MAINTENANCE SECURITY ACT OF 1971 (MISA)' WITH AMENDMENTS OF 1971

(MISA was amended by the Ordinance of June 29, 1975 and it was repealled by the amendment of the Act which came into Force on July 22, 1971)*

1. Short title and extent—(1) This Act may be called the Maintenance of Internal Security Act, 1971.

(2) It extends to the whole of India except the State of Jammu and Kashmir.

2. Definitions—In his Act, unless the context otherwise requires,—

(a) "appropriate Government" means, as respects a detention order made by the Central Government or a person detained under such order, the Central Government, and as respects a detention order made by a State Government or by an officer subordinate to State Government or as respects a person detained under such order, the State Government;

(b) "detention order" means an order made under Section 3;

(c) "foreigner" has the same meaning as in the Foreigners Act, 1946;

(d) "State Government", in relation to Union Territory, means the administrator thereof;

3. Power to make orders detaining certain persons—(1) The Central Government or the State Government may,—

(a) if satisfied with respect of any person (including a foreigner) that with a view to preventing him from acting in any manner prejudicial to—

---

* The Amended MISA was put in the 9th Schedule of the Constitution as Entry 92 of the Constitutional Amendment of 1975 w.e.f. August 10, 1975.

(i) the defence of India, the relations of India with foreign powers, or the security of India, or

(ii) the security of the State or the maintenance of public order, or

(iii) the maintenance of supplies and services essential to the community, or

(b) if satisfied with respect to any foreigner that with a view to regulating his continued presence in India or with a view to making arrangements for his expulsion from India, it is necessary so to do, make an order directing that such person be detained.

(2) Any of the following officers, namely—

(a) district magistrates,

(b) additional district magistrates specially empowered in this behalf by the State Government,

(e) Commissioner of Police, for Bombay, Calcutta, Madras or Hyderabad,

May, if satisfied as provided in sub-clauses (ii) and (iii) of clause 9a) of sub-section (1), exercise the power conferred by the said sub-section.

(3) When any order is made under this section by an officer mentioned in sub-section (2), he shall forthwith report the fact to the State Government to which he is subordinate together with the grounds on which the order has been made and such other particulars as in his opinion has a bearing on the matter, and no such order shall remain in force for more than [****] after the making thereof unless in the meantime it has been approved by the State Government:

Provided that where under Section 8 the grounds of detention are communicated by the authority making the order after five days but not later than fifteen days from the date of detention.

(4) When any order is made or approved by the State Government under this section, the State Government shall,

within seven days, report the fact to the Central Government together with the grounds on which the order has been made and such other particulars as in the opinion of the State Government have a bearing on the necessity for the order.

4. Execution of detention orders—A detention order may be executed at any place in India in the manner provided for the execution of warrants of arrest.

5. Power to regulate place and conditions of detention—Every person in respect of whom a detention order has been made shall be liable—

(a) to be detained in such place and under such conditions, including conditions as to maintenance, discipline and punishment for breaches of discipline, as the appropriate Government may, by general or special order, specify; and

(b) to be removed from one place of detention to another place of detention, whether within the same State or in another State, by order of the appropriate Government:

Provided that no order shall be made by a State Government under clause (b) for the removal of a person from one State to another State except with the consent of the Government of that other State.

6. Detention orders not to be invalid or inoperative on certain grounds—No detention order shall be invalid or inoperative merely by reason—

(a) that the person to be detained hereunder is outside the limits of the territorial jurisdiction of the Government or officer making the order, or

(b) that a place of detention of such person is outside the said limits.

7. Powers in relation to absconding persons—(1) If the Central Government or the State Government or an officer specified in sub-section (2) of Section 3, as the case may be, has reason to believe that a person in respect of whom a detention order has been made has absconded or is concealing himself so that the order cannot be executed, that Government or officer may—

(a) make a report in writing of the fact to a [7][Metropolitan Magistrate or a Judicial Magistrate of the first class having jurisdiction in the place where the said person ordinarily resides, and thereupon the provisions of Section 82 to 86 (both inclusive) of the Code of Criminal Procedure, 1973 (2 of 1974)], shall apply in respect of the said person and his property as if the order directing that he be detained were a warrant issued by the Magistrate;
(b) by order notified in the official *Gazette* direct the said person to appear before such officer, at such place and within such period as may be specified in the order; and if the said person fails to comply with such direction he shall, unless he proves that it was not possible for him to comply therewith and that he had, within the period specified in the order, informed the officer mentioned in the order of the reason which rendered compliance therewith impossible and of his whereabouts, be punishable with imprisonment for a term which may extend to one year or with fine or with both.

8. Grounds of order of detention to be disclosed to persons affected by the order—(1) When a person is detained in pursuance of a detention order, the authority making the order shall, as soon as may be, but ordinarily not later than five days and in exceptional circumstances and for reasons to be recorded in writing, not later than fifteen days, from the date of detention communicate to him the grounds on which the order has been made and shall afford him the earliest opportunity of making a representation against the order to the appropriate Government.

(2) Nothing in sub-section (1) shall require the authority o disclose facts which it considers to be against the public interest to disclose.

9. Constitution of Advisory Boards—(1) the Central Government and each State Government shall, whenever necessary, constitute one or more Advisory Boards for the purposes of this Act.

(2) Every such Board shall consist of three persons who are, or have been, or are qualified to be appointed as, Judges of a High Court, and such persons shall be appointed by the Central Government or the State Government, as the case may be.

(3) The appropriate Governments shall appoint one of the members of the Advisory Board who is, or has been, a Jude of a High Court to be its chairman, and in the case of a Union Territory the appointment to the Advisory Board, of any person who is a Judge of the High Court of a State shall be with the previous approval of the State Government concerned.

10. Reference to Advisory Boards—Save as otherwise expressly provided in this Act, in every case where a detention order has been made under this Act, the appropriate Government shall, within thirty days from the date of detention under the order, place before the Advisory Board constituted by it under Section 9 the ground on which the order has been made and the representation, if any, made by the person affected by the order, and in case where the order has been made by an officer, also the report by such officer under sub-section (3) of Section 3.

11. Procedure of Advisory Boards—(1) the advisory Board shall, after considering the materials placed before it and, after calling for such further information as it may deem necessary from the appropriate Government or from any person called for the purpose through the appropriate Government or from the person concerned, and if, in any particular case, it considers it essential so to do or if the person concerned desires to be heard, after hearing him in person, submit its report to the appropriate Government within ten weeks from the date of detention.

(2) The report of the Advisory Board shall specify in a separate part thereof the opinion of the Advisory Board as to whether or not there is sufficient cause for the dentin of the person concerned.

(3) When there is a difference of opinion among the members forming the Advisory Board, the opinion of the majority of such members shall be deemed to be the opinion of the Board.

(4) Nothing in this section shall entitle any person against whom a detention order has been made to appear by any legal practitioner in any matter connected with the reference to the Advisory Board, and the proceedings of the Advisory Board and

its report, excepting that part of the report in which the opinion of the Advisory Board is specified shall be confidential.

12. Action upon the report of Advisory Board—(1) In any case where the Advisory Board has reported that there is in its opinion sufficient cause for the detention of a person, the appropriate Government may confirm the detention order and continue the detention of the person concerned for such period as it thinks fit.

(2) In any case where the Advisory Board has reported that there is in its opinion no sufficient cause for the detention of the person concerned, the appropriate Government shall revoke the detention order and case the person be released forthwith.

13. Maximum period of detention—The maximum period for which any person may be detained in pursuance of any detention order which has been confirmed under Section 12 shall be twelve months from the date of detention.

Provided that nothing contained in this section shall affect the power of the appropriate Government to revoke or modify the detention order at any earlier time.

14. Revocation of detention orders—(1) Without prejudice to the provisions of Section 21 of the General Clauses Act, 1897 (10 of 1897 (10 of 1897), a detention order may, at any time, be revoked or modified—

(a) notwithstanding that the order has been made by an officer mentioned in sub-section (2) of Section 3, by the State Government to which that officer is subordinate or by the Central Government;

(b) notwithstanding that the order has been made by the State Government or by the Central Government.

15. Temporary relates of persons detained—(1) The appropriate Government may, at any time, direct that any person detained in pursuance of a detention order may be released for any specified period either without conditions or upon such conditions specified in the direction as that person accepts, and may at any time, cancel his release.

(2) In directing the release of any person under sub-section (1), the appropriate Government may require him to enter into a

bond with or without sureties for the due observance of the conditions specified in the direction.

(3) Any person released under sub-section (1) shall surrender himself at the time and place, and to the authority, specified in the order directing his release, or canceling his release, at the case may be.

16. Protection of action taken in good faith—No suit or other legal proceeding shall lie against the Central Government or a State Government, and no suit, prosecution or other legal proceedings, shall lie against any person , for anything in good faith done or intended to be done in pursuance of this Act.

17. Duration of detention in certain cases of foreigners—(1) Notwithstanding anything contained in this Act, any foreigner in respect of whom an order of detention has been made under this Act may be detained without obtaining the opinion of the Advisory Board for a period longer than three months, but not exceeding two years from the date of his detention, in any of the following classes of cases or under any of the following circumstances, namely—

(a) where such foreigner enters or attempts to enter the territory of India or found therein with arms, ammunition or explosives, or

(b) where such foreigner enters or attempts to enter a notified area or is found therein in contravention of Section 3 of the Criminal Law Amendment Act, 1961, or

(c) where such foreigner enters or attempts to enter the local limits or is found within the local limits of such area adjoining the borders of India as may be specified in an order made under Section 139 of the Border Security Force Act, 1968, without a valid travel document, or

(d) where the Central Government has reason to believe that such foreigner commits or is likely to commit any offence under the Official Secrets Act, 1923.

(2) In the case of foreigner to whom sub-section (1) applies, Sections 10 to 13 shall have effect subject to the following modifications, namely—

(a) in Section 10, for the words "shall, within thirty days", the words "may, at any time prior to but in no case later than three months before the expiration of two years" shall be *substituted;*

(b) in Section 11,—

   (i) in sub-section (1), for the words "from the date of detention" the words "from the date on which reference is made to it" shall be *substituted*

   (ii) in sub-section (2), for the words "the detention of the person concerned" the words "the continued detention of the person concerned" shall be *substituted;*

(c) in Section 12, for the words "for the detention" in both the places where they occur, the words "for the continued detention" shall be *substituted;*

(d) in Section 12, for the words "twelve months" the words "three years" shall be *substituted.*]

AMENDMENT OF 4 DECEMBER, 1971

SECTION 1: IN SECTION 1 PROVISO HAS BEEN ADDED:

"Provided that every person in respect of whom an order of detention made under the Jammu and Kashmir Preventive Detention Act, 1964 (J & K Act XIIX of 1964), is in force immediately before the commencement of the Act."

SECTION 2: CLAUSE (E) IS BEING ADDED IN SECTION 2 AFTER THE CLAUSE (D)

"(e) any reference in this Act to a law which is not in force in the State of Jammu and Kashmir shall, in relation to that State, be construed as a reference to the corresponding law, if any, in force in that State."

SECTION 3: SUBSTITUTION IN SECTION 3 SUB-SECTION (2) AFTER CLAUSE (E):

The words in brackets shall remain *substituted* for the words "may, if satisfied as provided in sub-clauses (ii) and (iii) of clause (a) of sub-section (1) during the continuance in force of Defence and Internal Security of India Act, 1971, *vide* its Section 6(6)."

SECTION 13: INSERTION AT THE END OF SECTION 13:

"or until the expiry of the Defence and Internal Security of India Act, 1971, whichever is later"

ADDITION OF NEW SECTION 17A AFTER SECTION 17:

"**17A. Duration of detention in case of detention on certain grounds**—(1) Notwithstanding anything contained in the foregoing provisions of this Act, during the period of operation of the Proclamation of Emergency issued on the 3rd day of December, 1971, any person (including a foreigner) in respect of whom an order of detention has been made under this Act, may be detained without obtaining the opinion of the Advisory Board for a period longer than three months, but not exceeding two years from the date of his detention in any of the following classes of cases or under any of the following circumstances, namely—

(a) where such person had been detained with a view to preventing him from acting in any manner prejudicial to the defence of India, relations of India with foreign powers or security of India;]

(b) where such person had been detained with a view to preventing him from acting in any manner prejudicial to the security of the State or the maintenance of public order.

(2) In the case of any person to whom sub-section (1) applies, Sections'10 to 13 shall have effect subject to the following medications namely—

(a) in Section 10, for the words "shall, within thirty days", the words "may, at any time prior to but in no case later than three months before the expiration of two years" shall be *substituted;*

(b) In Section 11,—
   (i) in sub-section (1), for the words "from the date of detention" the words "from the date on which reference is made to it" shall be *substituted;*
   (ii) in sub-section (2), for the words "the detention of the person concerned", the words "the continued

detention of the person concerned" shall be *substituted;*

(c) in Section 12, for the words "for the detention" in both the places where they occur, the words "for the continued detention" shall be *substituted;*

(d) in Section 13, for the words "twelve months", the words "there years" shall be *substituted.*]

AMENDMENT OF 25 JUNE, 1975 OF MISA OR COPEPOSA

SECTION 3 SUB-SECTION (3) SUBSTITUTION IN PROVISO:

this sub-section shall apply subject to the modification that for the words [twenty days], the words [twenty-five days] shall be *substituted.*

SECTION 15: IN SECTION 15 NEW SUB-SECTION (3A) IS BEING ADDED AFTER SUB-SECTION (3)

"[(3A) If the appropriate Government has reason to believe that any person who has failed to surrender himself in the manner specified in sub-section (3) has absconded or is concealing himself, that Government may make a report in writing of the fact to a Metropolitan Magistrate or a Judicial Magistrate of the first class having jurisdiction in the place where the said person ordinarily resides and thereupon the provisions of Sections 82 to 86 (both inclusive) of the Code of Criminal Procedure, 1973 (2 of 1974), shall apply in relation to such person as they apply in relation to a person who has absconded or is concealing himself so that a warrant issued by the Magistrate cannot be executed.]"

SECTION 15: IN SECTION 15 NEW SUB-SECTION (6) IS BEING ADDED AFTER SUB-SECTION (5)

"(6) Notwithstanding anything contained in any other law and save as otherwise provided in this section, no person against whom detention order made under this Act is in force shall be released whether on a bail or bail bond or otherwise."

ADDITION OF NEW SECTION 16A AFTER THE SECTION 16

"**16A. Special provisions for dealing with emergency**—(1) Notwithstanding anything contained in this Act or any rules of natural justice, the provisions of this section shall have effect during the period of operation of the proclamation of Emergency issued under clause (1) of Article 352 of the Constitution on the 3rd day of December, 1971, or the proclamation of Emergency issued under that clause on the 25th day of June, 1975, or a period of [14][twenty-four months] from the 25th day of June, 1975, whichever period is the shortest.

(2) The case of every person (including a foreigner) against whom an order of detention was made under this Act on or after the 25th day of June, 1975, but before the commencement of this section, shall, unless such person is sooner released from detention, be reviewed within fifteen days from such commencement by the appropriate Government for the purpose of determining whether the detention of such person under this Act is necessary for dealing effectively with emergency in respect of which the proclamations referred to in sub-section (1) have been issued (hereafter in this section referred to as the emergency) and if, on such review, the appropriate Government is satisfied that it is necessary to detain such person for effectively dealing with the emergency, that Government may make a declaration to that effect and communicate a copy of the declaration to the person concerned.

(2A) If the State Government makes a declaration under sub-section (2) that the detention of any person in respect of whom a detention order is made by an officer subordinate to that Government is necessary for dealing effectively with the emergency, this State Government shall be deemed to have approved such detention order and the provisions of sub-section (3) of Section 3, in so far as they relate to the approval of the State Government, and of sub-section (4) of that section, shall not apply to such detention order.

(3) When making an order of detention under this Act against any person (including a foreigner) after the commencement of this section, the Central Government or the State Government or, as the case may be, the officer making the order of detention

shall consider whether the detention of such person under this Act is necessary for dealing effectively with the emergency and if, on such consideration the Central Government or the State Government, or, as the case may be the officer is satisfied that it is necessary to detain such person for effectively dealing with the emergency, that Government or officer may make a declaration to that effect and communicate a copy of the declaration to the person concerned:

> Provided that where such declaration is made by an officer, it shall be reviewed by the State Government to which such officer is subordinate within fifteen days from the date of making of the declaration and such declaration shall cease to have effect unless it is confirmed by the State Government, after such review, within the said period of fifteen days.

(4) The question whether the detention of any person in respect of whom a declaration has been made under sub-section (2) or sub-section (3) Continues to be necessary for effectively dealing with the emergency shall be reconsidered by the appropriate Government within four months from the date of such reconsideration, it appears to the appropriate Government that the detention of the person is no longer necessary for effectively dealing with emergency, that Government may revoke the declaration.

(5) In making any review, consideration or reconsideration under sub-section (2), sub-section (3) or sub-section (4), the appropriate Government or officer may act on the basis of the information and materials in its or his possession without communicating or disclosing any such information or materials to the person concerned or affording him any opportunity of making any representation against the making under sub-section (2), or the making or confirming under sub-section (3), or the non-revocation under sub-section (4), of the declaration in respect of him.

(6) In the case of every person detained under a detention order to which the provisions of sub-section (2) apply, being a

person the review of whose case is pending under that sub-section or in respect of whom a declaration has been made under that sub-section—

(i) Sections 8 to 12 shall not apply; and
(ii) Section 13 shall apply subject to the modification that the words and figures "which has been confirmed under Section 12" shall be *omitted.*

(7) In the case of every person detained under a detention order to which the provisions of sub-section (3) apply, being a person in respect of whom a declaration has been made under that sub-section—

(i) Section 3 shall apply subject to the modification that for sub-sections (3) and (4) thereof, [the following] shall be *substituted,* namely:

"(3) When any order of detention is made by a State Government or by an officer subordinate to it, the State Government shall, within 20 days, [report the fact to the Central Government];

[(4) At any time after the receipt of a report under sub-section (3), the Central Government may require the State Government to furnish to the Central Government the grounds on which the order has been made and such other particulars as, in the opinion of the State Government, have a bearing on the necessity for the order];

(ii) Section 8 to 12 shall not apply; and
(iii) Section 13 shall apply subject to the modification that the words and figures "which has been confirmed under Section 12" shall be *omitted.*]

[(8) In the case of any person in respect of whom a declaration has been made by a State Government under sub-section (2) or a declaration has been made by a State Government or an officer subordinate to it or confirmed by the State Government under sub-section (3), or a declaration has not been revoked by a State Government under sub-section (4), the Central Government may, whenever it considers it necessary so to do, require the State Government to furnish to the Central Government the information and materials on the basis of which such declaration has been made or confirmed, or not revoked, as the case may be, and such other information and materials as the Central Government may deem necessary.

(9) Notwithstanding anything contained in another law or any rule having the force of law,—

(a) the grounds on which an order of detention is made or purported to be made under Section 3 against any person in respect of whom a declaration is made under sub-section (2) or a declaration or confirmation under sub-section (3) or the non-revocation under sub-section (4) of a declaration are based, shall be treated as confidential and shall be deemed to refer to maters of State and to be against the public interest to disclose and save as otherwise provided in this Act, no one shall communicate or disclose any such ground, information or material or any document containing such ground, information or material;

(b) no person against whom an order of detention is made or purported to be made under Section 3 shall be entitled to the communication or disclosure of any such ground, information or material as is referred to in clause (a) or the production to him of any document containing such ground, information or material]

(b) no person against whom an order of detention is made or purported to be made under Section 3 shall be entitled to the communication or disclosure of any such ground, information or material as is referred to in clause (a) of the production to him of any document containing such ground, information or material.]

ADDITION OF NEW SECTION 18 AFTER SECTION 17-A

18. Exclusion of common law or natural law rights, if any—No person (including a foreigner) in respect of whom an order is made or purported to be made under Section 3 shall have any right to personal liberty by virtue of natural law or common law, if any."

AMENDMENT OF 26 JULY, 1975

SECTION: IN SECTION 4 SUBSTITUTION

[6][Code of Criminal Procedure, 1973 (2 of 1974).]
Section 7: In Section 7 sub-section (2) is being inserted:

"(2) Notwithstanding anything contained in the Code of Criminal Procedure, 1973 (2 of 1974), every offence under clause (b) of sub-section (1) shall be cognizable."

SECTION 14: SUB-SECTION (2) IS BEING INSERTED AFTER SUB-SECTION (1)

"(2) the expiry or revocation of a detention order (hereafter in this sub-section referred to as the earlier detention order) shall not bar the making of another detention order (hereafter in this sub-section referred to as the subsequent detention order) under Section 3 against the same person:

Provided that in a case where no fresh facts have arisen after the expiry or revocation of the earlier detention order made against such person, the maximum period for which such person may be detained n pursuance of the subsequent detention order shall, in no case, extend beyond the expiry of a period of twelve months from the date of the detention under the earlier detention order or the expiry of the Defence and Internal Security of India Act, 1971 (42 of 1971), whichever is later."

AMENDMENT OF 31 JULY, 1975

SECTION 1: IN SECTION 1 SUB-SECTION (2) ADDITION IN PROVISO:

[Defence and Internal Security of India Act, 1971], shall continue to be governed by the provisions of that Act in respect of such detention as if this Act had not been extended to the State of Jammu and Kashmir.]

THE CONSERVATION OF FOREIGN EXCHANGE AND PREVENTION OF SMUGGLING ACTIVITIES ACT, 1974 (ACT NO. 52 OF 1974)

[*13th December, 1974*]

1. Short title, extent and commencement—(1) This Act may be called the Conservation of Foreign and Prevention of Smuggling Activities Act, 1974.

(2) It extends to the whole of India.

(3) It shall come into force on such [1] [date] as the Central Government may, by notification in the Official Gazette, appoint.

2. Definitions.—In this Act, unless the context otherwise requires,—

(a) "*appropriate Government*" means, as respects a detention order made by the Central Government or by an officer of the Central Government or a person detained under such order, the Central Government, and as respects a detention order made by a State Government or by an officer of a State Government or a person detained under such order, the State Government;

(b) "*detention order*" means an order made under section 3;

(c) "*foreigner*" has the same meaning as in the Foreigners Act, 1946 (31 of 1946);

(d) "*Indian customs waters*" has the same meaning as in clause (28) of section 2 of the Customs Act, 1962 (52 of 1962);

(e) "*Smuggling*", has the same meaning as in clause (39) of section 2 of the Customs Act, 1962, and all its grammatical variations and cognate expressions shall be construed accordingly;

(f) "*State Government*", in relation to a Union territory, means the administrator thereof.

(g) any reference in this Act to a law which is not in force in the State of Jammu and Kashmir shall, in relation to that State, be construed as a reference to the corresponding law, if any, in force in that State.

3. Power to make orders detaining certain persons—(1) The Central Government or the State Government or any officer of the Central Government, not below the rank of a Joint Secretary to that Government, specially empowered for the purposes of this section by that Government, or any officer of a State Government, not below the rank of a Secretary to that Government, specially empowered for the purposes of this section by that Government, may, if satisfied, with respect to any person (including a foreigner), that, with a view to preventing him from acting in any manner prejudicial to the conservation or augmentation of foreign exchange or with a view to preventing him from—

(i) smuggling goods, or
(ii) abetting the smuggling of goods, or
(iii) engaging in transporting or concealing or keeping smuggled goods, or
(iv) dealing in smuggled goods otherwise than by engaging in transporting or concealing or keeping smuggled goods, or
(v) harbouring persons engaged in smuggling goods or in abetting the smuggling of goods,

it is necessary so to do, make an order directing that such person be detained:

[2] [Provided that no order of detention shall be made on any of the grounds specified in this sub-section on which an order of detention may be made under section 3 of the Prevention of Illicit Traffic in Narcotic Drugs and Psychotropic Substances Act, 1988 or under section 3 of the Jammu and Kashmir Prevention of Illicit Traffic in Narcotic Drugs and Psychotropic Substances Ordinance, 1988.]

(2) When any order of detention is made by a State Government or by an officer empowered by a State Government, the State Government shall, within ten days, forward to the Central Government a report in respect of the order.

(3) For the purposes of clause (5) of article 22 of the

Constitution, the communication to a person detained in pursuance of a detention order or the grounds on which the order has been made shall be made as soon as may be after the detention, but ordinarily not later than five days, and in exceptional circumstances and for reasons to be recorded in writing, not later than fifteen days, from the date of detention.

4. Execution of detention orders—A detention order may be executed at any place in India in the manner provided for the execution on warrants of arrest under the Code of Criminal Procedure, 1973 (2 of 1974).

5. Power to regulate place and conditions of detention—Every person in respect of whom a detention order has been made shall be liable—

(a) to be detained in such place under such conditions including conditions as to maintenance, interviews or communication with others, discipline and punishment for breaches of discipline, as the appropriate Government may, by general or special order, specify; and

(b) to be removed from one place of detention to another place of detention, whether within the same State or in another State by order of the appropriate Government:

Provided that no order shall be made by a State Government under clause (b) for the removal of a person from one State to another State except with the consent of the Government of that other State.

5-A. Grounds of detention severable—Where a person has been detained in pursuance of an order of detention under sub-section (1) of section 3 which has been made on two or more grounds, such order of detention shall be deemed to have been made separately on each of such grounds and accordingly—

(a) such order shall not be deemed to be invalid or inoperative merely because one or some of the grounds is or are—

  (i) vague,

  (ii) non-existent,

  (iii) not relevant,

(iv) not connected or not proximately connected with such person, or

(v) invalid for any other reason whatsoever,

and it is not therefore possible to hold that the Government or officer making such order should have been satisfied as provided in sub-section (1) of section 3 with reference to the remaining ground or grounds and made the order of detention;

(b) the Government or officer making the order of detention shall be deemed to have made the order of detention under the said sub-section (1) after being satisfied as provided in that sub-section with reference to the remaining ground or grounds.

6. Detention orders not to be invalid or inoperative on certain grounds—No detention order shall be invalid or inoperative merely by reason—

(a) that the person to be detained thereunder is outside the limits of the territorial jurisdiction of the Government or the officer making the order of detention, or

(b) that the place of detention of such person is outside the said limits.

7. Powers in relation to absconding persons—(1) If the appropriate Government has reason to believe that a person in respect of whom a detention order has been made has absconded or is concealing himself so that the order cannot be executed, that Government may—

(a) make a report in writing of the fact to a Metropolitan Magistrate or a Magistrate of the first class having jurisdiction in the place where the said person ordinarily resides; and thereupon the provisions of sections 82, 83, 84 and 85 of the Code of Criminal Procedure, 1973 (2 of 1974), shall apply in respect of the said person and his property as if the order directing that he be detained were a warrant issued by the Magistrate;

(b) by order notified in the Official Gazette direct the said person to appear before such officer, at such place and within such period as may be specified in the order; and if the said person fails to comply with such direction, he shall, unless he proves that it was not possible for him to comply therewith and that he had, within the period specified in the order, informed the officer mentioned in the order of the reason which rendered compliance therewith impossible and of his whereabouts, be punishable with imprisonment for a term which may extend to one year or with fine or with both.

(2) Notwithstanding any thing contained in the Code of Criminal Procedure, 1973 (2 of 1974), every offence under clause (b) of sub-section (1) shall be cognisable.

8. Advisory Boards—For the purposes of sub-clause (a) of clause (4), and sub-clause (c) of clause (7) of article 22 of the Constitution,—

(a) the Central Government and each State Government shall, whenever necessary, constitute one or more Advisory Boards each of which shall consist of a Chairman and two other persons possessing the qualification specified in sub-clause (a) of clause (4) of article 22 of the Constitution;

(b) save as otherwise provided in section 9, the appropriate Government shall, within five weeks from the date of detention of a person under a detention order make a reference in respect thereof to the Advisory Board to make the report under sub-clause (a) of clause (4) of article 22 of the Constitution;

(c) the Advisory Board to which a reference is made under clause (b) shall after considering the reference and the materials placed before it and after calling for such further information as it may deem necessary from the appropriate Government or from any person called for the purpose through the appropriate Government or from the person concerned, and if, in any particular case, it considers it essential so to do or if the person concerned desires to be heard in person, after hearing him in person, prepare its report specifying in a separate paragraph thereof its opinion as to whether or not there is sufficient cause for the detention of the person concerned and submit the same within eleven weeks from the date of detention of the person concerned;

(d) when there is a difference of opinion among the members forming the Advisory Board the opinion of the majority of such members shall be deemed to be the opinion of the Board;

(e) a person against whom an order of detention has been made under this Act shall not be entitled to appear by any legal practitioner in any matter connected with the reference to the Advisory Board, and the proceedings of the Advisory Board and its report, excepting that part of the report in which the opinion of the Advisory Board is specified, shall be confidential;

(f) in every case where the Advisory Board has reported that there is in its opinion sufficient cause for the detention of a person, the appropriate Government may confirm the detention order and continue the detention of the person concerned for such period as it thinks fit and in every case where the Advisory Board has reported that there is in its opinion no sufficient cause for the detention of the person concerned, the appropriate Government shall revoke the detention order and cause the person to be released forthwith.

9. Cases in which and circumstances under which persons may be detained for periods longer than three months without obtaining the opinion of Advisory Board—(1) Notwithstanding anything contained in this Act, any person (including a foreigner) in respect of whom an order of detention is made under this Act at any time before the 13th December 1974 may be detained without obtaining, in accordance with the provisions of sub-clause (a) of clause (4) of article 22 of the Constitution, the opinion of an Advisory Board for a period longer than three months but not exceeding six months from the date of his detention, where the order of detention has been made against such person with a view to preventing him from smuggling goods or abetting the smuggling of goods or engaging in transporting or concealing or keeping smuggled goods and the Central Government or any Officer of the Central Government, not below the rank of an Additional Secretary to that Government, specially empowered for the purposes of this section by that Government, is satisfied that such person,—

(i) smuggles or is likely to smuggle goods into, out of or through any area highly vulnerable to smuggling; or
(ii) abets or is likely to abet the smuggling of goods into, out of or through any area highly vulnerable to smuggling; or
(iii) engages or is likely to engage in transporting or concealing or keeping smuggled goods in any area highly vulnerable to smuggling,

and makes a declaration to that effect within five weeks of the detention of such person.

Explanation.—In this sub-section, "*area highly vulnerable to smuggling*" means,—

(i) the Indian customs waters;
(ii) the inland area fifty kilometres in width from the coast of India falling within the territories of[3] [the States of Goa, Gujarat Karnataka, Kerala, Maharashtra, Tamil Nadu and the Union territories of Daman and Diu and Pondicherry];
(iii) such further or other Indian customs waters, or inland area not exceeding one hundred kilometres in width from any other coast or border of India, or such other customs station, as the Central Government may, having regard to the vulnerability of such waters, area or customs station, as the case may be, to smuggling, by notification in the official Gazette, specify in this behalf.

(2) In the case of any person detained under a detention order to which the provisions of sub-section (1) apply, section 8 shall have effect subject to the following modifications, namely:—

(i) in clause (b), for the words "shall, within five weeks", the words "shall, within four months and two weeks" shall be substituted;

(ii) in clause (c) for the words "the detention of the person concerned", the words "the continued detention of the person concerned" shall be substituted;

(3) The case of every person detained under a detention order to which the provision of sub-section (1) apply shall, within a period of six months from the date of detention, be reviewed [unless in the meantime a reference has been made in respect thereof to an Advisory Board constituted under clause (a) of Section 8 read with sub-section (2) or such order has been revoked] by the appropriate Government in consultation with a person who is, or has been, or is qualified to be appointed, as a Judge of a High Court nominated in that behalf by the Government:

Provided that where the appropriate Government is a State Government, that Government shall also consult the Central Government in the matter.

10. Maximum period of detention—The maximum period for which any person may be detained in pursuance of any detention order to which the provisions of section 9 do not apply and which has been confirmed under Clause (f) of section 8 shall be for a period one year:

Provided that nothing contained in this section shall affect the power of the appropriate Government in either case to revoke or modify the detention order at any earlier time.

11. Revocation of detention orders—(1) Without prejudice to the provisions of section 21 of the General Clauses Act, 1897 (10 of 1897) a detention order may, at any time, be revoked or modified—

(a) notwithstanding that the order has been made by an officer of a State Government, by that State Government or by the Central Government;

(b) notwithstanding that the order has been made by an officer of the Central Government or by a State Government, by the Central Government.

(2) The revocation of a detention order shall not bar the making of another detention order under section 3 against the same person.

12. Temporary release of persons detained—(1) The Central Government may, at any time, direct that any person detained in pursuance of a detention order made by that Government or an officer subordinate to that Government or by a State Government or by an officer subordinate to a State Government, may be released for any specified period either without conditions or upon such conditions specified in the direction as that person accepts, and may, at any time, cancel his release.

(1-A) A State Government may, at any time, direct that any person detained in pursuance of a detention order made by that Government or by an officer subordinate to that Government may be released for any specified period either without conditions or upon such conditions specified in the direction as that person accepts, and may, at any time, cancel his release.

(2) In directing the release of any person under sub-section (1) or sub-section (1-A), the Government directing the release may require him to enter into a bond with sureties for the due observance of the conditions specified in the direction.

(3) Any person released under sub-section (1) or sub-section (1-A) shall surrender himself at the time and place, and to the authority, specified in the order directing his release or cancelling his release, as the case may be.

(4) In any person fails without sufficient cause to surrender himself in the manner specified in sub-section (3), he shall be punishable with imprisonment for a term which may extend to two years, or with fine, or with both.

(5) If any person released under sub-section (1) or sub-section (1-A) fails to fulfil any of the conditions imposed upon him under the said sub-section or in the bond entered into by him, the bond shall be declared to be forfeited and any person bound thereby shall be liable to pay the penalty thereof.

(6) Notwithstanding anything contained in any other law and save an otherwise provided in this section, no person against whom a detention order made under this Act is in force shall be released whether on bail or bail bond or otherwise.

12-A. Special provisions for dealing with emergency—(1) Notwithstanding anything contained in this Act or any rules of natural justice, the provisions of this section shall have effect during the period of operation of the Proclamation of Emergency issued under clause (1) of article 352 of the Constitution of the 3rd day of December, 1971, or the Proclamation of Emergency issued under that clause on the 25th day of June, 1975, or a period of twenty four months from the 25th day of the June, 1975, whichever period is the shortest.

(2) When making an order of detention under this Act against any person after the commencement of the Conservation of Foreign Exchange and Prevention of Smuggling Activities (Amendment) Act, 1975, the Central Government or the State Government or, as the case may be, the officer making the order of detention shall consider whether the detention of such person under that Act is necessary for dealing effectively with the emergency in respect of which the Proclamations referred to in sub-section (1) have been issued (hereinafter in this section referred to as the emergency) and if, on such consideration, the Central Government or the State Government or, as the case may be, the officer is satisfied that it is necessary to detain such person for effectively dealing with the emergency, that Government or officer may make a declaration to that effect and communicate a copy of the declaration to the person concerned:

Provided that where such declaration is made by an officer, it shall be reviewed by the appropriate Government within fifteen days from the date of making of the declaration and such declaration shall cease to have effect unless it is confirmed by that Government, after such review, within the said period of fifteen days.

(3) The question whether the detention of any person in respect of whom a declaration has been made under sub-section (2) continues to be necessary for effectively dealing with the emergency shall be reconsidered by the appropriate Government within four months from the date of such declaration and thereafter at intervals not exceeding four months, and if, on such reconsideration, it appears to the appropriate Government that the detention of the

person is no longer necessary for effectively dealing with the emergency, that Government may revoke the declaration.

(4) In making any consideration, review or reconsideration under sub-section (2) or (3), the appropriate Government or officer may, if such Government or officer considers it to be against the public interest to do otherwise, act on the basis of the information and materials in its or his possession without disclosing the facts or giving an opportunity of making a representation to the person concerned.

(5) It shall not be necessary to disclose to any person detained under a detention order to which the provisions of sub-section (2) apply, the grounds on which the order has been made during the period the declaration made in respect of such person under that sub-section is in force, and, accordingly, such period shall not be taken into account for the purposes of sub-section (3) of section 3.

(6) In the case of every person detained under a detention order to which the provisions of sub-section (2) apply, being a person in respect of whom a declaration has been made thereunder, the period during which such declaration is in force shall not be taken into account for the purpose of computing—

(i) the periods specified in clauses (b) and (c) of section 8;

(ii) the periods of "one year" and "five weeks" specified in sub-section (1), the period of "one year" specified in sub-section (2) (i), and the period of "six months" specified in sub-section (3), of section 9.

13. Protection of action taken in good faith.—No suit or other legal proceeding shall lie against the Central Government or a State Government, and no suit, prosecution or other legal proceedings shall lie against any person, for anything in good faith done or intended to be done in pursuance of this Act.

14. Repeal.—The Maintenance of Internal Security (Amendment) Ordinance, 1974 (11 of 1974) shall, on the commencement of this Act, stand repealed and accordingly the amendments made in the Maintenance of Internal Security Act, 1971 (26 of 1971) by the said Ordinance shall, on such commencement, cease to have effect.

ENDNOTES

1. 19th December, 1974, vide GSR 690 (E), dated 16th December, 1974.
2. Added by Act No. 46 of 1988 (w.e.f. 4-7-1988).
3. Subs. by Act. No. 23 of 1987 (w.e.f. 2-7-1987).

APPENDIX-II

DELHI JUDGES LISTEN TO WORLD JUDGMENTS ON HUMAN RIGHTS

THE TIMES (LONDON), FEBRUARY 17, 1976

Delhi Feb. 16.—The "unfettered and unguided" powers claimed by the Indian Government to suspend fundamental rights under the internal state of emergency, are in direct conflict with the constitution, the United Nations Charter, and international law, the Supreme Court was told here today.

Dr. N.M. Ghatate, a counsel arguing on behalf of people jailed without trial under the seven-month-old emergency, told the five judges on the bench, that the state was bound, under the constitution, to act in accordance with international law and treaty obligations.

After successful petitions in various high courts by some detainees, the central Government and some state Governments have appealed to the Supreme Court to uphold their powers of arrest and detention of people without trial or recourse to habeas corpus.

Dr. Ghatate read out provisions of the United Nations Charter, the Universal Declaration of Human Rights, the 1950 Nuremberg Principles, the International Covenant on Civil and Politics Rights and other documents to show that the right to life and liberty was a fundamental human privilege.

He argued that all United Nations members had to show respect for, and secure and guarantee, human rights.

He asked the court to interprete the presidential suspension of fundamental rights last June in line with India's international obligations relating to life and liberty.

The power claimed by the state on the basis of the order by President Fakhruddin Ali Ahmed amounted to the destruction of the right to life and liberty, not its suspension, and this was beyond the powers given in the constitution, he said.

APPENDIX-III

EDITORIAL IN THE NEW YORK TIMES APRIL 30, 1976

FADING HOPE IN INDIA

If India ever finds its way back to the freedom and democracy that were proud hallmarks of its first eighteen years as an independent nation, someone will surely erect a monument to Justice H.R. Khanna of the Supreme Court. It was Mr. Khanna who spoke out fearlessly and eloquently for freedom this week in dissenting from the Court's decision upholding the right of Prime Minister Indira Gandhi's Government imprison political opponents at will and without court hearings.

Indian democrats are likely to remember only in infamy the four judges who obediently overturned the decisions of a half-dozen lower courts scattered across India, which had rules in defiance of the Government that the right of habeas corpus could not be suspended, even during the emergency that Mrs. Gandhi declared last June. But they will long cherish the lonely judge who said, in words reminiscent of other enduring declarations for freedom:

> "The power of the courts to issue a writ of habeas corpus is regarded as one of the most important characteristics of democratic states under the rule of law. The principle that no one shall be deprived of his life or liberty without the authority a law is rooted in the consideration that life and liberty are precious possessions."

For his colleagues, who held the Government's actions in jailing thousands of its political opponents without trial or even detailed charges to be "legal" under the sweeping emergency powers granted by the Constitution, Mr. Justice Khanna had a tart and hurting reminder:

> "In a purely formal sense, even the organized mass murders of the Nazi regime qualify as law."

It is a reminder that ought somehow to force its way into the consciousness and thence onto the conscience of the stubborn woman who, for the last ten months, has behaved more in the manner of an empress or a vicereine than like the daughter of Jawaharlal Nehru. The submission of an independent judiciary to absolutist government is virtually the last step in the destruction of a democratic society; and the Indian Supreme Court's decision appears close to utter surrender.

A defeated lawyer was close to the truth when he said, after that decision: "This case was out last hope, and now that hope is gone".

APPENDIX-IV

ANALYSIS: JUDGMENTS OF THE DELHI AND BOMBAY HIGH COURTS

A. JUDGMENT OF THE DELHI HIGH COURT

The detenue before the Delhi High Court Bench of Justice S. Rangarajan and Justice R.N. Aggarwal, was Kuldip Nayar a well-known journalist. The grounds of detention were not furnished to him, nor did he have the right to make a representation to the Advisory Board because the Government had made the declaration under Section 16-A of MISA that his detention was necessary for the successful implementation of the Emergency. Kuldip Nayar thus had a heavy burden to prove *prima facie* that the detaining authority could not possibly have any material before it to warrant a valid and *bona fide* satisfaction that his detention was necessary.[1]

His *habeas corpus* application was filed on his behalf by his wife Mrs. Bharti Nayar giving a detailed statement of his background as a reputed journalist, author and the various responsible positions held by him.

It was also stated in the petition that he had always been a peaceful citizen. He had never been a member of any political party, nor participated in any political demonstration, and had not done a single act which could possibly lead to the satisfaction by the detaining that he was likely to commit an act prejudicial to public order to warrant his detention. It was further stated that Nayar had only written a private letter to the Prime Minister Indira Gandhi in which he had merely expressed an opinion that pre-censorship of the press was undesirable. This private expression of contrary opinion could not be a basis for his detention.

V.M. Tarkunde, appearing for the detenue, contended that the press censorship order did not cover private communication and therefore a private letter could not form the basis of any detention order. Citing the averments in the petition and the arguments advanced by Tarkunde, Justice Rangarajan, who delivered the judgement came to the conclusion that the detaining authority "might have made a mistake about the scope of his power under the MISA." It weighed with him in ordering Kuldip Nayar's release that the detaining authority did not even know that Nayar was a journalist nor had the detaining authority controverted the significant assertions stated in the *habeas corpus* petition, namely, he had never been a member of any political party; he had never participated in any political demonstration; he had not even committed any ordinary breach of the law; he had been holding positions of great responsibility; he was a professional journalist with an international reputation for his objective reporting; and lastly, that the censors had not objected to his publications, even after the declaration of Internal Emergency, in foreign papers. The detaining authority had merely made an assertion that he had report of "specific facts" about the detenue without disclosing these facts of the Court. The Court therefore held that it was not possible to understand "how assessment was made or can be made" that the detention was justified.

This judgment laid down a principle that if the *prima facie* burden is discharged by the detenue, then the onus shifted on the detaining authority to furnish facts satisfying the detention order.

This judgment however, had limited value. The whole case of Kuldip Nayar was that he was a political and responsible citizen. His pen was so restrained that government never objected to his writings. He expressed contrary opinion only in private correspondence. In other words, a wholesome constitutional right of expressing contrary opinion in public was neither claimed nor exercised by him.

But most of the persons detained during the Internal Emergency were either political or social workers, who conscientiously opposed the government's authoritarian measures and found it their duty to create public opinion in their favour. They, therefore, could not and did not adopt the stand Kuldip Nayar had taken in the Court to obtain his release.

This raises an important question that if a detenue demonstrated that he was a responsible, peaceful citizen but was a member of a political party and had participated in a peaceful demonstration, would he get relief? This question squarely came up before the Nagpur Bench of the Bombay High Court and again before the same bench of the Delhi High Court.

B. JUDGMENT OF THE BOMBAY HIGH COURT[2]

The detenues before Justice C.S. Dharmadhikari and Justice C.T. Dighe of the Nagpur Bench of the Bombay High Court belonged to the Jana Sangh and the Rashtriya Swayamsevak Sangh (R.S.S.)[2]. Like Justice Ranganathan, Justice Dharmadhikari, who delivered the judgment in the case also employed the theory of shifting onus but came to the conclusion that the detenues had not made out a *prima facie* case that there was no material before the detaining authority to warrant their detention. The reasons for this conclusion were twofold: certain admissions made and facts mentioned in the *habeas corpus* petitions and the ratio of the *Machindra Shivaji's Case.*[3]

Before analyzing these reasons, it is necessary to state that these petitions were filed not by the detenues but by their near relatives or friends who swore affidavits as to the facts and grounds contained in the petitions. They were ditto copies of the *habeas corpus* petitions filed on behalf of Atal Bihari Vajpayee in the Karnataka High Court.[4] As such, these petitions contained the history of political developments from Proclamation of emergency in 1971 following the Indo-Pak War to the imposition of Internal Emergency in 1975, and the banning of the R.S.S. on July 4, 1975. This factual history was given to substantiate the contention that the continuation of the Emergency in 1971 and the Proclamation of Emergency in 1975, was unconstitutional and a *mala fide* abuse of power.

Each petition, however, narrated personal data of the detenue such as date and time of his arrest, details of his membership of Jana Sangh or R.S.S. as the case may be. Each petition also asserted that the detenue or his organization had never indulged in any violent or subversive activity and there could be no material before the detaining authority to warrant his detention on these grounds.

When these petitions came up for hearing, V.R. Manohar who led the arguments on behalf of the detenues gave up the larger questions regarding constitutional validity of the Emergency of 1971 and Emergency of 1975, the 38th and 39th Constitutional Amendments and amendments to MISA made during the Emergency. The challenge to the order of detention was confined only to the grounds of non-compliance of the provisions of MISA and malice in law. Therefore on the direction of the Court all the averments mentioned in these petitions regarding political developments and constitutional challenges were withdrawn in writing and specifically deleted from these petitions.

Nevertheless Justice Dharmadhikari in his judgment observed:

> Though the challenges based on various averments and allegations made in the petitions are given up, in our opinion, the same are indicative of the attitude and inclination of the detenues towards the political life and various happenings. It also indicates the nature and sphere of their political activity as well as their association and affiliation with political parties and banned organizations.

One fails to understand how averments and allegations made in the petitions could be held to be indicative of attitude of the detenues towards the political life and various happenings in contrary because all these petitions were filed not by the detenue but by their relatives and friends. Secondly, all these petitions on their face were identical regarding political developments immediately preceding the declaration of Emergency. Assuming that the facts mentioned in petitions were sworn on affidavit by the detenues which was not the case, was there anything wrong in knowing about the political happening which were narrated in these petitions? Or holding a particular view on these developments and stating so in the court of law? The purpose of giving these facts was also to substantiate the averments that the detaining authority had detained them not on his own satisfaction but on the instructions of higher authorities (as hundreds of persons were detained all over the country on June 25-26, 1975) which was not permissible under MISA.

The High Court erred in inferring about the attitude and inclination of the detenues on the basis of averments made and political history narrated by someone else in the petition. Nor was it justified in holding that these facts and allegations could be the basis for satisfaction of the detaining authority to warrant the detention of detenues because they were stated in the writ petitions, which were filed *subsequent* to detentions. The law requires that there must be material before the detaining authority for arriving at a satisfaction *prior to* issuing the order of detention. Moreover, mere "attitude" and "inclination" in the absence of any prior violent activity by detenues could not be a basis for valid detention, especially when in the *Ram Bahadur Rai's Case*[A] the Supreme Court had held that "peaceful protests and voicing contrary opinion are powerful and wholesome weapons in the democratic repertoire" and cannot be a valid ground for putting a peaceful protestant behind bars.

No doubt none of the detenues belonging to the RSS or Jana Sangha denied their association or affiliation with these organizations. On the contrary, this was specifically admitted in these petitions. But it was also stated that neither Jan Sangh nor RSS had ever advocated violence there was no evidence with the government that these organizations indulged in violence. There were also specific averments that the detenues personally believed in democracy and had never advocated, but had always condemned, violence.

But since the Central Government had by notification banned the RSS and declared it to be an "Organisation whose members are indulging in activities prejudicial to internal security, public safety and maintenance of public order" the High Court merely on that basis held that there was a *prima facie* enough material before the detaining authority to warrant detention that the detenue had indulged or was likely to indulge in activity prejudicial to public order or security of state because the "Central Government" was "satisfied". This reasoning however was erroneous on more than one count.

Section 3 of MISA required that the detaining authority must be *personally* satisfied about the need to detain a person. The central government notification was of a general character to justify the ban on RSS and other 25 organizations. It was not in regard to each and every member of the banned organization. To hold otherwise was against the time tested cannon of justice that guilt by association of alien to civilized law. This reasoning in the judgment itself lent support to the allegations in the petition that the detaining authority was acting not on the basis of his own satisfaction but that of some higher authority, which could not be a valid ground for detention under Section 3 of MISA.

In the absence of material furnished by the detaining authority to justify its assertion that he was personally satisfied of the need to issue detention orders, the High Court should have shifted the burden on the detaining authority and on its failure to discharge the same it should have quashed the detention orders. This is because when a person is detained on the ground specified in the statute, the onus of proving that there existed facts to justify detention is on the detaining authority. The Supreme Court in the *S.K. Nizamuddin's Case* has held that when a show cause notice is issued, it is an obligation on the State to place all relevant facts before the Court.[6] When an assertion was made that the detenue had not done any violent act, the detaining authority was required to satisfy the court about such acts, what they were etc., to justify that detention was necessary to prevent their petition as held in the *Lal Kamal Das's case.*[7] The High Court should have seen that the requirement of filing a proper affidavit was not a mere formality.[8] In the absence of a clear and complete affidavit that detention was necessary, it should have held, as the Supreme Court had held in the *Dulal Roy's Case* that the order of detention was mechanically passed.[9]

In the absence of a clear and complete affidavit by the detaining authority, the High Court should have called for the file containing grounds and particulars as it did subsequently, in the *habeas corpus* petition filed in the *Matka Gamblers Case.*[10]

Instead, the High Court relied on the Federal Court's decision in the *Machindra Shivaji's case* wherein the detention order was held to be valid because of his association with the

Communist Party of India.[11] The High Court erred in applying this case for two reasons. Firstly, acts of this case were entirely different. In that case the detenue was supplied with grounds of detention according to which the Communist Party of India to which he belonged was said to be "spreading the doctrine of violence, fomenting industrial strikes, rendering life and property insecure and trying to seize power by violence." Furthermore, he was assisting and associating with the party leaders "who had gone underground and that he himself was likely to go underground and from there guide various subversive activities of the Communist Party."

In that case, the detenue had not contradicted the allegation regarding subversive activities. While in the cases before the Bombay High Court the allegation of violence was emphatically denied. No serious allegation trying to seize power by violence or likely to go underground to direct subversive activities, could be inferred. No specific statement relating to such past activity by the detenue was made by the detaining authority; no such facts or grounds were made available. The counter affidavit was in the nature of denial of assertions made in the petitions. All that the detaining authority asserted in a parrot-like style in each case was that after considering the activities of the detenue prior to Internal Emergency he was satisfied that his detention was necessary to prevent him from acting prejudicial to the security of india but claimed privilege from producing any material. These assertions were mere repetition of the language of Section 3 of MISA, the Proclamation of Emergency and the order banning RSS and therefore, the High Court fell in error for taking the shadow for substance, especially when privilege for producing the material was claimed.

The High Court was not correct in relying on *The Machindra Shivaji's Case.*[11] This decision turned on its own facts and it is not an authority for a ratio that mere association with a party alleged to be engaged in subversive activity is relevant for arriving at a satisfaction for detention. At best the principle that can be deduced from this decision was that "satisfaction" as Justice P.N. Bhagwati observed in the *Khudiram Das Case*, must be grounded "on materials which are of rationally probative value".[12]

The High Court, however, allowed the petitions of the detenues who were not active members of any opposition political party or banned organizations. It followed the judgment in the *Kuldip Nayar's case* which was an authority to obtain release for those detenues who were apolitical and were not guilty of exercising their democratic right of voicing contrary opinion.

In fact, when the *habeas corpus* petition of Nanaji Deshmukh, who was then the General Secretary of the Jana Sangh and the Sangharsha Samiti organized by Jayparakash Narayan, came for hearing before the Division Bench of the Delhi High Court, Justice Rangarajan himself exclaimed, "How could my judgment in *Kuldip Naryar's Case* apply to a person like Mr. Deshmukh?" At the request of the government he adjourned the hearing of this and all other pending petitions of detenues who belonged to opposition parties, until the decision of the Supreme Court on the maintainability of *habeas corpus* petitions which then were pending before the Supreme Court.

C. SECOND JUDGMENT OF THE BOMBAY HIGH COURT[12]

The Nagpur Bench of the Bombay High Court however did order the detaining authority to produce information, material and grounds on which detention was ordered under MISA. This order was made in a batch of *habeas corpus* petitions filed by the detenues who were detained for gambling activities namely 'Worli Matka'. Since the Government had made a declaration under Section 16-A of the MISA that their detention was necessary for implementing emergency, the right of receiving grounds of detention or making representation to the Advisory Board was denied to them. The Division Bench consisting of Justice V.S. Deshpande and Justice C.S. Dharmadhikari after perusing the pleadings found that the detenue had made a *prima facie* case that detention was not in compliance with MISA, and passed the Order on 8th December, 1975, directing the detaining authority to produce for perusal of the Court the file containing grounds and information on which orders of detention were based.[9] Justice Deshpande, who delivered the judgment upheld the validity of Section 16-A of MISA according to which all the material was to be treated "as confidential and shall be deemed to refer to matters of State and to be against public interest to disclose except as provided under the Act." But this provision, according to Justice Deshpande, could not defeat the High Court's power of judicial review under Article 226. According to him the fiction created by this provision could only operate when grounds and material related to Section 3 of MISA under which the detention order was passed. The provision did not create a further fiction that material in possession of the detaining authority "indisputably and necessarily" pertained to the condition on which detention was ordered. Mere claim to that effect by the detaining authority could not be conclusive when the section did not say so, and when there have been instances apart from abuse of power when the detaining officer's notion was found by courts to be misconceived.

In this case the High Court further held that for the purpose of deciding the claim of privilege about whether material in the files was relevant, the court itself could look into it and this would not amount to disclosure. The High Court relied on the Supreme Court judgment in the *State of U.P. Vs. Raj Narayan;* that even if the matter was considered to relate to the affairs of State under Section 162 of the Evidence Act, the Court was competent to look into the documents.[13] On the same reasoning the High Court ought to have called for the files of detenues belonging to the Jana Sangha and RSS.

The High Court refused the Government leave to appeal to the Supreme Court as it was following the laws settled by the Supreme Court. But the Government went in appeal and a Bench presided over by Chief Justice Ray granted leave and stayed the production of records ordered by the High Court.[15]

ENDNOTES

1. *Mrs. Bharti Nayar vs. UOI & Ors.*, Writ Petition (Crl.) No. 121 of 1975. Judgment cited 15 September, 1975. This judgment was censored by then government and could not be reported.
2. *K.M. Ghatate vs. Union of India and Others*, A.I.R. 1975 Bombay, p. 324.
3. *Machindra Shivaji vs. The King*, AIR 1950 FC 129.

4. On my way from Bangalore to Delhi I had stopped in Nagpur and given them the copy of the petition to the petitioners and subsequently had sent these copies for the benefit of detenues all over the country.
5. *Ram Bahadur Ravi vs. State of Bihar and Ors.*
6. *Sk. Nizamudding vs. State of West Bengal*, 1975 (3) SCC 395.
7. *Lal Kamal Das vs. State of West Bengal*, AIR 1975 SC 753; 1975 (4) SCC 62.
8. *Mohammad Alam vs. State of West Bengal*, 1974 (3) SCR 379; 1974 (4) SCC 463.
9. *Dulal Roy vs. Distt. Magistrate Burdwan and Ors.*, 1975 (3) SCR p. 186; 1975 (1) SCC 837.
10. *Machindra Shivaji vs. The King*, AIR 1950 FC 129.
11 *Khudiram Dass vs. State of West Bengal & Ors.*, 1975 (2) SCR p. 832; 1975 (2) SCC 81.
12. Judgment of Bombay the High Court (Nagpur Bench) dated 5, 6 and 8, 1975 in Criminal Application Nos. 95, 97, 99, 109, 115, 116, 168 and 171 of 1975.
13. *State of U.P. vs. Raj Narain and Others*, 1975 (3) SCR 333; 1975 (4) SCC 428.
14. The Rajasthan High Court also took a similar view and ordered the detaining authority to produce the file in its judgment dated 12 December, 1975, in Crl. habeas corpus No. 1606 of 1975. This order was also stayed by the Supreme Court and both the appeals were allowed along with other appeals of the Government in the *A.D.M. Jabalpur etc. vs. Shivkant Shukla etc. Case.*

INDEX